UP
and
RUNNING

THE JAMI GOLDMAN STORY

UP
and
RUNNING

BY *Jami Goldman* AND *Andrea Cagan*

POCKET BOOKS
NEW YORK LONDON TORONTO SYDNEY SINGAPORE

POCKET BOOKS, a division of Simon & Schuster, Inc.
1230 Avenue of the Americas, New York, NY 10020

ISBN-10: 0-7434-2421-2
ISBN-13: 978-0-7434-2421-9

First Pocket Books hardcover printing September 2001

10 9 8 7 6 5 4 3 2 1

POCKET BOOKS and colophon are registered trademarks of
Simon & Schuster, Inc.

For information regarding special discounts for bulk purchases,
please contact Simon & Schuster Special Sales at 1-800-456-6798
or business@simonandschuster.com

Printed in the U.S.A.

to My Family,

especially the Fab Four,

Poppy, Grandma, Mom, and Dad

Acknowledgments

I WOULD LIKE TO THANK . . .

Beau, for unconditional support and love in my life.

Jason, for being the greatest brother ever.

Lisa, for being my partner in purgatory, my strength in recovery, and my friend.

Brittney, my closest friend and confidante.

Michael and Jake Estes, for saving my life.

The people who made this book possible and believed in me: my lawyer, William Jacobson; my book agent, Paul Fedorko; my editor, Emily Bestler.

My doctors, without whose genius I wouldn't be walking: Dr. James Malone, Mr. Joe Leal, C.P.

The loving staff of Scottsdale Memorial Hospital.

Richard Plattner, my lawyer, who worked unselfishly for three long years to stand up for what we all believe is the truth.

Barbara Ferrell-Edmonson, my brilliant coach, who taught me to keep my legs underneath me.

The Challenger Athlete Foundation, Athletes Helping Athletes, Adidas, and 24-Hour-Fitness.

Ossur Flex-Foot, RGP Prosthetic & Research Center, and Michael Stull, without whom I wouldn't be running.

All the extended members of my family who live forever in my heart.

Pearl Jam, for inspiring me by creating the song "Alive."

And Andrea, my writer. When I first faced delving into my painful past, I wondered how I would manage. With your comforting and easygoing personality, I was able to open up completely, which made this project so true to my heart. In a process more gentle than counseling, your presence, your warm heart, and your caring soul made this book come alive. Thank you.

Introduction

ON DECEMBER 23, 1987, I LEARNED THAT A SEEMINGLY INSIGNIFICANT mistake can change the course of a person's life forever. I was driving home from a ski trip to spend the holidays with my family when I took a turn onto a seldom traveled road. That should have been no big deal. People get lost every day with repercussions no more serious than being late for an appointment. In my case, however, getting stuck on a back road that the state barricaded without first searching for travelers in distress wound up being costly beyond my wildest imagination.

After sliding into a snowbank on a deserted back road in Arizona in the middle of a blizzard, a friend and I were stranded in a red Chevy Blazer for eleven days without a telephone, heat, food, or water, besides small handfuls of snow we melted whenever the sun came out in bursts. When the intensity of the storm diminished, three days after we got stuck, we tried to escape by foot. Our plan was quickly thwarted when we fell into snow up to our knees. After pushing our way through the snow for a short distance, we were forced to retreat and take refuge back in the car. Little did I know that those were the last steps I would ever take on my own two feet. By the time we were found, we were half-delirious, freezing, frostbitten, thirsty beyond description, and wondering if we had been left for dead.

In another twenty-four to forty-eight hours, we would have died of dehydration, so as random and irreversible as my mistake was, when I open my eyes each morning and see my husband sleeping in bed beside me, I feel immensely grateful that I survived to tell my story. My friend, Lisa Barzano, a year younger than I, with whom I shared this life-altering experience, paid a tough price. After thirteen surgeries and the partial loss of several toes, she is in daily physical pain and is still healing from the emotional scars of those difficult days when we were lost, freezing and deprived. I bore a more dramatic physical burden. At age nineteen, after a painful and fruitless three-week therapeutic battle, I had both my legs amputated five inches below the knee. And yet, through the extraordinary love, caretaking, and steadfastness of my family, my friends, and my husband, Beau, I have healed emotionally, adjusted to life as a double below-the-knee amputee, and become a decorated sprinter who sets world records and wins gold medals, and I am enthusiastic about my future.

Thirteen years after the fact, my original ordeal feels more like a dream than reality. Following seven weeks in the hospital, I returned home and deliberately placed the details of the accident into the background, as I had a daunting task ahead of me that required my full attention: learning to release what could have been, and to embrace life as a double amputee. I am grateful that human beings forget trauma faster than pleasure, but I have learned that we make peace with our past only when we achieve complete healing in the present. In this way, we can embrace the future with hope, joy, and strength of purpose.

Personal healing was a part of my motivation to write this book, but when I tried to recall my ordeal, the details had become vague in my memory, mainly because so many positive events had taken their place. And so I had to confer with the people who searched for me, found me, nursed me back to health, got me up on legs immediately, forced me to go to the gym, fitted me with prosthetics, taught me to walk again and finally to run like the wind, in order to spark my memory of the accident and the recovery period following.

Even more difficult was writing about the trial that happened several years after I was found. When I sued the state for negligence in an attempt to secure my uncertain future, I was confronted with an emotionally debilitating nightmare, an unthinkable betrayal while I was struggling to make sense of a daily existence turned upside down. Arizona is a "comparative negligence" state—even if a guilty verdict is reached and a sum of money is awarded to the victimized party, the jury is required to compare the negligence of both parties and adjust the award accordingly. And so, although the fated eleven days were found to be the state's fault owing to an annual closure of the road upon which we mistakenly had stumbled and gotten trapped, Lisa and I were viewed, in large part, as comparatively guilty for the catastrophe. In a ferociously nasty trial, an ordeal more abusive than amputation, the fact that we saved our lives under adverse, sometimes torturous conditions was not good enough for the judge or the panel of jurors. I was shocked to find myself being degraded and blamed for not getting away soon enough to save my legs.

No one will ever completely understand Lisa's and my eleven-day struggle for survival, or the massive adjustments that were required of me to reenter society as a whole woman. It's not that I consider my challenges to be more or less difficult than anyone else's. We all have our trials to bear in this life and mine have been considerable. But if the saying is true that living well is the best revenge, I have achieved my goals and then some. Each day, when I get up in the morning, put on my legs, and face a new day, I feel like one of the luckiest women in the world. My future children will, no doubt, agree.

Many years ago, during one of my first speaking engagements, a child stood up and asked me, "Do you want your legs back?" The truth is that, at the time, I would have given every penny I had or would ever attain, as well as all my material possessions, to feel my real legs beneath me. That was before I started running. Now I have a different point of view. I have found my purpose in life as an athletic amputee, an inspirational speaker, a role model for children and adults alike, and I wouldn't change a thing. When I'm sixty years old with my own grown kids and there is some groundbreaking surgery out there, I might decide that having legs would make life easier for me. For now, it's important for me to wake up and put on my prosthetics every day, because that defines who I am and where I'm going.

In a world where healthy young people are suffering body-image problems and starving themselves, sometimes to death, in order to "fit in," I hope that my story will provide some inspiration and sanity along the way. In the final analysis, although my detour on "the road not taken" robbed me of my legs and changed my life forever, it gave me the unexpected gift of fully embracing and appreciating my life and myself, exactly as I am. In the pages that follow, my intention is to inspire and motivate you to embrace your life and the body that God gave you in the same way that I have learned to embrace mine.

In the immortal words of the late great American poet, Robert Frost:

> *I shall be telling this with a sigh*
> *Somewhere ages and ages hence:*
> *Two roads diverged in a wood, and I—*
> *I took the one less traveled by,*
> *And that has made all the difference.*

> —*"The Road Not Taken"*

PART ONE

Purgatory

1

The Privilege of Running

I STOOD AT THE STARTING LINE, CHECKING MY BLOCKS TO MAKE SURE they were in exactly the right positions. As naturally as I took to running right from the beginning, those starting blocks were not my friends and they still aren't. Not yet, anyway. I just can't seem to come off them as fast as I need to, but I'm working on it every day. That's what running is all about, practicing your strengths and your weak points over and over, and making every race count.

For a quick moment, I glanced upward into the stands at the immense crowd of people, ablaze in bright summer colors. It made me almost dizzy, there were so many of them. I heard my coach's voice as if she were beside me, reminding me to keep my mind on the race, to breathe, to focus, not to get distracted. I brought my attention back to the track in front of me, a much safer place.

It was midafternoon in July 2000, at the Olympic trials in Sacramento, California. I'd been training and waiting for this day, and now that it was here, I couldn't have been more excited. The buzz of more than twenty-five thousand people, alive with anticipation, was in the air, as they milled around, talking loudly and making predictions, trying to steal a look at their favorite superstar track athletes, who were all gathered in one place to qualify for the upcoming Olympic games in Sydney, Australia.

My fellow disabled runners and I were there too, but for us, this was an exhibition race, not a qualifier. For me, personally, I hadn't been lucky enough to nab one of the seventy-one slots that were available for U.S. disabled athletes to compete in the Paralympics in Sydney. I had trained really hard and could have gotten a slot if the other double below-the-knee (BK) amputees and I had been given our own races. But because there weren't enough of us, I was up against people who were missing only one leg. I can't beat an elite runner with one leg, and it's not fair to expect me to, but fairness is not the theme of this book or of my life. I've learned not to think in those terms. It's much more about rising to meet your circumstances, overcoming adversity, and appreciating yourself exactly as you are, along with the gifts that life keeps offering you.

This was not my first exhibition race, but it was definitely the most exciting. The sheer number of spectators and the importance of what the greatest athletes in the world were here to do reverberated all over the stands and on the track. Runners in warm-up clothes pretended to ignore probing television cameras while they stretched and jumped around, partly to keep their muscles supple and warm, partly to control the adrenaline that was shooting through their bodies. The great female athlete Marion Jones was running in the next qualifier. I couldn't see her yet, but she was probably on the sidelines somewhere warming up. With her extraordinary talent, her impeccable work ethic, her speed, and her determination, she was a modern-day hero to all women runners. I could hardly believe that when my race was over, I would get to watch her qualify for the hundred-meter sprint, the same distance I was about to run. Her goal was to win five gold medals in the Olympic games; mine was to finish this exhibition race in a strong time and to get through the rest of my life.

Butterflies danced in my stomach, bumping into my bladder over and over again. I felt like I had to pee, even though I'd done it five minutes before. That always happens to me right before a race starts, whether my intention is to improve my time, set a world record, win a gold medal, or run an exhibition race in front of an Olympic audience. The feeling that my stomach is about to splatter just seems to come with the territory, whether I'm competing against myself or other runners. Whatever race I'm in, whether I expect to come in first or last, competing always feels important to me, just because I'm able to play the game at all. I derive immense satisfaction from knowing that I've conquered some really tough obstacles in my life to get me to the starting line. Win or lose (I've done both), competing is a huge privilege, finishing is its own reward, and winning is icing on the cake.

I crouched down in the blocks, looked at the ground, and did a few practice starts. I looked across the line at eight other women, all pretty revved up. doing the same thing. I knew these women really well; I knew their idiosyncrasies, their strengths and weaknesses, and their best times for the different distances, just as they knew mine. It's part of our training to study each other, to know who we're running against, what shape everybody else is in and what they're capable of, so we can determine where we're likely to place on any given day. I watched them with affection as they jogged in place, breathing and trying to calm their nerves. We were all amputees and we had such a tight bond, although only five of us had been competing internationally for the last year and a half. The other three women were just starting to train, but although this was their first time running in front of people and they were here for the fun and excitement, we all needed each other. If even one of us had been missing, there would have been no exhibition race. The Olympic committee felt that only filling all eight lanes would create a strong enough showing to make an exhibition race worthwhile.

I jumped up and down on my "cheetah legs," my carbon flex sprinting prosthetics made by Flex-Foot, the most innovative prosthetic company in the world. When I wear them, especially when I run, they make me feel more like a robot than a human being. Going into this exhibition race, the silicone sleeves felt good and tight over my sockets, my limbs were sunken down perfectly into their socks, and the new cleats on the bottom of the cheetah feet were sharp and ready to dig into the earth.

"Runners to your marks!" I heard the voice boom over the loudspeaker.

I walked over to lane eight, the outside lane I'd been assigned. It's not considered a great lane, but at least there would
be nobody on one side of me for this hundred-meter sprint. Most
runners feel more control in the middle of the pack, where they
can keep an eye on everyone else. I generally do too, but I don't
mind the outside for the hundred meters, since it's a clean
straightaway. For the two hundred meters, location matters more.
You have to start out low and stay that way, rising gradually, working the curve by leaning into the lane. It's hard to execute that
balancing technique in the two hundred meters, to keep that
lean on, especially on cheetah legs. But this was not the two hundred meters.

I stepped in front of my blocks, jumped up and down twice,
and did a few stretches. That's the extent of my rituals before I
begin; I have no talismans, charms, or strange routines I perform,
but I've found that jumping and stretching are good psychological tools to keep me from getting into the blocks too early. For a
runner with both legs intact, relaxing your body while you tighten
your muscles to stay steady in the blocks is tough enough. With
prosthetics, it's almost impossible, and you can end up wasting
energy and strength that should be conserved for running. It's
best to wait until the last possible moment. The idea is not to
crouch all the way to the ground when I start, the way an able-
bodied athlete would. I have discovered, as have other double
BKs like myself, that if I put my hands on the ground and try to
start from there, I can lose a good second and a half getting up
on my legs, balancing, and then taking off. That's an eternity in a
fifteen- to seventeen-second race, the difference between winning
and losing. The only way to save time is to start low, go out at an
angle like an ascending airplane, and come up gradually as I
move forward.

I crouched one last time and exhaled. Everybody down the
line did the same thing. Nobody was moving.

"Set!"

Although there is no predetermined amount of time after the
starter calls out "Set," it takes from two to four seconds for the
gun to go off. In fact, every starter's timing is different, so a huge

part of the training is mastering the takeoff. On that day, I anticipated the gun. An instant before I heard it, I moved. False start— a runner's nightmare. I apologized to the other women while we all jogged forward for ten to twenty meters, turned around, and headed back to the blocks. If you get a sense you're about to flinch or move before the gun goes off, you're supposed to raise your hand. They stop the race, call everyone up, and you get another chance with no penalties. But a runner isn't always in control enough to raise her hand and avoid false starting, which is irritating to everyone, both psychologically as well as physically. It takes a lot of practice to sync it all together, to have your body trained so automatically that there's no thought. The ideal timing is that when the gun goes off, you're moving—not before, not after, but at the same exact time. That takes mastery.

I looked down the line of women, preparing to start again. Nobody was pissed off at me; anticipating the gun happens to everybody and we're trained to move right on. I cleared my head, waited until the last possible moment, and crouched down again, determined not to move early. One more false start and I'd be disqualified; wait too long for the gun and I'd lose time. I was not about to let either of those things happen—not in a race this crucial.

I looked down at the ground in front of me, completely focused, waiting for the cracking sound that would start my legs moving and send me flying across the field. I had images of my training, my coach clapping her hands suddenly behind my head to help me get familiar with the gun. My cheetah legs were in position, I could hear my own breath, I could smell the track. Thirteen years ago I was stranded on a lonely, deserted back road in Arizona in the middle of a blizzard; who could ever have predicted that I would be here today, able to walk, able to run, able to compete fiercely in an athletic event? When you consider the way circumstances unfolded, the fact that I'm alive at all is a miracle in itself. . . .

2

The Cinnamon Roll from Purgatory

IT WAS A WEEK BEFORE CHRISTMAS, 1987, WHEN I TALKED MY BROTHER Jason into trading cars with me. I was planning a ski trip in Colorado with Lisa Barzano, my boyfriend Mike's sister, and we needed a four-wheel drive in case of heavy snow. Mike was living in Gallup, New Mexico, where he'd gotten a pretty decent job working with a friend, while I was attending college in Tempe, Arizona. That was about a five-hour ride and he was usually the one who commuted, spending a few days each week at my place. This time, Lisa and I would be driving to New Mexico to pick up Mike and his roommate, Adam. Then we'd all go skiing together in Colorado.

Although Lisa and I attended the same school, she was a year younger than I, so we were in different classes. I didn't know her all that well, but she lived in Scottsdale, a short distance from my one-bedroom apartment in Tempe. She had skied with me once before, she'd liked it, and she wanted to go for a second time. And so, on Saturday, December 19, 1987, I gave Jason my Dodge Daytona, while Lisa and I loaded up his red Chevy Blazer with ski equipment and our warmest clothes, and headed out from Arizona to Gallup, New Mexico. Final destination: Purgatory.

Despite its ominous name, Purgatory, Colorado, is magnificently beautiful country. I loved to see the sun shining on the abundant aspen and spruce trees, while snow-covered mountain ranges rise in all directions, waiting to be conquered by enthusiastic sports nuts on skis, snowboards, and snowmobiles. For people inclined toward quieter sports, there was cross-country skiing and old-fashioned horse-drawn sleigh rides during the winter months along with good hearty food. The air in this Rocky Mountain range was clear, skiing was good, and before that winter, I associated the name "Purgatory" with beauty, playfulness, and snow-filled vacations. By the time January 1988 had rolled around, however, I'd learned the dictionary definition of purgatory: a condition of spiritual cleansing and temporary suffering.

I skied pretty often in my teenage years, even though I wasn't what you'd call the athletic type. Back then, going to the gym and working out was something for other people, but I loved the feeling of going fast. When I first started to ski, I didn't bother practicing moguls because I wasn't patient enough for anything that disciplined. For me, skiing was about having fun and moving like the wind, so I went straight for the intermediate runs, where I could fly down the mountain and get high on the speed.

Lisa and I didn't take a map with us when we left for New Mexico. We figured we didn't need one, because Mike had given us detailed directions to his house. At one point, when we reached an area called the Mongolian Rim, which always received the heaviest snowfall, we put the car in four-wheel drive and I took the wheel. It was no big deal; I'd skied a lot and I was accustomed to driving through snow. The plan was to drive the five or so hours to Gallup on Saturday and spend the night with Mike and Adam. Then Lisa, Mike, myself, and Adam (his dad had a cabin in Purgatory) would leave Sunday morning to go skiing. Lisa and I had timed the trip so we would have two and a half days on the slopes, drop the guys back off in New Mexico, and head home early in the morning on the twenty-third. That way, we'd be back by 3 P.M., in time for Lisa to work her afternoon child-care program at the YMCA in Scottsdale.

Mike's directions were great; we arrived at his house on Saturday, just as we'd planned. Purgatory was about a four-hour drive from there, so we all got up Sunday morning with the intention of getting in a solid half day on the slopes. I left Jason's Blazer at Mike's and we piled into Adam's truck, but unfortunately, it slid on some ice and we got stuck in a cow track. When we got out of the car to assess the situation, a tire had blown. Lisa and I went back to the house (we were still within walking distance) while Mike and Adam waited for the tow truck. By the time they were out of the cow track and had changed the tire, it was afternoon. We considered skipping Purgatory altogether, but since we'd only lost a half day, we decided to forge ahead. Two days of skiing were better than nothing.

We left late that afternoon and arrived in time to get a good night's sleep. Monday morning we hit the slopes early. The sun was warm, the weather was ideal, and by that night we were all in a terrific mood. We got up on Tuesday morning, skied until late in the afternoon, and drove back to Gallup, where we fell into bed, deliciously tired.

Lisa woke me up at about 6 A.M. on Wednesday the twenty-third, because we had to be back in time for her to get to work. I remember being a little grumpy because I hate getting up early, but it was part of our deal. We grabbed a six-pack of Diet Pepsis from Mike's fridge and a huge cinnamon roll that I'd bought the day before in Purgatory, in case we got hungry. Then we drove for about an hour until we got to Holbrook, catching a magnificent sunrise which changed my attitude. Since we had limited time, we stopped at a drive-through, a Jack in the Box, for some fast food, but the line was so long, we decided to find another one. We settled for some French toast sticks from Burger King and we were on our way. We felt good, we were on schedule, and we were ready to backtrack our route from a few days prior. Lisa took the wheel and we thought we were heading toward home.

Two hours later, neither of us recognized anything. We looked out onto an area of tall, reedy grass that we had not noticed on the way there. It was all unfamiliar territory. We had no idea where we were, but one thing was for sure—we were not where we were supposed to be. When we saw a sign that said we were entering a town called St. John's, with an arrow pointing toward Springerville, Lisa became upset. We were lost and she was afraid she wouldn't make it to work. We decided to stop at the first gas station to buy a map and get our bearings.

The moment we arrived in Springerville, although the sun was still out, the weather turned freezing cold. If I had been superstitious, I might have called it an omen, but I've never been the superstitious type. We found a gas station pretty quickly, that was the good news, and while Lisa went inside to get a map and some directions, I went to the rest room. A few minutes later, I wandered into the office to see how she was doing. Not all that well, apparently. An elderly couple was in the office right then, picking up a few snacks, and Lisa was poring over a map taped to the wall, listening to the attendant, who was pointing and explaining something to her. She looked confused.

"What's wrong?" I asked her. "Why didn't you buy a map?"

"They don't have any maps for sale," she said. "Jami, I think we really screwed up. Can I talk to you for a minute?" She motioned me toward the door, out of earshot of the others. "You need to take over," she said. "This guy talks like a hillbilly and I can't understand a word he's saying." She pointed to my watch. "It's already eleven."

She left the office to go to the rest room while I studied the map on the wall. The attendant started explaining to me exactly where we were; we appeared to have gone southeast instead of southwest. Lisa came back into the station.

"We're at least four hours from where we're supposed to be," I said.

Lisa looked distraught. We were running out of time, and we were almost back at the New Mexico border. Retracing our steps would take us much too far out of the way. The couple, who had joined in our discussion, lived in Ahwautkee, a suburb of Phoenix, and were traveling to their cabin up north for the holiday. They knew the area well. Instead of going back to where we started, which would take hours, they knew of another highway that cut across the state and would land us pretty close to home.

The man said, "Get back on Route 260 and go to 73, it's a ways from here, and you'll be behind the Sunrise Ski Resort. When you come off that road, you can go through Pine Top and head home that way. You might even make it in time if the weather holds."

The sky looked ominous; dark clouds were hovering, threatening a storm. Lisa took the wheel. She was concerned about how much time had passed, and even though we knew our timing was borderline, she decided not to call her boss. When we got closer, if it looked impossible, we'd stop along the way and she could make the call then. Once again, we thought we were heading home, but now we had very little time.

We'd been driving for about ten minutes when we spotted a highway decal that read **273,** in bold black letters. "Is that what they said?" Lisa asked me. "273?"

"That's what I remember," I answered. I didn't recall them saying it was this close, but the closer, the better. Right? We turned onto the back road into a sudden blustery wind. I shivered—it had gotten really cold and windy—and I turned up the heat. The skies were darkening, a light snow started falling, and within fifteen minutes it was coming down very hard. That was when visions of Dorothy and Toto battling the winds and running for cover came into my head—the storm was that sudden and severe. We put the car in four-wheel drive and I took the wheel. We slowed to five miles an hour. Now it was impossible to tell where we were, and stopping was not an option since we couldn't see three feet ahead of us. My hands and feet were tense. I felt anxious and determined to get us home, no matter how bad the storm became. I drove on into a strange stillness, as if we were climbing into the center of a bright, cold, stagnant world.

Lisa looked out her window. She could see absolutely nothing. Only one car had passed us from the other direction since we'd taken the turn. "I haven't seen a car for a long time," she said. "Are you sure we're on the right road?"

"I'm not sure of anything," I said, squinting through the glowing whiteness to try and see in front of me. "Should I pull over to the side of the road?" I asked. "Just until it lets up a little?"

"I don't know," Lisa said. "The storm doesn't look like it's going to let up anytime soon."

A heavy veil of snowflakes hung over us like a dreamy shroud as we drove farther into the unending white maze. We fell silent, each thinking our own fearful, disjointed thoughts. When we had driven for about thirty minutes (we hadn't covered much ground because I had to drive very slowly in the snowfall), our hypnotic reverie was interrupted by a sliding sensation beneath the tires. After we slid for a moment, we hit a snowbank. We stopped dead on a road that we couldn't see and there we sat. The engine revved as I tried to put the car in reverse. The wheels spun, the car teetered for a moment as if at the edge of something. We felt ourselves slipping forward and down a couple of inches. Then it was over. We were standing still. Much later, we learned that we had stopped in the center of the highway, and we were straddling the white line, facing in the wrong direction on a solid sheet of ice.

I tried to rock the car by switching it from drive to reverse and back to drive. It wouldn't budge. I turned the engine off. "Lisa," I said, "I know the snow is coming down hard, but we have to get out and try to move this car ourselves. Maybe we can chip the ice or something."

Lisa nodded, grabbing a ski pole to try to break up the ice under the tires. I stayed behind the wheel in case she made some headway, so I could drive the car forward. When nothing happened, I got out with my ski pole too, to try to break up the ice with her. It was solid; we weren't going anywhere, and still we tried. After about forty-five minutes of shivering and chipping unsuccessfully at the impenetrable ice block, we were freezing, soaking wet, and discouraged. It wasn't working. We got back in the car, our teeth chattering and our bodies shaking. I turned on the heater. Exhausted, we stripped off our wet clothes, put on some dry ones, and looked out the window to determine where we were. We knew which road we'd taken, it had been about an hour since we left the gas station, and now we were staring at a blinding cloudlike veil covering a blackened sky. We could have been anywhere in the world right then, the horizon was so foggy and nondescript.

Lisa looked scared. "What's going on?" she said. "What are we gonna do?"

"I guess we'll have to wait here for a snowplow," I said. We'd seen a number of them a few days ago, clearing the roads way up high on the Mongolian Rim, when we were headed in the opposite direction. It had been snowing then, but not this hard. "A plow'll be here any minute," I said, trying to reassure her.

"Yeah," Lisa agreed reluctantly. "I'm sure you're right, but I can forget getting to work today. I can't even call. I hope they're not too upset." Lisa had a reason to be nervous. She was on a tight budget and if she lost her job, it would set her back.

Any signs of testiness disappeared between us in the seriousness of the situation. I could see Lisa trying to control her panic. I knew I had to stay calm as we sat in the idling car, blasting the heat for a few minutes until we stopped shivering. Then I said, "We have to turn off the car now. If we use up all the gas, we won't be able to drive out of here when the plows come."

It was about one in the afternoon when we put down the backseat and climbed over the divider into the back area of the Blazer. Now we had some room to move, and we grabbed several sweaters, sweatshirts, and a couple of fresh pairs of socks. It was getting colder all the time and my feet felt slightly numb. I pulled on dry socks and a few extra layers of clothing, and climbed back into the front and sat. What wouldn't we have given for a cell phone? Thirteen years ago most people didn't have cell phones, so we never even thought about it. And then, the road we were on was so far off the beaten track, we might not have been able to get a line. I'm sure I was scared but I didn't allow myself to feel it fully or to admit it. What good would that have done?

We discussed our situation, asking each other if we were making the right decision to stay put. Finally, what else could we do? We were two young girls stuck in our car in unknown territory in the middle of a freezing blizzard. We turned the engine on at intervals during the day, warming ourselves for a few minutes and then turning it back off again, keeping our eyes and ears alert for signs of motion outside the car. We weren't mechanics, but we knew we needed to save the battery and any remaining gas.

By the time it got dark, it was still snowing and no one had come, not a snowplow or a patrol car. We began to feel hungry.

That was when I remembered the cinnamon roll from Purgatory that I had stashed in my bag. I found it, unwrapped it, broke it in half, and divided the half evenly. Thank goodness this is so large, I thought, munching away. I got thirsty and reached into the back for the soft drinks. I grabbed one and tried to open it. It was frozen solid. We looked at each other, dismayed. We were in for a very cold night, with half a cinnamon roll left, and a six-pack of frozen Diet Pepsis. I took my keys and sliced through the tin of one of the cans, scraping a little frozen soda off the top. I sucked on it. It was sweet and cold. This was not what I had in mind, but it was all there was.

"Lisa," I said, "I have to tell you something."

"What is it?"

"It looks like we're spending the night here."

Lisa looked at me with terrific fear in her eyes and I watched the panic begin to take over. Her breathing became shallow, tears poured down her cheeks, and she wiped them away quickly. It was so cold, she didn't want them freezing on her face. I tried to start the car again, to give her a little heat to calm her panic, but the engine wouldn't turn over. It never did again.

A few scattered trees were vaguely visible in the distance, camouflaged behind a blur of falling snow. Besides that, I could see nothing. I climbed into the back to look at what we had with us. We had gloves, parkas, long johns, ski pants, several sweatshirts, and a couple of sweaters. I decided to take out my contact lenses. My vision is somewhat blurry without them but my eyes were bothering me and I didn't need them because there was nothing to see. I stashed them carefully in their container of saline solution, and grabbed another pair of sweatpants to pull up over my jeans. Then I climbed into the front, where we spent the night, dozing a little bit, shivering, and holding each other for warmth. We didn't consider stretching out in the back to sleep. It might have been more comfortable but we wanted to be prepared for a patrol car or a snowplow. It must have been in the very early hours of the morning when we both fell asleep, and we opened our eyes at exactly the same moment. The sky was dark. I glanced at my wristwatch. It had a neon dial that lit up in the dark and the numbers were large enough to read without my lenses. It was 6:30 A.M. on December 24, Christmas Eve day, and the weather had gotten worse, if that was possible.

Shivering, we stared at each other blankly. What now? We climbed into the back and took out every article of clothing we had. We put them all on. I felt a little warmer now, except for my feet. They had never completely warmed up from yesterday. I had packed my makeup and cotton balls in Baggies, so I grabbed one from my makeup case, emptied it, and peed in it. I gave Lisa a Baggie and she did the same thing. Now it was time to get a clear view of where we were. I found my lens case and opened the container. I couldn't believe it; my contacts had frozen in the night, right in the saline solution, becoming so brittle, they cracked the moment I touched them. Great! Now I was stranded in a car in a howling blizzard with no heat and I couldn't see. I tossed the lens case back in my bag in frustration. There was nothing I could do, so I climbed into the front. Even though we were facing a ton of problems, there was no point in dwelling on them, because right here, right now, there were clearly no solutions.

When I tried to open my car door to throw my used Baggie out into the snow, it wouldn't budge. A solid block of ice had formed around my door and it was stuck closed. Thank God Lisa could get her door open a little bit. We tossed our Baggies into the snow and pulled her door shut. Then I climbed into the back again to look over our shoes. We each had a pair of ski boots and a pair of tennis shoes. They wouldn't do us a whole lot of good in the snow, but from the looks of things, we weren't about to do much walking. Three feet of snow must have fallen overnight. I wished we had some blankets with us, but no such luck.

I took what was left of the cinnamon roll, broke it in half, and we finished it off. I scraped at some Diet Pepsi and rolled the icy sweet stuff in my mouth, turning it into slush before I swallowed it. I wished we had brought water with us, and then I realized that even if we had, it would be frozen and there was no way to melt it. We got back in the front seat to wait. I was wearing so many clothes I felt like the abominable snowman. When my parents eventually saw me, I thought, they would probably laugh. I wondered what they were doing right then. I was in the habit of phoning them when I got back from a trip, to let them know I'd arrived safely. What were they thinking when there was no call? They must have phoned Mike, and he hadn't heard from me either. I knew how worried they had to be. I imagined climbing into my warm bed and falling into a deep sleep, but my throat was too dry to allow my mind to slip too far into such a comforting fantasy.

I looked outside again. There was no way to know how much it had snowed overnight; the windshield was a frozen sheet of ice, and the windows were automatic, so we couldn't have opened them if we wanted to. I wondered if the car was covered. Maybe we were buried alive. If we were, how would anyone ever find us to rescue us? What would we drink? Maybe we would have to eat snow until someone found us.

"I need to wipe off the top of the car," Lisa said, reading my mind. "If we're buried, how will anyone spot us?" She looked like she was in shock, ready to start crying again any second. She put on her ski boots and squeezed through her door opening, clutching a ski pole. The snow was up to her knees and the wind nearly knocked her over, blowing snow into her eyes. She struggled to sweep off the hood and roof of the car. What would have happened if her door hadn't opened? We'd be stuck in a freezing cold prison cell—buried alive. I shuddered and erased the thought from my mind. I needed to stay calm since Lisa looked panicky, like she would burst out crying at any moment, and she was shivering out of control. Anyway, it was only a matter of hours before we'd be found. I needed to hang on.

Lisa fell back into the car as if the wind had blown her in, her teeth chattering so hard, I got worried. I held her for a few minutes until she stopped shivering. It was dark and the wind was blowing so hard, we couldn't even consider walking away at this point. Then we sat, hardly moving the whole day. My thoughts kept returning to my parents. I could imagine them calling everyone they knew, trying to locate me. There was no way they could know that we had taken the wrong road. I had a really good sense of direction; I almost never got lost, but now, although we knew we were on 273, we had no idea where that was. I hoped my folks weren't suffering too much, but soon we would all be out of our misery. In a matter of a few hours, we'd be dry and warm, drinking hot chocolate. I kept seeing my father's face in front of me; he was the emotional one, but both he and my mother had to be worried sick.

3

Obstacles

WHEN I FAILED TO CONTACT MIKE THAT WEDNESDAY AFTERNOON, he'd called my mother in the late evening. We'd been gone overnight, and my mother was already sensing something—moms are like that, especially when it comes to trouble. I guess there was plenty of that when I was growing up, especially when I was a teenager. I was a decent student, I got mostly B's and a few C's, and I was a pretty wild kid, sneaking the car out at night while my parents slept, tormenting Jason, my younger brother, partying and carrying on—no worse than other kids my age, but definitely no better either. And yet, although my mother, Robin, and I were like oil and water, there was a bond between us, an unspoken love and loyalty that neither of us ever questioned. We just knew it was there, a powerful sense of connection that never wavered. While I sat in the car, stranded and freezing in the midst of that never-ending blizzard, my parents were foremost in my mind. I knew they were upset, but I had no idea the extent of it. In fact, until recently, I couldn't have fathomed the nitty-gritty of what my family and friends went through while I was missing. Not all of it. Now, thirteen years later, as we reminisce and review the events for this book, here's what I found out:

Mike's phone call clinched my mother's discomfort. She was terrified for me but she decided not to wake up my father until

she determined the seriousness of the situation. They owned
and operated a commercial photo lab, and since my dad worked
the early-morning schedule, my mother let him sleep. Jason got
home late that night and found my mother up, watching television in the living room. My mother told him she hadn't heard
from me, but he avoided any in-depth discussion. He was sixteen, it was Christmas vacation, and he and his friends had been
"partying hearty." Since he didn't want our mother to smell al-
cohol on his breath, he scurried off to bed, relieved that his rev-
elry had gone undetected, unaware of the implications of my
absence.

My mom paced the living room all night long, finally speaking to Lisa's mother, Bernadine (affectionately known as Bunny).
She called her at about five A.M. on Christmas Eve day, to learn
that there had been no sign of Lisa either. When Michael, my
dad, woke up to go to work, my mom was still up. She told him
what was going on. He drove the twenty minutes or so to Phoenix
to open the shop, but once the help was there, he came right
back home. In the meantime, my mom called the police to report
us missing, whereupon she encountered her first stunning obsta-
cle, with many more to follow. The police were unsympathetic
about our disappearance, reminding her that at eighteen and
nineteen years old, Lisa and I were adults. That meant they
couldn't launch a search for at least forty-eight hours. Not unless
there was evidence of foul play, which there wasn't. Besides, what
made them think we hadn't stayed away voluntarily? We were
grown-ups, maybe we didn't want to come home for Christmas
Eve, they suggested. These things happened all the time.

"Jami isn't like that," my mother told the officer at the other
end of the line. "We're close. She always calls me whenever she
gets home from a trip."

"Did you have any fights or misunderstandings?" they asked.

"No," my mother said adamantly. "Jami wouldn't dream of
spending Christmas Eve anywhere else."

The policeman was unimpressed. My mother hung up the
phone frustrated, and took off for work. She cried all day and she
called my answering machine over and over while my dad and my

uncle Peter got into a four-wheel drive, retracing the route we should have taken. They drove up into mountain country, where it snowed most of the winter, passing beneath the Mongolian Rim, taking the various tributary roads that veered off from Phoenix. When they arrived in Payson, Arizona, a small mountain town an hour and a half northeast of Phoenix, the weather stopped them. The snow was so treacherous, even a four-wheel drive couldn't get through, so they stopped at the police station, where they got the same resistance as my mother: We were adults and we were entitled not to come home. I was probably a teenage runaway, the police officer said, but I was too old for them to chase after. He added that if a few more days went by and my parents still hadn't heard from me, they would start looking. Just because my dad claimed I was so close to them, the officer said, how did he know I felt the same way? He wondered why every parent thought their kid was some kind of saint.

My dad assured them I was not a saint, but I was not a runaway either. The police were jaded, they had seen too many unsuspecting parents with kids who couldn't wait to be old enough to get away. Besides, Christmas was coming and it was snowing hard. This was no time to launch a search, especially when they weren't convinced that we were missing. My dad left the police station angry, and he and my uncle continued driving through the heavy snow as best they could, pulling off the sides of the road, looking down into ravines in case we'd crashed, stopping at motels to see if we'd been spotted.

While my mother put our friends and family on the alert, she had someone run off a flyer of Lisa and me, with our pictures and the word MISSING printed across the top. The flyer included our names, ages, and descriptions and a description of the car: a 1986 red Chevy Blazer truck with a luggage rack, license plate number DFR164. The flyer also reported when we were last seen and it gave a police contact number in New Mexico as well as the number of the criminal investigation unit of the Department of Public Safety in Arizona. My mom had called the Gallup police, since that was our last known sighting, to let them know she had a situation.

They'd given her the same story: Without evidence of foul play, the police were not authorized to do anything besides distribute bulletins. They would make an "attempt to locate," but beyond that, they were powerless. My mother was forlorn; she knew something terrible had happened. She decided at that moment that if the police were not willing to begin a search, she and my father would launch one of their own.

Family members and friends began to congregate at our house on Christmas Eve. At four the next morning, after another sleepless night for my mother with no word of encouragement from anywhere, my father grabbed a handful of flyers and left the house with his brother-in-law to drive up north. This time, he headed all the way to Gallup, our city of departure. He showed our faces around at all the local markets and gas stations and he asked questions. Had anyone seen us? What about the car? We had to have eaten and gotten gas somewhere. Why didn't anyone remember us? One gas-station attendant was accommodating enough to go through all his receipts from the last several days, but our names didn't show up.

My father got a few vague responses. Someone here or there thought they had seen us but they couldn't recall if it had been before or after our ski trip. Someone even said they thought they might have spotted us in a truck, but they had no more details. While other friends took their cars out to search adjoining roads, my dad and my uncle continued all the way to Flagstaff on Route 40, stopping everywhere they could along the way, turning up nothing.

My mother's brother, Mark, and my aunt Tona, who lived next door, were in St. Louis, Missouri, for the holiday. They had a three-month-old baby boy named Tyler, and they were visiting Tona's parents. My mother decided not to call them; what good would it do to worry them? When they returned, she would know more and they could join the revolving-door chaos that was forming in our living room. When Tona and Mark returned a day or so later, Tyler had an intestinal flu, so my aunt alternated between the doctor's office and the doom and gloom of my parents' house. It was a rough time for everyone.

Meanwhile, my grandparents arrived from Chicago. I think I should take a moment here to tell you about my mother's father, Seymour, the patriarch of the family. Seymour (we all called him Poppy) and I were very close. I created his nickname when I couldn't say "Poppa," and the whole family picked it up and ran with it. A greatly revered member of our tight-knit family, Poppy was a real Colin Powell type, a "take charge" kind of guy who showed up whenever there was a crisis, ordered the troops, and the rest of us obeyed without question. He was someone who didn't buckle under pressure, refused to show signs of weakness, and no one had ever seen him cry, not even my grandmother . . . until Christmas of 1987. For the first time in the history of our family, Poppy walked through the door of my parents' house hunched over, looking ancient, and he fell into my mother's arms, sobbing. His distress careened the family into profound feelings of helplessness and insecurity, as it was terrifically unsettling to see the patriarch so devastated. They had always looked to him for strength. My mother was anticipating the arrival of her dad, the family rock, solid and steady and filled with hope. Instead, the rock was crumbling right before her eyes.

Poppy's wife, my grandmother Shirley, took out her frustrations in the kitchen. Looking straight ahead, she made vast amounts of food for the circus gathered in the living room, never allowing herself to think the worst as people came and went, day after day. One regular visitor was Cheryl, a woman with a parrot on her shoulder who gave everybody psychic messages and, later, gave massages at the hospital. Grandma cooked for everyone, nonstop, feeding the masses, including the children playing all over the house and the adults who were answering phones, offering moral support, and keeping up on the latest news.

On Christmas afternoon, the presents lay unopened next to the fireplace. Channel 10, one of the local TV stations, was good enough to put my mother and Bunny on the ten-o'clock news, so the story was out, which kicked the police into gear—somewhat. They actually didn't show up fully until a week later, shamed into doing a search by continuous press coverage. No one understood why they were so reticent. On January 5, 1988, several days after we were found, the *Arizona Republic,* a local newspaper, published a critical article, admonishing the police department for dismissing my parents' early cries for help.

The article begins:

> When the word goes out that someone is lost in the desert or stranded on a mountain, little expense is spared to mount a rescue. The emergency squads move into high gear, indifferent to whether the individual's predicament was caused by outside forces or was brought about by inexperience or stupidity.
>
> What happened then, in the case of two young valley women—Lisa Barzano . . . and Jami Goldman . . . who were reported missing two days before Christmas? Because of an apparent absence of official concern, they endured [eleven] days of numbing cold, stranded in a snowbank in the White Mountains.
>
> Officials showed no sense of urgency. Their attitude can best be described as cavalier. Despite pleas from the parents of the two missing women, nearly a week elapsed after their disappearance before the Department of Public Safety made any attempt to coordinate a statewide search.

Why the authorities dragged their feet, no one knew. Thirteen years later, we still don't. Why my parents had to hire a private investigator to do what the police should have been doing, I also have no idea. I only know that it shouldn't have been that way. We shouldn't have spent Christmas freezing, thirsty, and stranded on a road that three hours prior had been open to the public, officially designated by the U.S. Forest Service as a Christmas-tree-cutting area. Our parents shouldn't have suffered and we shouldn't have suffered either, but we did. "Shouldn't" can be such a useless word.

4

When Hell Froze Over

I SPENT CHRISTMAS EVE STRETCHED OUT IN THE BACK OF THE BLAZER. When I awakened to a painfully dry throat on Christmas morning, nothing had changed except that a network of icicles had formed on the inside of the car, like stalactites on the roof of a cave. It was Day Two and no one had come, not the police, not a snowplow, and there were no signs of Santa or any reindeer tracks. Lisa and I climbed over into the front seat and started talking. It's funny how self-centered you become when you're stuck in one place with no distractions. I'm not a patient person to begin with, and as we talked about our fears and frustrations, I found myself irritated and disappointed. Where was everyone? Why hadn't they found us? It's not like we were in some godforsaken hick town in the middle of nowhere, or that nobody knew we were gone. We were less than an hour away from the gas station, we'd driven at only five miles an hour, and three people knew we had taken this road. We had to be close enough to be found. In fact, the couple and the attendant had suggested we go this way, so why hadn't they contacted the police? Didn't they care? Where were the snowplows, the helicopters, the Sno-Cats that rescue people who get stuck in storms?

It snowed the whole day long and into the night. It was endless darkness; I only knew it was daytime because my watch glowed in the dark. Once or twice during that long cold day, I detected a slight glare in the sky—the storm had let up, but not for long. The darkness quickly returned. From time to time, we thought we heard aircraft overhead, and one of us got out of the car intermittently to brush off the hood and the top. It was tough; the cold stung our faces and took our breath away, the wind nearly blew us over, and the driving snow made it impossible to see.

The biggest problem for both of us was our throats; we were so thirsty, we could hardly swallow. Once I grabbed a handful of snow and ate it. It almost sizzled on the warmth of my tongue when I swallowed it hungrily, but it did nothing to quench my thirst. In fact it made it worse. I discovered later that for some unknown reason, eating snow always made people more thirsty, but I didn't know that at the time. I went back to Diet Pepsi slush. As I patiently scraped the soda with a key and swallowed the sticky brownish slush, I thought of the old expression "When hell freezes over." I guess this was it. Hell had frozen over and Lisa and I were stuck in the middle of it.

We had a backgammon game with us, the small, traveling kind, and we played a few rounds, but it was hard to stay interested. Then we discovered my brother Jason's baseball cards. He was a bona fide baseball nut and his trading cards were scattered all over the floor of the Blazer, so we gathered them. We found enough to make up a deck of playing cards; we wrote suits and numbers on them and played War and Rummy 500. It made us feel better, just to forget for a minute, but mostly, we stared into the emptiness and imagined being rescued. The day inched forward with no changes, no movement, no nothing. It was just Lisa and me, sitting, playing cards, talking, hoping, silently despairing, dozing, waiting—for something, anything. We stared at the red interior, the same color as the paint on the outside of the car. Everything including us was dark and red and gloomy and nothing happened.

Toward the evening of the third day, I was dazed, disoriented, and very, very cold. But my thirst overpowered everything else, even hunger, and kept me unaware of how cold and numb my feet were becoming. Toward the end of the day, I checked my watch, my lifeline to the outside world. Night had fallen. Another day had come and gone and no one had found us. We climbed into the back area, cuddling close together for warmth. Where were we? How long would the storm keep up? Where were my parents and why hadn't they done anything? Was this a dream? Would I wake up in the morning and it would all be over? Surely something had to change tomorrow.

I comforted myself with the sound of Lisa's breath. It was a sign of life in a bleak empty world devoid of movement or noise. What would the morning bring? How would I quench this savage thirst? It was inconceivable to me that nobody had come. We're right here, I thought, where *is* everyone? I wondered for a moment if I was thinking it or saying it out loud. I'm here, Mom and Dad, in this car in the middle of a blizzard. That was my last thought before I drifted into a dreamless sleep, as dark and empty as the day had been.

On December 26, when I awakened, I was immediately aware of my nagging thirst. That was the same as yesterday, but something was different. I forced my eyes open and then shut them quickly. It was the sun—it had come out, and the world had shifted from darkness to a blinding brilliance that reflected in prisms off the dripping windshield. The ice was melting. I struggled to become conscious and to accustom my eyes to the light. I felt a rare surge of joy as my hope surfaced. It was like somebody had switched on the light for the first time in three days and the gloom had lifted. If the sun was out, we could get out of here. I peed into a Baggie to discover I'd gotten my period overnight. What a bad piece of timing! I shuffled around in my bag and found a box of tampons. Thank goodness for that.

I shook Lisa. She was awake, looking almost relieved. It was the light. I climbed over to the front, leaving Lisa alone to do her own morning ritual, and I slid onto a soaking wet seat. Yuch! The icicles on the inside of the car had melted in the warmth of the sun. I wiped off Lisa's side and she joined me in the front.

"Nobody's coming," she said.

"Yeah," I agreed. "Let's get out of here. But we need to leave a note," I suggested, "in case somebody finds the car while we're walking away."

Lisa had a Day Planner so she tore out a page, took out her pen and wrote a note. I don't know what finally happened to it—neither of us have it—but it went something like this:

We are Jami Goldman and Lisa Barzano. We've been in this car since Wednesday, December 23rd. We're stuck here on Highway 273 and we're walking toward the beginning of the road, following the path that got us here. We can't see very well and we don't know where we are, but we think we're walking in the same direction we drove. We're leaving now, at 10 A.M. on Saturday morning.

We took off our ski pants, we put on every article of clothing we had, and we pulled our ski pants on top of all of it, as well as our jackets, gloves, and ski boots. My feet hurt pretty badly right then but I didn't say anything. I knew we had to press on. Whatever was wrong, my parents would help me once I was back home. I grabbed a ski pole to help me walk and I tried my door. It was still frozen solid, even in the sun. Lisa's door worked, though, maybe because we'd been opening and closing it. I placed the note on the dashboard and climbed over Lisa's body. Since she was much smaller than I, we decided I would go first. She could walk behind me and if she started to fall, she could use my tracks to steady herself. I looked her in the eye, as if to ask if she was ready. She offered me a weak smile, which I returned. We were going home. I squeezed out the door and took my first step outside in the sunlight.

I fell into snow up to my knees. I took another step and stopped, breathless. Now the snow was up to my thighs. It was worse than I'd imagined. The heaviness of my ski boots was no help at all; they felt leaden, they tilted my feet at a weird angle, and they didn't bend. They were not built for walking, but they were better protection than tennis shoes. The cold hurt my face so much, it felt like it was cutting through my skin. I couldn't ever remember feeling such biting cold, not when I was skiing or at any other time. I learned later that when the sun comes out after a long, intense blizzard, the air currents travel in such a way as to cause the temperature to plummet. That morning when we tried to walk out, the temperature was 21 degrees below zero, much colder than it had been previously and the coldest it would be that entire winter.

I looked back at Lisa. I was trying to make a path for her and she was following in my footsteps as best she could. With each step, the snow was so high, I could only see the top part of her body. Neither of us had any idea how much snow had fallen in three days, and I could see that Lisa was working really hard and that she was terrified. I looked in front of me at a blank sheet of white. I didn't know where the road was. Our tire tracks from three days prior had been covered with freshly fallen snow. I could see what looked like trees way off in the distance, but I had no idea how far it was to the end of the road—or if there was an end at all. As it later turned out, the car had twisted when we stopped abruptly, and we were facing in the wrong direction, so which way to walk would have been anybody's guess.

It was still worth a try. I walked forward a few more steps. It was agonizingly slow going, because it was up to my thighs and I was weak from lack of food and water. I stopped to catch my breath. I took another step or two; maybe I had covered a hundred yards when I looked back to check on Lisa, only to watch her collapse in the snow. I couldn't see her anymore and I carefully made my way back to her, using my own tracks for walking. She lay there, not moving, but when I stood over her, she looked up at me, sobbing hysterically. Her breath was shallow, as if something was gripping her throat. "I can't do this, Jami," she managed to gasp out. "I don't have enough strength. If you want to go ahead, you can, but I can't go on. I'm sorry."

I looked at the infinite blanket of coldness that spread out in front of me, uninterrupted as far as I could see. Lisa coughed hard, rasping. She couldn't stop until she spit blood onto the snow, destroying the purity of the monochromatic scene—obscene red paint splattered on a whitewashed canvas with no beginning or ending. There was no way I could leave her like this. She continued to cough up blood and mucus as I grabbed her and supported her under the shoulders and we trudged back through the freezing powder toward the car. She held on to me with as much strength as she could muster. I wondered if I could have kept going on my own. I doubted it; we hadn't even lost sight of the car and I was exhausted. With no idea where the road was, there was very little chance of finding anyone to help. The thought of dying out in the middle of a deserted snowbound valley was too awful. I continued to put one foot in front of the other, dragging Lisa with me. I was unaware that my steps back to the car held great significance—they were the last ones I would ever take on my own two feet.

We squeezed back into the passenger side of the car. I climbed over Lisa into the driver's seat and there we were again. As if we'd never left. The note sat on the windshield, right where I'd left it. I yanked it off, discouraged. The only thing that had changed was that our feet were now hopelessly soaked and so were all of our socks. Lisa was crying and coughing; her eyes were bloodshot and watery. I felt so helpless. I wished there was something I could do to make her feel better. I remembered some cough drops in my backpack. I found them and as soon as she sucked on one, she felt a little bit better and she stopped crying.

"Maybe I should try to walk out of here without you," I said. "It might be our only hope."

"I don't know," Lisa answered. "I don't think we should separate."

"But I could bring someone back to help you," I said.

"No." She was adamant now and her voice held an edge of panic. "What if you don't make it back? I couldn't do this by myself. Could you?"

The answer was no. We had gone through this together and had gotten strength from each other. Alone, I wasn't so sure. What if I wandered off into the wilderness, saw no one, and then I couldn't find my way back to the car? What if I ran out of strength and couldn't go on? I was extremely depleted from lack of food and water. It was better for us to stay together. Besides, now that the sun was out, we could melt snow and try to quench our terrible thirst.

We each ate a cough drop. I rifled through my bag and found my contact lens case. I certainly didn't need it for my lenses any-

more. When I pulled the lid off and emptied the case, I had a perfect receptacle to melt snow. I stretched across Lisa, opened her
door, and scooped up a fistful of clean snow, stashing it in a plastic bag. Then I put a small amount of snow in the lens case and
placed it on the dashboard to melt in the sun. We put our feet on
the dashboard, reveling in the warmth, and waited. I expected
the snow would melt quickly, the sun felt so warm, but it didn't. It
took close to an hour to get one sip, and then there was the task
of sharing it. We were so thirsty, each time a tiny amount of snow
melted, we could barely stop ourselves from drinking it all right
down, but we had to share. Caring for each other was just as important to our own survival as caring for ourselves. Once or twice,
when we swallowed more than a sip, it made us as thirsty as eating
a handful of snow, so a sip at a time was the right recipe. The
process took up most of the day as we melted and sipped, grateful
for something to do.

An hour or so later, Lisa was the first one to notice her feet. I
can easily call it the saddest moment of the ordeal when she took
off her socks. I'd felt pain and tingling in my own feet since the
first day when we walked outside in tennis shoes to try to break up
the ice. Our feet never had really warmed up, but the pain wasn't
too bad because they'd gotten so numb, it was easy to overlook
them. Now Lisa noticed that her feet were hideously discolored
and swollen.

"Jami," she said, "take your socks off."

"What?"

"I want to have a look at your feet."

"Why?" I said.

"Just do it."

She sounded frightened so I took off my socks. My feet were
thick, blue, and purplish, the veins were extended, and they
looked bruised and puffy, like they were retaining liquid, particularly on the toes and insteps. Just like Lisa's. I checked my hands.
They were okay and so were Lisa's, but our feet most definitely
were not.

"I think we have frostbite," I told her.

"What's frostbite?" she said, almost angry. "What in hell are you talking about?" Lisa had moved to the Arizona desert when she was eight. Nobody in Arizona got frostbite.

"When your feet get really cold, they freeze. That's frostbite."

Enough said. Besides, that was all I knew about it. Now we had to do something. We both climbed into the back and started massaging each other's feet. Then we massaged our own but the color didn't change. In retrospect, I don't think our feet were totally frostbitten yet, I expect it was a gradual deterioration process. The trouble was that over the many days to follow, even though we kept our feet on the dashboard whenever the sun was out, it wasn't warm enough to reverse what had taken hold. We kept our feet in the sun anyway, not for any sort of instant gratification, it didn't even feel all that wonderful. It just felt like our duty to keep our feet as warm as possible, in order to survive.

We tried sitting on each other's feet for a while, thinking our backsides would provide more warmth than our hands could. I still remember staring across at Lisa's long brown hair stuffed into a ski hat, while we played cards and tried to sit on each other's feet. Our knees banged together and it was almost impossible to balance, so we didn't stay in that position for very long, but the attempt set us into our only bout of laughter I can recall in the entire eleven days. It might have been the only time we smiled. The rest of the time, we lived in a constant state of sadness.

And so it went, day after uneventful day. The foot incident marked a switch in our emotional roles. I didn't panic or sob or scream, that wasn't my way. Instead, I slipped into a state of depression and dread, turning so far inward, it must have felt to Lisa like I disappeared. She recognized what was happening to me and she rallied to help, offering any comfort and soft words she could think of. It was all a lesson in survival that we learned by trial and error, as we fell into rituals that we performed unemotionally—as if they were our unspoken duties.

It went like this:

Each morning, after trying to sleep cuddled up for warmth in the back of the Blazer, we would get up and pee into a Baggie. We were peeing only once a day because we were so dehydrated (Lisa got her period, also), and we had no bowel movements after the first day because we weren't eating anything. We would climb into the front, dump the Baggies, gather snow, and start melting. Fortunately, it didn't snow again. We got warmth from the sun in the front seat and our lives took on the rhythm of survival as we cried, holding on to each other, hardly sleeping, waiting and watching and wondering what was to become of us. Neither of us had any dreams we could remember. We never slept deeply enough for that.

When I felt like talking, I told Lisa stories about my extended family. She was amazed by all my aunts and uncles and cousins, and she talked about her family, too, which was a small unit. While we reminisced and told our tender and silly stories about our loved ones, we silently wondered if we would ever see these people again. We didn't say that out loud, we tried to stay positive and strong for each other, but we both wondered on a daily basis if we would get out of there alive.

And yet, we never screamed or hit the walls of the car. We didn't do anything that dramatic, at first because we expected to get found any minute, and later because we had no energy to do anything besides melt snow, warm our feet, and visualize our rescue. We certainly each did our share of crying, but to our credit, we never had a breakdown at the same time. It wasn't something we planned, it was just what happened. If I cried or got upset, Lisa kept her shit together until I was through. I would ask through my tears, "Where's my mom? Where's my dad? Where are Mike and Adam? Why aren't they out looking for us?"

She would hug me and say, "They're looking for us, Jami. They're gonna show up any minute." And I would do the same for her.

My family and I had planned a trip to Mexico the day after Christmas. When I was in my deepest despair, I imagined they'd gone without me and were having a wonderful time. Lisa assured me they would never do that. When she cried for her family, I comforted her, reminding her that this was the day we'd be found. We gave each other the strength and the faith not to lose hope, even though we were always thirsty, hungry, cold, and disappointed.

Over the years, as I think back about that frozen frame of

eleven days, my mind plays tricks, forgetting the bad and holding on to the good, so it's a challenge to remember the details. What I do recall is that we repeated certain patterns each day that made us feel secure. For example, we always sat in the same seats on the same side of the car; I was behind the wheel and Lisa was in the passenger seat. We melted snow in the same way, we talked for certain periods of time and observed silence for others, without ever discussing it. I guess in my case, these rituals offered me a sorely needed sense of structure and stability, something familiar that grounded me and allowed me to feel I was caring effectively for myself and for Lisa. I felt protective of her all the time, partly for her, partly for my own selfish reasons. If she died, I didn't think I could make it. One of my worst nightmares was an image of me sitting next to a dead body in the front seat of the car. I simply could not have done that. I don't think I could have dumped her body out in the snow, either. It's a terrible thing to think about, but it's something I considered, especially toward the end. I bet she thought about it, too, but I never believed we would die out there. Not really. I just couldn't accept that as a possibility. I had too much left to do and too many people whom I cared about—which, I believe, is a good part of the reason I am here today to tell my story.

The days were long, the nights were much longer, and they all blended together. I awoke each morning wrapped up in close to half a dozen T-shirts, a couple of sweatshirts, a ski jacket, and every pair of pants I had, knowing exactly where I was. I never was disoriented and, at the same time, I always was with my family. Or to be more accurate, they were with me. Not physically, of course. It was more like a vivid imagining, seeing my parents' and grandparents' faces looking at me, soothing me, reassuring me. I reassured them too, as I knew they were beside themselves with grief. It's not that I spoke out loud to them, there was no communication like that. But I felt them with me all the time, reaching out to me, letting me know they were doing everything in their power to find me. It was as if my spirit flashed my loved ones' faces in my mind's eye constantly, protecting me by making sure I never forgot who they were and how much we loved each other.

5

The Spook

JUST AS LISA AND I FELL INTO A RHYTHM OF SURVIVAL DURING THOSE stressful days, so did my parents. My father went to bed early at night, got up at four each morning, opened the lab, came back home, and went out searching. My mother stayed up most of the night drowning in anxiety, caught a few hours of sleep on a good day, got up when my father got home from work, and went to the office, unless she sat for a TV interview. She did TV, my father did radio, and they had very little time alone with each other, partly because they were living different schedules, partly because they didn't want to discuss the horror of what might be. One night, though, they sat on the couch together and broke down, sobbing, asking each other out loud what in hell was going on. What could have happened and what were they missing? When they were suddenly interrupted by Jason and a friend who came walking out of his room, they pulled it together. They didn't want their son to see them like that, so they snapped out of it and didn't go back there again.

The next day, Jason contacted a friend whose dad was vice-president of a multimillion-dollar real-estate corporation. When he offered my parents the use of a helicopter, the pilot and an assistant went on a search over the areas where we possibly could have been. Between that search and the private detective my par-

ents found in the yellow pages (it was tough getting hold of anyone over the Christmas holiday), there was a lot of action. But
no results. It was as if we had disappeared off the face of the
earth without leaving a trace. There were no accident reports
from the police that matched our description, the private detective found nothing, the air search revealed the same. And so my
father was surprised when he called my mother from across the
state during a long day of land searching. "Just checking in,
Robin," he said.

"Oh, Michael," my mother said, "thank God you called. Please
come home right away."

"But I just got up here. I'm not through looking yet. What
happened?"

"Please," she said, "don't ask any questions."

"Why? What's going on?"

"If you love me, just come home."

He agreed and got back in the car. When he got home, the
pain and sorrow of my parents' dilemma was about to take a leap
into the realm of the bizarre. It seems that a family friend knew
someone who knew someone who was connected with the CIA
who would be willing to help. This vague "someone" supposedly
knew about a drug ring in Colorado and New Mexico that abducted young girls on weekend ski trips, drugged them, and sold
them into white slavery and prostitution. Or they murdered them
in the New Mexican desert. These horrific scenarios were only
the beginning in a series of perverse possibilities this man described. He had contacts all over the West, people in shadowy
places who were part of the underground. If something of this nature had happened to Lisa and me (he was pretty sure it must
have, since there were no signs of us or the car for five days), he
would find out the truth. In fact, during their first phone call this
man said he would be willing to meet with my father and discuss
what could be done. But no cops. From the moment my uncle
Les heard about this strange character, he labeled him the Spook
and the name stuck.

The police had finally kicked in, launching a search when we
were still gone after nearly a week. But my parents felt no loyalty

toward them since they had done so little to help from the start. They never thought of looking for us in the area where we were stuck, not during the blizzard or after. My mother felt that we must have been abducted, what else could possibly have happened, so they had a day of clandestine phone calls while they made arrangements. Every strange thing occurred as the Spook set up a private meeting at his home; he even backed out once, calling to say that he'd changed his mind. He no longer wanted to pursue this thing owing to a sudden falling-out with the people who had referred him. It was something about them giving my parents his direct phone number without his consent. That's when my mother got on the line to beg and plead with him not to abandon them. He was their only hope. After my mother assured him that the people with whom he was feuding could easily be left out of the loop, the mysterious man acquiesced. The meeting was on.

My dad and my uncle Les got in the car and headed for a modest, unremarkable house in West Phoenix, to meet a strange man in whom they were suddenly placing all their hopes. Although he still says little about it, I know that meeting was far more difficult than my father will ever let on. I can only imagine how it felt to sit at a kitchen table with a gray-eyed fiftyish man in cowboy boots, worn jeans, and a flannel shirt (the Marlboro man with a hard edge), while he espoused nauseating scenarios about what happens to young unsuspecting girls who do drugs with bad people. He even accused my boyfriend, Mike, of being involved in my disappearance. Amid a backdrop of photos of himself with celebrities like Ronald Reagan and other famous politicians, the Spook gave few instructions and didn't volunteer his name. He took no notes and offered no encouragement. He asked for a four-wheel drive and $7,500 in cash.

After an unsuccessful attempt at convincing this man that neither Lisa nor I were drug addicts, my father agreed to return the next day with the cash and the car he had requested. He assured him no authorities would be contacted, but would he mind telling them where he intended to go and what he intended to do? The Spook was not big on details. He would only affirm that he needed the car to cover back-road territory, and he needed the money for expenses like food and motels, and to pay people off for information. He said he would follow my trail wherever it went, that there were no guarantees, but if I was alive he would find me. He also added that if he did indeed successfully track me down, he wanted an additional $20,000—whether I was alive or dead. He would give them twenty-four hours to bring him the supplies he requested, and all terms were nonnegotiable.

When my father got home, he and my mother gathered the family into the living room to debate the situation. Needless to say, it seemed unreal, like something out of a bad TV docudrama, so far-fetched it might have been laughable. But no one had seen a sense of humor in days. They were desperate, the police were doing next to nothing, the family already was in enormous pain and they didn't want to create more. But something had to be done. They were leaning toward hiring this man as a last resort, but what if he was not who he professed to be? What if he took off with the money? What if they ended up needing the authorities later, and secretly hiring this man created a greater rift between them and the police? Suddenly, Poppy, who had been silent and brooding since the beginning, stood up. Everyone went silent. He began by saying that the Spook had his full support; at least he was offering something tangible. Then he went around the room, asking each person for a vote. When they got to the end, it was unanimous. They would hire the Spook.

To this day, my father cries when he remembers how willing everyone was to help, no matter what he needed. When he arrived at the door of his friend Jim and asked for his four-wheel drive for a week, Jim handed him the keys, no questions asked. After assuring Jim that whatever happened to the car, they would take care of it, my parents went to West Phoenix the next morning with the car and the money in hand. Although the Spook asked them to say nothing about *him* to the press, he encouraged my parents to get as much publicity as possible while he was out searching for the next few days, as it would discourage kidnappers from harming us. Then he took off, promising to call if he came up with anything at all. Strangely, the family felt a release. It wasn't that they were comfortable with the situation or any of the possible outcomes. It was just that something was finally being done, and the Spook's sense of certainty and the way he'd taken charge offered them a short respite from their ceaseless anxiety.

During this time, my mother got an extra phone line installed, since our home had become "Search Central." It generally takes weeks after placing such an order to have it okayed and then get on the installation schedule, but my aunt Vicki took charge. She was a cracker; the phone line was connected in twenty-four hours. Again, the kindness of people and their efforts to help was overwhelming.

My parents did no physical searching for the next three days, something that my father came to regret, but he needed a break. Instead, they concentrated on daily TV and radio appearances, while they fielded a variety of disturbing rumors. Many of my friends, along with my best friend, Brittney, who lived in the same apartment complex as I did, posted MISSING flyers at bus stations, train stations, and anywhere else they could think of. From then on, calls started coming in to the police and my parents from all over the state, reporting Jami and Lisa sightings, all fraudulent, often grisly and deeply disturbing.

We were seen in Phoenix, Scottsdale, and Flagstaff, in truck stops, diners, and coffee shops, all at the same hour. We were spotted at the state border twice, each time with an unidentified male driver supposedly at the wheel of our Blazer. Brittney heard that we had been seen eating in a diner with an older man, but she knew in her heart that it wasn't true, that if we were with someone, it would have been against our will. That would rule out the possibility of our calmly eating a meal with our abductor. One of the more convincing reports was that we had been spotted in Kingman, Arizona, getting into a truck with a rough character and taking off with him. The report had not mentioned whether or not we appeared willing to be with him, and it was impossible to discern who he was or where we'd gone.

On the seventh day, after constant criticism and prodding from my parents on local TV news reports, a task force was formed, headed by the Department of Public Safety (DPS), to search for us. Senator John McCain from Arizona appeared on the news, informing people that he was contacting the FBI to join the search, now that sightings had gone beyond the confines of the state line. Their efforts would include Arizona, New Mexico, Nevada, and California, eventually spreading through the entire western half of the United States, which only brought more rumors to light. Additional sightings were reported—while we sat in the car, somewhere in the middle of the White Mountains, a red speck in a vast white wilderness, along a stretch of an impassable rural highway that was covered in a blanket of fresh snow.

Amid the rumors, there was a real sighting of a red Chevy Blazer in the snow somewhere, but it wasn't ours. Someone managed to spot another red car in the snow as well, but it was quickly identified as a sedan of some sort. They also found a red car on its back in a remote area called Salt River Canyon, but it turned out to be a red pickup truck that had been in a wreck a year and a half prior and was never removed. The worst of all was when the police called my father and told him two girls had been found dead in a car, and they suspected it was us. Before they met my dad at the morgue, would he please send them my dental records? Devastated, my father kept the information between himself and my mother, loath to unnecessarily upset the rest of the family until he knew for sure. They ordered my dental records and thank goodness, they didn't match. It was just one more agonizing false story during that excruciating period of time—the worst torture they ever had gone through.

From all that they have told me, it seems that the agony of not knowing was worse psychologically than what Lisa and I were going through. Granted, we were trapped, freezing and thirsty, but at least we knew where we were. It got so bad for my dad, he took a risk one day and called a friend on the Phoenix police force while the Spook was still out searching. "I have to know something," he said, "but please, just answer the question and don't ask me to elaborate."

His friend agreed.

"Is there really a drug ring in Colorado, Arizona, and New Mexico, that abducts girls who ski?"

"Yes, there is," he answered quite simply.

Three days after the Spook had gone out, he called and asked my parents to meet him at his house. The ride there was hellish; neither of them said a word. When they finally were sitting at the Spook's kitchen table once again, he reported on his mission. He had followed our supposed route, going off the beaten track at intervals and meeting with a variety of anonymous people along the way. He had visited back alleys and bars deep in the heart of the Indian reservations, he'd spread the money among winos, junkies, pushers, pimps, and the rest of his extensive underworld grapevine connections, all with the same result. Nothing. Yes, there really was a drug ring and no, we had *not* been abducted. If we had been, he would know, of that he was certain. He turned over a list of his expenses including motel rooms, food, a new set of tires, and gas. Then he handed my father more than half the unused money and he fell silent.

"What's the bottom line?" my father asked.

"I think the girls are probably dead," he said. "If they weren't, I would have found them."

That was the first time anyone had spoken the *d* word out loud. My parents' drive home was another silent one. On one hand, they felt relieved to know that I hadn't been abducted or worse, that was their belief, but they also felt an odd kind of disappointment. When they'd believed that the Spook was on to something, it was a matter of waiting for a solid answer. Now that he'd come up empty, here they were again—not knowing. Back to Square One.

6

We're Here

A VIBRATING SOUND OVERHEAD INTERRUPTED OUR SOLITUDE SOME-
time at the beginning of the second week. The sun was high,
we were in our usual positions, our feet thrown up on the dashboard, dozing in delirium while snow melted in a variety of con-
tainers: my contact lens case, the top of a hair spray container,
and a couple of extra plastic bags. It looked like a strange little
snow-melting lab. When I heard the roar overhead after hearing
next to nothing for days, adrenaline shot through my body. This
was it! They'd found us! I figured I'd better get out of the car and
make sure the top was cleared off.

I reached into the back for my ski boots and tried to pull
them on. It was hopeless, we obviously had our skis with us, but
there was no way we could have skied out. My feet were too
swollen and I couldn't step into thigh-deep snow in my socks or
my tennis shoes—if I could even get into my tennis shoes. Feeling like Cinderella's big-footed stepsister, I handed my boots to
Lisa. Her feet were as bad as mine but they were smaller, so
hopefully, she could fit them into my boots. It worked; she pulled
them on, but it hurt a lot. She opened the car door, winced from
the pain in her feet, and squeezed through as if she were about
to do a space walk. I handed her a ski pole to make sure the top
of the car was swept sufficiently to be seen from above. Thank

goodness the car was red. What if it had been white or cream-colored?

"It's a helicopter!" she yelled. The next thing I knew she was scrambling up the side of the car, standing on the roof, screaming and waving her arms through the air. "We're here, we're here," she shouted as loudly as she could from her raw throat.

The chopper continued roaring overhead and kept on going. She didn't stop waving until it was totally out of sight. Why was it leaving? We could see it clear as day, so why couldn't it see us? We were both devastated as Lisa quickly got back in the car and sobbed. The chopper had been flying too high. Whoever it was must not have been looking for us. Later, we found out that they had indeed sent helicopters to find us, but not in that area. We were too far off the beaten track.

The last four or five days were a maze of confusion; I can hardly separate one from the next. We stopped playing backgammon and cards, we were delirious most of the time, and we spoke very little. I withdrew into myself so completely, I couldn't bear to be touched. If we were climbing over the seat at the same time and Lisa brushed my body even the tiniest bit, I yelled out. It hurt me that badly. I barely moved or spoke and neither did Lisa, except when we heard a roar outside. Each time, she diligently got out of the car and waved her arms. She didn't always climb on the roof or the hood, but we never gave up trying to grab the attention of air traffic, all to no avail. After a plane or a helicopter disappeared from sight, Lisa would get back in the car as fast as she could (it was between 7 and 11 degrees below zero out there) and she cried. Not that it was much warmer inside but it was less exposed. I felt so helpless; I couldn't get out of the car at all since my feet were so swollen. All I could do was melt snow for us and try to stay dry.

When the sun went down, we managed to climb over the seat (toward the end it took most of our energy) and we fell into a slump in the back. The nights were a terror; it was always freezing, I was always shaking, and all my extremities were cold: my ears, my nose, my hands. We had no sleeping bags or blankets, just lots of clothing, and I tried to sleep with my head covered. We tucked in as closely to each other as we could manage, my hands clasped together in the fetal position between my thighs, wearing gloves, scarves, and hats. Anything I could find.

The early mornings were not much better. Staying dry was a constant challenge because intricate icicle networks formed on the doors, windows, and along the sides of the car overnight. If we didn't remember to sweep our clothing and our travel bags into the center of the back area when we tried to sleep, everything was soaked in the morning sun when we woke up.

To make matters worse, we were plagued at every moment by a thirst that would not be satisfied. It was much worse than hunger, which was ever-present as well, but overpowered so much by thirst, it was easy to forget about it. A few days before the ordeal was to end, I opened one of the ash trays, probably for lack of anything else to do, and I discovered hidden treasure—half a bag of salted peanuts. I thought it was a miracle, but when I stuffed a peanut in my mouth, chewed and swallowed it, the salt was so intense, it made my thirst even more unbearable, something I thought couldn't possibly happen. Lisa ate one or two peanuts also, and she had to discard the rest of them as I did, because of the salt. It was like a bad joke in hell.

How much can a person take? That's what we constantly asked ourselves. It's extraordinary when you consider how strong the body is and how powerful the will to survive. The truth is that for some odd reason, I knew I would see my family again, so fear was not in the foreground. But intermittent bouts of anger arose, perhaps covering the fear, as I silently railed against everyone I could think of, with no energy left to speak the words out loud. What the hell were they doing? I wondered. Had they given up on us? Where were the people who had directed us here—the gas station attendant and the couple? They knew we'd come this way. How could they have let this happen to us? I had a great deal of aggression; I suppose it was a defense mechanism, which I leveled toward the people who should have found us, but so far hadn't. As if they didn't care and had abandoned us on purpose.

Above all else, Lisa and I were there for each other. We never argued, not one time. Instead, we supported each other, we spoke about our family and friends, and we got to know each other in a way that never would have happened otherwise. We explained where we came from, what our relationships were like, who we cared about. Lisa was just about to begin college, so she talked about that. At one point, we discovered that her brother, Mike, she, and I all had been born in the same hospital in Illinois. The truth is that Lisa and I had few similarities between us, and we were fine with that. Three or four months before this trip, when Mike had first moved to Gallup, Lisa and I had gotten to know each other somewhat. We were very different, we understood that, but now our differences kept our minds occupied during those endless days of cold, thirst, and sorrow.

During the last forty-eight hours, profound sadness permeated our every waking moment. We had stopped talking, there was little left to say, and Lisa had almost completely stopped writing in her day planner, except for a short sentence or two like: We're still here. Where is everyone?

As delirium set in, I imagined my family sunbathing in Mexico without me. When I was sixteen, my parents had flown Jason and me there with them during Christmas, a luxury vacation that I had bitterly opposed in the spirit of a self-centered teenager. "You're ruining my life," I'd told my mother, "taking me away from my friends over Christmas break."

"Do it for me, then," she said wisely, knowing it would get better. "Let this be your gift to me."

I soon changed my tune and apologized, since I ended up having one of the greatest trips I could remember. We had tried to return there last year, but an earthquake in Mexico City had stopped us. I was so looking forward to returning this year, and when I thought of my family having a great time without me, it infuriated me. Of course, they'd canceled the trip and were holed up in the house, living out their own nightmares, pleading with the phone to ring, bargaining with God, agonizing, despairing, going to extreme measures to find me in the most bizarre scenarios, which I would learn about much later. Even Jason was housebound, too upset to go anywhere, but when I lost control of my mind in that car in the middle of nowhere, I imagined my family forgetting all about me and getting on with their lives. That was the worst thing I could imagine, and how could I know the exact opposite was true?

Lisa and I kept to our routine, rapidly losing weight, trying to avoid dehydration. Gratefully, the cold kept our feet numb enough to mask the full impact of the pain, and we both projected most of our frustration on the people who gave us the wrong directions and the ones who hadn't found us. The car is red, we'd say to each other, and the snow is white. Why can't anybody see us? Where are the helicopters? And then, each time we heard one, it passed overhead and was gone. We heard other mechanized noises, too, but we had no idea that they were snowmobiles. We looked around when the silence was broken, expecting someone to come walking up to the car. Each time nobody showed up, we cried. And still, we never lost control at the same time. One of us would have a day with continual breakdowns, and the other showed up strong. Then we switched.

Between helping each other and relying on our strong faith in ourselves, in God, and in a benevolent universe, we went to sleep on the ninth night, believing we would be rescued in the morning. In the middle of the tenth day, I heard a motorized sound but I hardly thought anything of it. Reality and fantasy had merged; I couldn't discern if I were imagining the sound or if it were real. I thought it seemed closer than the ones I'd heard previously but I couldn't be sure. I sensed that something had been there and then it was gone, just like all the other times, but maybe it had been closer. When it left, Lisa and I looked at each other and laid our heads back against the seat to doze.

I knew that starving to death or dying of dehydration were possibilities. We'd gotten pretty skinny by then, but we didn't know how extreme it was, since it was never warm enough to take off all our clothes. I didn't feel hungry any longer, that was always overpowered by thirst, so I was hardly aware that I hadn't eaten. I didn't know how long a person could survive without food, and we weren't monitoring our intake of water. There was no way to do that, we had no education about it. We kept waking up in the mornings, so we were obviously drinking enough to stay alive. Beyond that, I only knew that my pants were so loose, it was a joke, that nobody ever came, and that all we had was our strange little red universe that consisted solely of me, Lisa, and the interior of a Chevy Blazer.

By the eleventh day, Lisa was sure no one would find us. She was wondering, silently of course, how long a person could live under these conditions, with no heat, no food, and no water, as we both drifted in and out of consciousness. When I managed to climb into the front seat that morning, the warmth from the sun inspired a kind of euphoria in me and I relaxed into a state of semi-awareness. My mind was quiet, there was nothing to think about, and I saw my family's faces stronger than ever before. They were hovering nearby, I felt them, and I knew that the situation at hand was completely out of my control. I sent a mental message to my mom and dad, telling them I was okay, and then I surrendered into a state of peace. My feet throbbed, my stomach churned, my throat ached, my body shivered, and it was as if those things were happening to somebody else.

As I sat there with my feet on the dashboard, melting into the warmth of the sun, I sensed a presence that had not been there before. The angel of death, perhaps. I looked over at Lisa, whose eyes were open. She'd felt something, too. We both looked to the left and if my mouth could have managed it, I would have laughed at what had to be a hallucination. There stood a boy and a man on a pair of snowmobiles, looking in the car window, holding a Dr Pepper and a Snickers bar.

7

Return of the General

I RECENTLY FOUND AN OLD BOX OF MEMORABILIA MY MOTHER STASHED in a garage closet. A cassette tape marked "Jami's Message" was in there, the greeting from my answering machine that my mother called several times a day while I was lost. Although she never admitted it, she wasn't sure she would ever hear my voice again. She took comfort listening to the recording in her private moments when everybody had gone home for the night and my father had retreated into a dark, heavy sleep.

In the meantime, she worried about Jason, her sixteen-year-old son, who was getting lost in the shuffle. Jason was so upset during my disappearance, he hardly knew what to do with himself, and his hours at home were boring and endless. No one deliberately ignored him, he wasn't being pushed aside, but his home was being invaded every day by a load of people, he wasn't old enough to go out searching, and he had no idea where he fit into this insanity. Since the trip to Mexico had been canceled and he had no other plans for the holidays, he opted to stay home for the entire Christmas vacation, holed up in his room with a friend or two, trying to stay out of the way as much as possible.

My family awakened in the morning on December 31, 1987, and I was still gone. What was New Year's Eve supposed to mean?

How could they possibly celebrate? The day crawled along like the one before and the ones before that, until the early evening, when my mother literally shoved my brother out of the house to go to a New Year's party with his friends. He went, albeit reluctantly, but very soon she faced another intense challenge. Jason had been out only once since my disappearance to go to a local TV station to be interviewed. Now that he had emerged, after being at the party for a few hours he called my mother to ask her permission to go on a ski trip to Flagstaff with his friends. She agreed, on the condition that he would call her each morning before he hit the slopes and each evening when he got back. My mother's friends thought she was crazy to let him go. She didn't want to, but what was the alternative? Was she supposed to get overly protective of Jason now, and make his life even more miserable than it already was?

New Year's Eve that year was strange, to say the least. Nobody felt like celebrating, but everyone gathered in my parents' living room anyway. My grandmother cooked as usual, and the atmosphere was depressed and awkward. The family ate, cleaned the kitchen, watched TV, and silently acknowledged that midnight had arrived. Ten minutes later, they all went home. They wanted to be together and to support my parents, and for some odd reason, although nobody knew why, they felt they couldn't leave until after midnight.

In Brittney's world, all she could do was think about Lisa and me. She'd reluctantly attended a baby shower during that week (she thought she should) but she missed me terribly the whole time. On New Year's Eve, she dragged herself to a gathering at a friend's house, but her heart wasn't in it. Suddenly a news flash about us appeared on TV. The bustling room went silent as they listened to the newscaster. At this point, the anchors were speaking more openly about the possibility of foul play or murder, or our being buried in the snow. When the report was through, they resumed their party, all except Brittney. She just couldn't shake her depression. Her friends tried to pull her out of it. "You don't have to be unhappy all the time," they told her. But she was. I feel so sad when I think about the pain and grief my disappearance caused family and friends, but what could I do? I wanted to be found as much as they wanted to find me.

On January 1, my father still hadn't given up. He got on the phone and hired a new private detective to get on the case. Then he met a reporter from Channel 10, the local TV station, to do a helicopter air tour, retracing our steps. My father was about to start the new year by facing one of his greatest fears. He always had hated flying, he was afraid to fly in commercial jumbo jets, so when he was confronted with boarding a private chopper, he was terrified but determined. Before he went up, he did an interview. "You think to yourself, how can this happen?" he said. "This is not a dream or a nightmare, this is real, and I intend to keep looking until I find my daughter." Then he bit the bullet, strapped himself in, and got over his fear of flying forever.

He and the pilot/reporter flew all the way to Gallup and back. Once again, they returned with nothing. When my father headed home at the end of a very long, discouraging day, the pilot reminded him, "If there's anything you need, we're here." My dad thanked him and cried, always astonished at the degree of help that strangers were offering him. Little did he know he'd be taking this man up on his offer very soon.

While my dad was in the air, my mother contacted a psychic who'd been referred by a friend. She figured there was nothing left to do, so she brought her to my apartment. Talk about last resorts. This woman listened to my voice on the answering machine, walked around, and touched some of my things. "The girls are still alive," she said with certainty in her voice. "I see them in a truck, surrounded by white." At least she didn't say we were dead, but where we were and how they could get to us was still a mystery.

On January 2, the eleventh day, my father was home at around noon and my grandmother was in the kitchen—you guessed it—cooking. The usual suspects—my mom, my grandfather, and my aunt—were at the table and my other aunt was on the way over. Lunch was a somber affair. It was an exceptionally quiet day, there had been no calls all morning, and it seemed that with each passing day hope was fading and despair was taking its place. When the phone rang, my mother slowly went to answer it, expecting it to be a relative or a well-wisher.

"Mrs. Goldman?" the voice said.

"Yes."

"This is the sheriff of the Springerville Police Department. I'm pretty sure we have your daughter. We found her in Big Lake, twenty miles south of Springerville, in the car. They're both alive."

"Hold on," my mother said. "I'll get my husband." There had been so many false alarms, she was on alert. And yet, something was different about this call; she knew it was real, she felt the hysteria rising in her, and she couldn't trust her brain to process the information correctly. "Michael," she called out in a controlled voice. "Can you come here?" Shaking, she handed the phone to my father. "They found her," she said.

My father spoke to the sheriff for a minute or two, hung up the phone, and, without a word, dialed Channel 10. He spoke with the pilot who had offered his help the day before. "A man named Estes and his son just found them," my father said. "I need a favor. I haven't talked to anybody else, you can have an exclusive on this if you can fly me to the White Mountain Community Hospital right now in Springerville. The girls are on their way there."

"Meet me in a half hour," the reporter agreed.

Michael put down the phone. Phase One was over. Phase Two was about to start. As he walked back into the living room, cheers rose up and Poppy stood. We were not the only ones who had been found. My grandfather's broken demeanor had been shed in one second flat and he was ready to resume his rightful place as patriarch, a dynamic force barking orders and gathering the troops, never again to return to what he had become in the face of unacceptable loss. We were back—and so was the general.

8

Getting Found

NEITHER OF US HAD HEARD A SOUND; I GUESS WE WERE THAT CLOSE to oblivion. As I stared at a man and his son standing beside their snowmobiles, looking in through my window, it could have been the Twilight Zone. It was that surreal.

"Oh, my God," I said, touching Lisa's arm lightly. She burst into tears instantly, while this man tried to open my door. The ice block was still there; it hadn't melted or budged a bit since it formed during the three-day blizzard. He walked to the other side of the car and pulled at Lisa's door, which opened a little bit. She became hysterical, crying and grabbing on to him, saying, "I love you, I love you." That was all she could say. I just smiled, I couldn't imagine where Lisa found the strength to cry like that. In quiet determination, I took the extreme effort to climb over the seat to start packing up my things. It was over, we were getting out of here. It felt no more dramatic than that.

"Who are you? What are you doing here?" the man asked.

"We're Jami and Lisa," I said over Lisa's sobbing. "We've been here since the twenty-third."

His eyes lit up. "My Lord, are you the two girls from New Mexico? You've been all over the news."

Those were shocking words, but not as shocking as the next thing he said. "I'm sorry, but I can't take you out of here."

Lisa moaned "No!" and I stopped clearing up the back of the car. "Why not?" I said.

"Because I have to get the law," he stated firmly. "I'm afraid if I move you, I'll hurt you," he said as an afterthought. "I need to go get someone. We'll come right back."

Lisa tightened her grip on his coat. There was no way he was leaving her here, not for a second, and she would use her last breath to make that clear. The young boy, Jake, watched, fascinated. We discovered later that we actually had this twelve-year-old boy to thank for our rescue. The motorized sounds we'd heard the day before came from snowmobiles on which Jake and his father, Michael, had been riding. They'd seen the car from a distance, but hadn't come closer to look inside. It wasn't irresponsible of them; abandoned cars were nothing out of the ordinary around there. This was a designated Christmas-tree-cutting area and unsuspecting people from all over the state came to chop down trees, got stuck, and had to leave their cars. It happened every year.

For some reason, at dinner that night, the young boy couldn't get the red Chevy Blazer off his mind. "Dad," he'd said, "let's go back tomorrow and check out that car. I have a funny feeling about it."

Michael Estes, the man with the same first name as my father, had done as his son suggested, and here we all were.

"You can't leave us here," Lisa pleaded. "I'm afraid you won't come back."

"I'm not going to leave you here for long," he said. "I just need to go get the law."

What that was all about, I had no idea, but I had no energy to argue. "Okay," I said.

Lisa continued to cry and hold on to Michael for dear life, as if he would disappear if she let go.

"Lisa," I said. "He's not going to leave us here. Let him go and he'll come back. Look, he has a little boy. He isn't going to abandon us. We're alive and we're okay. Let him find someone to get us out of here. What are we gonna do, get on their snowmobiles? Come on back here with me and get your stuff together. By the time we're done, they'll be back. Right?" I asked our saviors.

"Yup. I just have to get the law," Mike repeated. He handed Lisa the Snickers bar and the Dr Pepper. She loosened her hold on him, took the food, and they were gone.

We each took a bite of the candy bar, a swig of the soda, and spent the next few minutes doubled over, waiting for the stomach cramps to pass. We never did finish them off, the taste was so overpowered by the pain the sugar created in our stomachs. We kept the provisions in clear sight, though, just to reassure us that we truly had been found. Lisa calmed down and joined me in the back. It looked like we'd had a weeklong sleep-over back there, with our stuff strewn all over the place, remnants of our attempts to stay clean and warm during our unexpected confinement. We'd done our best to take care of ourselves, cleaning our faces, brushing our teeth, putting on deodorant, doing whatever it took to simulate a real life.

The vibration of those snowmobiles returning an hour and a half later was as sweet as any birdsong I'd ever heard. There they were again, just like they'd promised, the father and his son. I looked beyond them to see who they'd brought with them. They were alone. I looked at them questioningly.

"We couldn't get anyone to help get you out," Mr. Estes said.

I got angry. "Are you telling me that we've been stuck here for eleven days," I said, "and there's no one to get us out? What are you going to do, leave us here?"

Lisa cried out.

"Of course not. We're taking you out ourselves," Michael said. He motioned to his son. "On our snowmobiles."

I could hardly believe my ears. I'd joked about that a moment ago and now it was happening.

"But we're all packed," Lisa said. "What about our things?"

Michael looked at our large suitcases that were all ready to go. "We can't manage those on a snowmobile," he said. "Take a few things in a small bag, only what you need. Someone'll come back to get the rest."

I didn't ask any more questions and neither did Lisa. We opened our suitcases, took out some cosmetics and a change of underwear, and transferred them to an overnight bag. Mike Estes picked Lisa up, carried her to Jake's snowmobile, and sat her down on it. Then he came back, picked me up, and sat me on his own. There was no way we could get our feet into boots or shoes, so we held on to our bags, our stockinged feet dangling over the sides. The snowmobiles purred like a heavenly choir as I wrapped my arms around my rescuer and we took off, never looking back.

The eight-mile ride to the gate was a combination of some of the most conflicting emotions I ever remember feeling. Elation was on top, we were free and we were going home, but something else was creeping in. It was something powerful and unavoidable, that would escalate for the next three weeks until it was utterly unbearable. It was pain—my feet were out in the elements for the first time in eleven days and it was only the beginning.

When we arrived at the gate, it began to dawn on me what had happened. A padlock held two sides of the gates together, posted with a red STOP sign and another that said, ROAD CLOSED. When we passed through the gate the first time, it had been physically open, even though the road had been officially closed a couple of hours earlier. A flash of anger surged through me, even in my state of delirium. No wonder there were no snowplows. The road was barricaded the whole time, no motorized vehicles had been allowed entry, and only snowmobiles could have made it through. I didn't think about it a whole lot right then, though. I had other things to deal with, like the police who were standing on the other side of the gate, "the law," to which Mike Estes had referred so many times. Next to them, Mrs. Estes was waiting in an idling Suburban station wagon with a gaggle of kids (there were seven counting Jake), ready to drive us away from hell.

I tried to step off the snowmobile by myself but I fell. A surge of pain shot from my feet up through my legs, as a police officer picked me up and put me in the back of the Suburban beside Lisa. Four Estes kids were in the back, too, staring at us shamelessly, as if we were some kind of freaks. I didn't think much of them, either, but I took a doughnut one of the young girls gave me. I bit into it, slowly this time. I'd learned from the Snickers bar. My stomach cramped, less severely now, and I chewed methodically. It felt foreign—I hadn't chewed for a long time—and I sipped some hot chocolate somebody handed me. The sweet warmth traveling down my throat was a fine feeling. I would be okay. I hadn't a clue that my feet were damaged beyond repair and I was as dehydrated as a person could be and still draw breath. All I could think about was taking a nice long shower and going home. But that was not the plan.

"We'll be there real soon, girls," Mrs. Estes said reassuringly from the front seat.

"Where?" I asked.

"White Mountain Community," she said.

"What's that?" Lisa said.

"The hospital."

"What for?" Lisa and I asked in unison.

"To have you examined and treated," she said.

"We don't need to go to the hospital. We're fine," I informed her rather indignantly. "Please just take us to your house so we can take a shower." Besides my family, all I could think of was warm water pouring over me. I wanted to shave my underarms and my legs, and to clean up the endless days of dirt and fear that had almost become a part of me. I definitely didn't want to meet anybody looking or smelling like this. Not even doctors or nurses.

"I'm sorry, honey, I can't do that," she said.

"Why not?" Lisa said.

"I just can't," she said. For the moment, I was aware of a dull ache in my feet that was getting worse by the minute, but because my body was beginning to shut down, I thought I was fine. But we were on our way to the hospital in Springerville, where the real pain was about to begin.

I didn't know that I couldn't walk. I didn't have a chance to try, because in a minute we pulled up to a tiny hospital where Lisa and I were carried out of the Suburban and put into a couple of wheelchairs. I stared at Lisa, the only person I had seen for close to two weeks. This felt so chaotic; there was so much action and everybody around me seemed to be rushing. Why is everybody in such a hurry? I thought, unaware that in forty-eight more hours at the most, I would have been dead. I vaguely remember being hooked up to an IV, probably a morphine drip and something to reverse the dehydration. Then we both got wheeled into a steamy room with a huge silver vat in the center that looked like a trash can. I watched, almost from above the scene (the pain medication must have been working), while they switched us from regular wheelchairs to very tall, movable chairs, also with wheels. We were wheeled to the rim of the vat. Now I felt like Alice in Wonderland sitting in an oversized chair as the steam rose up into my face, my purple swollen feet throbbing and dangling over the edge of the hot water.

"Put your feet in the whirlpool," a nurse directed us.

We did as we were told and let out simultaneous screams. I crashed back into my body, the last place I wanted to be. The pain was excruciating, morphine and all, and we cried our way through that entire whirlpool bath. There was a great deal of conflicting information about frostbite at the time and we were never certain if the hot bath helped or damaged our feet further. They did not know much about it at White Mountain Community Hospital—there were no frostbite experts—but I know for sure that the ride on the snowmobiles in the bitter cold without shoes did not help at all.

At least we're alive, I kept reminding myself, something I wasn't so pleased about as my semi-frozen feet were being thawed in aggressive, swirling water that was heated to over a hundred degrees. Death seemed like a plausible alternative in that moment, the pain was so bad. We screamed and cried all the way through it and yet neither of us pulled our feet out of the water. We wanted to do what would be best for us, but the truth was that nobody knew. At the end of the foot bath from hell, when they wheeled our same tall chairs into a room with individual showers, I understood that my feet were in big trouble.

At some point, my dad and Lisa's mother arrived at the hospital. When my father had gotten to the helicopter pad, they'd had room for only one person among the camera crew, the reporters, and all their equipment. That was okay with my mother, since I would be flown to Scottsdale later that night. She let my dad go on his own after he promised to call her as soon as he laid eyes on me. At the same time, Bunny had flown to Springerville separately in a single-prop jet. It scared the daylights out of her, but she was there, too.

A nurse helped us soap up our bodies and shave our underarm hair, which had grown very long. She washed my hair—that felt really good—and by the time I saw my father, I was clean. But I was also infuriated. Between the unbearable pain, the physical depletion, and the medication that was coursing through my bloodstream, I remember yelling at him, "Where were you? What were you doing for the last two weeks? Why didn't you find us?" I was grateful to be alive, but the pain made me feel mean and angry and I didn't mind letting my father know.

He swears he doesn't remember me yelling at him. My voice, as angry as it was, was music to his ears, so even if he did remember, I'm sure he wouldn't have cared. His daughter was back and all he could do was laugh and cry at the same time. He knew that I was a complainer by nature and that I was feisty, so anything I had to say was fine, just as long as I was alive and able to talk. After he hugged me and kissed my face a hundred times, he went to the wall phone to call my mother with his first positive report in many, many days.

PART TWO

Recovery

9

The Torture Chamber

I'VE BEEN ASKED MANY TIMES IF I PRAYED WHEN I WAS LOST. LISA prayed all the time, and I suppose I did, too, but not in the conventional sense. I'm not a particularly religious person, but I spoke to God in my own way and I firmly believe that if He had wanted me to die in the middle of a stark white wilderness, I would have. Since I didn't, I have come to envision God and destiny as integral parts of each other. The way I see it, God Himself shapes this thing called destiny, forever interweaving the two for eternity. I believe that the mere fact that I survived means that I had a higher calling in this life, as did Lisa—a purpose to remain on this earth. I believe it was my soul's task to stick around and that God had an influence on that. Why else would those angels on snowmobiles have found us?

When I was growing up, I always felt that I was earmarked for something particular, something that would define my daily existence in more expansive terms than going to school, getting married, having children, and perhaps choosing a career when the kids were grown. It's not that I consider any of those things to be less than honorable. Quite the opposite. I always wanted them for myself and I still do. And yet, I believe that living on the edge of death for so many days was about more than simple survival. It was a large part of what shaped my future, it was obviously God's will, and I can accept that. But when I get to the other side, He and I need to have a long discussion about those three weeks of unrelenting pain in the hospital.

I was already feeling it, medication and all, when they shipped us out of Springerville on a medical plane called an Air Evac. Our parents had us flown to Scottsdale Memorial Hospital, because they have a hyperbaric oxygen chamber which is crucial in treating frostbite. It was close to where we lived, too, so it was the obvious place for treatment, but Lisa and I had to be transferred out of White Mountain Community Hospital into Scottsdale Memorial by a participating doctor. So far, we didn't have one. Once again, our friends saved us. Somebody's father was a foot surgeon, Dr. Kerry Zang, who worked out of Scottsdale Memorial, and was glad to immediately oversee our transfer.

Lisa and I landed at Sky Harbor Airport in Phoenix at about nine that night, where my father met us. A seasoned flyer by now, he had left Springerville a little bit ahead of us in a single engine four-seater Channel 10 news plane, and he was waiting there when we arrived, along with a ton of press. It wasn't only the local stations anymore; CNN had showed up and our story was about to go global.

When we were switched from Air Evac to an ambulance under the scrutiny of swarming reporters, my feet were throbbing pretty badly. It's kind of a blur, but I remember telling my father how much I loved him and asking him when I would see my mother. He assured me she was already at Scottsdale Memorial. In fact, Poppy had insisted that they leave for the hospital the second they knew we were on our way. The only thing my mother stopped to do was tear up one of the MISSING posters, a symbolic gesture that the waiting was over. Then she, my grandparents, and several other family members headed to the hospital, where they'd been waiting for a good three hours when we pulled up.

I don't recall how many friends and family members were gathered to see us; I only know that our house started filling up with people the moment the word was out. It was still chaotic, but the mood was completely different than during the weeks prior.

The celebratory atmosphere missing throughout the holidays hit full force. People cheered and ran around in circles, crying, laughing, making plans to get to the hospital hoping to catch a glimpse of us. They'd heard we had frostbite, but nobody, including me, had any idea how severe it was. They were only focused on the fact that we were back and our lives were no longer in jeopardy. That was something to celebrate.

Jason was in Flagstaff at the tail end of his ski trip when he got the news. He was sitting in the back of an SUV while one of his buddies was on a pay phone, telling his mom they were on their way home. Suddenly his friend came running to the car, yelling, "Jason, Jason, they found your sister! She was on the side of the road somewhere, in the car. She's alive! They're both alive! They're on the way to the hospital right now!"

Jason had a weird reaction. "Shut up!" he said, thinking his friend was playing with his head. He had resigned himself to the bizarre fact that I'd been kidnapped—he was still waiting for the Spook to come up with something—so this sounded too simple. "You better not be lying to me," he warned his buddy, trying to break out of numbness to accept the truth. It didn't take long for his excitement to burst through and they sped home as quickly as possible, joking all the way that if they got pulled over, for once they had a really good excuse for speeding.

Brittney had been at the mall with a friend, halfheartedly returning some Christmas gifts, when we surfaced. She was pulling into her driveway and her mother came rushing toward her, screaming, "They found them, they found them!" Brittney ran into the house and got my mom on the phone.

"Robin, is it true?" she asked.

"Yes, it's true," my mom said. "They're found. I can't talk right now."

Brittney put down the phone and burst into tears. Her mother had a dream the night before that we were in the snow, and we were very, very cold, which she'd shared with Brittney. But since the search had been so extensive and so much time had passed, just about everyone had concluded that we were either abducted or lying dead somewhere, maybe at the bottom of a

snowdrift. Brittney got right back in her car and headed straight
for the hospital.

A couple of my parents' close friends, Bob and Nancy Huber,
had been standing in the home-electronics department at Wal-
Mart when news of our discovery appeared on two long rows of
televisions, all at the same time. They jumped up and down and
cheered, right in the middle of the store. Then they rushed out to
their car to come and join the huge mob scene that was gathering
at the hospital. A CNN camera crew was there, along with crews
from all the local TV stations, waiting for a peek at us and hoping
they could get some interviews. The press had been so helpful all
along the way, especially Channel 10—publicizing our disappearance, shaming the police into searching, and flying my father to
see us on a moment's notice—that my parents were more than
happy to oblige them. Lisa and I, of course, didn't speak to anyone. We were dazed and drugged, fighting pain and dehydration,
getting wheeled and flown from place to place.

When I look at film of me heading into ICU on a gurney,
hooked up to an IV, holding a stuffed animal over my chest, it
seems like it was somebody else. The only people I remember seeing are my mother, my father, and my grandparents, who kissed
me and cried. But I must say that the staff at Scottsdale Memorial
were amazing. Nancy Reagan had used them in the past, so not
only were they the best in their fields, they also knew how to handle the press. This was crucial, since we were a highly publicized
case and it wasn't over. The staff was masterly at keeping the press
at bay while offering just enough information to keep them
happy.

They gave me an epidural before I got to ICU, to block out
pain. If it really worked like they say it did, then I'd rather not
imagine how I'd have felt without it. The initial examination revealed that there was no pulse in my feet below the ankles. This
was not good news. The doctors informed both Lisa's parents and
mine that although they would do everything to avoid it, amputation was a very real possibility for both of us. To their credit, the
doctors never lied, they were careful to cite worst-case scenarios,
they pulled no punches, while at the same time they began to ad-

minister aggressive treatment in the hyperbaric oxygen chamber to save our feet.

A hyperbaric chamber (they might as well call it a torture chamber, as far as I'm concerned) looks like a cylindrical, transparent glass coffin. It feels like one, too. It's terrifically confining, especially after being confined in a car for eleven days. You can take nothing in there with you except a hospital gown, a pillow, and a set of headphones. I couldn't even take a tissue with me to dry my tears or blow my nose. I'm not especially claustrophobic, but there you lie, immobilized inside a tight glass shell-like covering, while valves force highly pressurized oxygen onto your damaged tissue. It hurts like hell, that's all I can say, and I had to grin and bear it. You can bet there wasn't much grinning going on.

During this time, my mother and I became experts on frostbite. Here's the simple version of what we learned:

When a person's skin becomes frostbitten, the blood vessels that supply oxygen and nutrients necessary to keep the skin alive have been frozen. If the skin continues to lose the blood supply, it will die. The hyperbaric chamber tries to combat this by increasing the concentration of oxygen in the tissues, which also increases the blood supply to the feet. Three sessions a day, an hour and a half each, were doctor's orders, combined with mild medications to thin out my blood in order to decrease the possibility of clotting. I learned that any kind of treatment for frostbite is delicate; too little will produce no results at all, while too much too soon can traumatize even partially damaged tissue.

They took good care of me when I was inside the chamber; there was always a nurse or a family member there with whom I could speak, and I could watch television or listen to music through the headphones. But it was hard to concentrate on anything besides rising above the pain, which I was not accomplishing particularly well. All in all, it was a highly unpleasant, pain-producing therapy. They even drilled a hole in my eardrum to relieve pressure in my ear while I was in the chamber, of which I'm happy to report I have no memory. I suppose I must have been in so much pain, it was difficult to discern one source of pain from the next and it all blended together. Perhaps they did the drilling while I was asleep. I only know that I disliked the chamber intensely and everything connected to it (what was there to like about it?), but I did it anyway, hoping it would bring my feet back.

"Pain is a good sign," the doctors said. "It means some of the nerves and tissues are still alive." If that was true, I should have healed completely, but I didn't. One of the reasons was that my feet had frozen, thawed, frozen, and thawed again, several times during the ordeal. This thawing and freezing process creates ice crystals (not unlike the ones that formed a network in our car each night and melted each morning), increasing cellular damage and injury. We learned this from a frostbite expert, Dr. James Beauchene, a surgeon from Canada who recently had moved to Arizona. He never imagined he'd be treating frostbite in the Arizona desert, but everything about my story was and continues to be outside the norm. I'm only grateful that my hands didn't suffer damage. They peeled when I was in the hospital—so did my nose—but they didn't freeze like my feet, maybe because most of the time I wore ski gloves that threw off moisture and I covered my face while I slept.

My parents stayed at the hospital all that night with me. At seven in the morning, when they finally went home to catch a few hours' sleep, the phone didn't stop ringing. People called with congratulations and words of encouragement, which was a blessing, but my folks had to return to the hospital at 11 A.M., to face another nightmare. There they met a team of seven doctors, each a specialist in his field, who were assigned to our case. They wanted to let my parents know that they would do everything within their power to save my feet, but at that point, it was probable that I'd require amputation.

Nobody knew why I fared worse than Lisa. We'd been in the same situations all along the way, but during those days in ICU, the frostbite on Lisa's feet was reversing, although her flesh retained its dark color for a long time. Mine were making little to no progress at all. I pity my family; they had to watch me suffer and they felt so helpless. They were always looking for things to do, and I remember my grandma bringing me a special feather pillow for the hyperbaric chamber after I complained about how uncomfortable the hospital pillows were. It helped a little bit, and I know everyone was doing whatever they could, but nothing could make the pain go away. Nobody would talk about it yet in certain terms, it wasn't time, but the inevitable was fast approaching.

10

Passing the Buck

WHEN I WAS MISSING, ALL MY MOTHER COULD THINK ABOUT WAS having me home, being able to sleep again, and returning to some semblance of her normal routine. Now that I was back, she thanked God every day for answering her prayers, but my return had done nothing to restore normalcy to her life. In fact, her sleeping didn't improve much (there was too much to worry about) and her days became more demanding than before as she went to work each morning for as long as she could, and then spent the rest of the time in the hospital with me. Her jobs there included running interference with the nurses, reassuring me, placating the rest of the family, and studying my condition until she knew as much as, if not more than, the doctors.

My mother is one of the strongest women I know and she loves me unconditionally. She's opinionated but she's also very empathetic and she shows up for me in the most easygoing, friendly way. Over the years, whenever I've turned to her for advice on the most important issues in my life, she hasn't judged and she's always told me the truth, whether I wanted to hear it or not. During this terrible time, she was my greatest comfort, even though everybody else was present and willing to help in any way they could, especially my grandparents.

They were at the hospital every single day, hoping to offer

their own daughter some time off for herself, but I wanted my mother with me as much as possible. I often put on a positive face for the rest of the family. I didn't want them to take on the weight of my troubles; I was afraid it was too much stress for them. But because of my mom's inner strength, I was able to fall apart with her. I guess I knew she could take it and I had to do it somewhere, so I unloaded on her, day or night, as my emotions careened into the stratosphere. I called her whenever I was really upset, it was sometimes two or three in the morning, and I refused to enter the "chamber of horrors" without her close by.

At first, I'd shown the slightest improvement above the ankles, but my feet were getting progressively worse. That meant the pain was escalating and without a powerful dose of medication at the right time, I simply could not endure the hour and a half of agonizing therapy in the hyperbaric chamber. My mother worked out a medication schedule with the nurses: Whoever was on duty would administer the pain medication at a specified time, then roll me in, and it would kick in while I was inside. That was the only way I could bear it. One day, however, when a nurse timed it incorrectly and tried to put me inside the glass coffin without administering the meds at the right moment, my mother went ballistic when she heard my screams. You can bet that never happened again. Besides that one time, though, I don't remember her ever yelling at nurses or doctors, and she doesn't remember it either, because they did such a good job, she didn't need to. The staff at Scottsdale Memorial were angels walking the earth and they took extremely good care of me, under very difficult circumstances.

I tried everything to manage my pain, but if someone as much as touched the bed, the motion sent shock waves of agony throughout my body. Lisa was having the same experience; frostbite is no fun. One day, a woman came to see me with relaxation tapes I could listen to while I was in the hyperbaric chamber. I tried, but they really didn't help. By the time they'd moved me out of ICU into a private room in the children's ward (an easy location to accommodate my large number of visitors), my feet were still bruised, they were red, blue, and purple, and they were so swollen, there was almost no separation between my toes. I spent as much time sleeping as possible, just to escape. More than once, my mother arrived from work and found my door closed with my grandmother and a friend or two sitting outside my room. I hurt too much to talk so I closed everyone out—even Mike, my boyfriend. I saw him a few times but I had nothing to give. He was good about it, he kept coming back to see me, but I know my indifference upset him.

They say that we forget physical discomfort as time passes, but whoever "they" are have not had frostbite. The unrelenting agony of those three weeks is the only clear memory I have of that time. Living in constant pain and being heavily medicated, day in and day out, does something to a person. It brought out the worst in me, and although my father interpreted my feistiness and complaining attitude as a sign of healing, I think the opposite was true. Although I did my best to be a "good" patient, I had some choice words for the nurses when they inadvertently brushed up against one of my feet. It sent me through the roof and I let them know about it.

I also let them have it when they needlessly woke me up in the mornings. Sleep was my only escape from my feet, which were beginning to turn black, and for some reason I wasn't able to sleep in the nighttime. Besides the throbbing, if I tried to turn over, searing pain woke me up, so when I finally dropped off into a drugged sleep in the early hours of the morning and some nurse tapped on my shoulder at 6 A.M. to take blood, I was pissed. What did they need blood for, and why did they need it at six in the morning? It would be exactly the same blood at nine or ten. I never understood why they insisted on disturbing me during my only moments of oblivion.

While we waited to discover whether or not I would keep my feet, an interesting development was unfolding in the media. News reports were still going strong, citing details of our rescue and the people who found us and offering progress reports on Lisa's and my recoveries. But a new focus had taken hold. Everyone agreed that staying with the car had saved our lives, but why had it taken so long for us to be found? This is what the reporters were all asking. Why had the police waited five days before they even began searching, and why was it a full week before a task force was formed to scour the outlying areas where we might have been stranded? Why hadn't the Department of Public Safety (DPS) contacted the counties that were adjacent to Gallup, particularly Apache County, the last place we'd been seen? If they had, they surely would have found us and saved us a great deal of misery. What if we had died? They would have been in deep trouble, a lot more than they were in right now.

A sergeant from the Apache County Sheriff's Department appeared on the news to say that they had received no official notification from DPS citing our disappearance. Since statistics showed that most teenage missing persons turn out to be runaways, the police had said they couldn't launch a full-scale search for every teenager reported missing. However, if they had received an official "Missing Persons Report" from DPS, that would have prompted an organized police search of the area where we were stranded. They called it a lack of common courtesy on the part of DPS.

At the same time, DPS swore up and down that they'd sent the report in question, not only to Apache County but to all the neighboring counties. When the Gallup police weighed in, they insisted that the ROAD CLOSED sign already had been posted on the gate when we drove through. It hadn't, and the gates had been left open, only to be closed, posted, and locked a few days after we were stranded. Now the Gallup police were pointing fingers at the Arizona Department of Transportation for closing the road without searching it first. This supposed gap in communication all around was a classic case of passing the buck. Nobody would assume responsibility and everybody's fingers were pointing in every direction but back at themselves.

To add to the criticism, Mike Estes, our rescuer, said that he and Jake had been forced to take us out of the area on their snowmobiles, exposing our socked feet to more of the bitter coldness and wetness, because the police were moving too slowly. In interviews, he said he had called the Apache County Sheriff's Department right away, but he was dissatisfied with their lack of response. Mike didn't know if they had a new dispatcher or what, but when he reported finding us, she'd been quite blasé, acting as if she didn't believe him. "If it had been one of my kids," he said, "I would have wanted more action than that." So he took things into his own hands.

The sheriff from Apache County appeared on the news in response to Mike's comment, assuring citizens that the dispatcher would be disciplined. Then he opened up on the DPS again, criticizing them for not ordering a task force sooner. While the agencies were busy throwing blame at each other, some of it started landing on us. As we lay in our hospital beds, writhing in pain, we heard our accident described as the result of an alleged joy ride. Believe me, if we'd been looking for some fun, we wouldn't have chosen a blizzard, eleven days in a car with no heat or food, and a frozen six-pack of Diet Pepsis to achieve our goal. Nobody is that stupid!

The following segment is part of an article from January 5th in the *Arizona Republic:*

> From the evidence at hand, it appears that right up to the instant that the women were found, the official assumption was that they were off on a lark. Only this explains the foot dragging at the outset and the persistent failure to mount anything like an intensive search.
>
> It was possible, to be sure, that these young women, returning from a skiing trip, might have decided to extend their outing without letting their families know. But nothing known about them suggested anything of the kind. Every indicator suggested two mature and responsible young women who were looking forward to being home with their families for Christmas.
>
> As it turned out, the indicators were correct. The women had taken a wrong turn in a snowstorm—the sort of mistake a hiker or a mountain climber might make—and, without heat for more than a week, suffered undetermined injuries from frostbite. What a pity the authorities dismissed their parents' early cries for help.

By week two, my feet were not improving. In fact, they were getting much worse. Lisa and I were in separate rooms; it was a bit disorienting after all we'd gone through together in such close proximity, and it took some adjustment for us to be apart. I couldn't leave my bed—neither could she—but they rolled us into each other's rooms occasionally so we could check up on one another's progress. I was happy for her improvement. The original diagnosis was that her entire feet were frozen, but the hyperbaric treatments were helping. She might have to undergo some form of partial toe amputation, but it looked like her feet would be saved. She had gotten out of ICU several days before I did and they were looking at a date for her release.

In my case, however, no pulse whatsoever had returned to my feet. Dr. Leonard Bodell, the microvascular hand surgeon overseeing my case, had become pessimistic. My feet were not revascularizing, he said, and the concept of amputation was becoming ever more present. Meanwhile, the media were clamoring for a press conference—they were stimulated by the constant reports of wrongdoing by the state—and my parents had been advised to seek legal counsel before they made statements of any sort. If what the media were reporting was true, the state was heavily at fault here. If we intended to sue, they would need to be careful about anything they said publicly. Amid exposure of bad performance by the authorities, unsuccessful pain management, and evidence of gangrene eating my flesh, a new angel entered the scene: Richard Plattner, Attorney at Law, one of the first lawyers to be certified as a specialist in injury and wrongful death litigation.

Everybody knew my story. It had been plastered all over the newspapers and on every local television station for the last three weeks, so when Richard was contacted, he knew exactly who I was. He was at the driving track the day a friend phoned him at my parents' request, engaged in a high-performance-driving training course. When the call came, they literally dragged him out of his car and he responded immediately, making arrangements for a runner to bring him the initial client documents. That night, he met us at the hospital.

He told us that at first glance, he saw a good reason to question the state's conduct. Of course he would need some time to study the details, but it appeared that there were solid grounds for a lawsuit. He was quite excited and nervous about taking my case. It was so high profile, what lawyer wouldn't want it? But he also was aware of the work ahead of him. My parents liked him immediately. His peaceful demeanor, his habit of looking a person in the eye when he listened, and his straightforward manner of speaking instilled confidence in them. As for me, I wasn't in any condition to evaluate anything or anyone by then. I only knew he didn't offend me, as my life revolved around pain, therapy, and figuring out how to get through a day.

I know there were times I gave Richard a bad time; I was like Dr. Jekyll and Mrs. Hyde, depending on whether the medication was working or was wearing off. For our first meeting, he sat at my bedside scribbling notes for about an hour. I acted like myself at the onset of the interview; the meds had kicked in before he arrived and I answered his questions as best I could. Toward the end of the hour, though, as the pain began creeping back in, an issue arose with my parents about what I was going to eat for dinner. My appetite was diminishing in direct proportion to the gangrene growing in my feet and I could hardly digest anything. I was losing weight rapidly, and when my mother showed up with a dinner tray while Richard was still there, I'm afraid he got to see a side of me that was not pretty.

Hoping I could eat something, I'd requested a meal from a restaurant called Don and Charlie's, a rib house where I'd been a part-time hostess during my high-school days. My order had arrived, my mother was holding a huge plate of ribs and a baked potato, but I caught one whiff and yelled, "Get out of my room and take this with you right now! It's horrible. Eat it yourself or give it to the nurses. I don't care what you do with it, just take it away from me."

"Do you want something else?" my long-suffering mother asked.

"No! Just leave me alone!" I yelled.

I knew it was awful, but I couldn't seem to control myself. I'm sure that Richard left my room that night with great trepidation as to whether he was making a mistake in taking my case. What kind of client would I be? To his credit, he didn't give up on me, and we were the lucky ones. He advised my parents well and guided them through the press conference that the media was demanding. It turned out that for the next few years, as my family and I rode the hard-breaking tides of a rising swell of legal and emotional challenges, I couldn't have had a greater champion by my side than Richard Plattner.

11

The Silver Lining

LISA WAS DISCHARGED FROM THE HOSPITAL WHILE MY CONDITION was still in question. She was far from fine—the muscles, tissues, tendons, and nerves in her feet were permanently damaged and ached all the time—but the hyperbaric treatments had helped a lot. The black was still there but the tissue was healing, and while she was still in constant pain, there was nothing left for her to achieve by staying in the hospital.

Upon her release, she gave a press conference, thanking everyone for their support while we were missing and in the hospital. She expressed her sincere wishes that I would be following her soon and she headed home. Still her ordeal was far from over. A month or two after her release, since the tips of three of her toes were still black on her right foot, she was forced to undergo partial amputations. She would require ongoing physical therapy and many additional operations during the next several years on hammered toes that the doctors could not seem to straighten. She also needed surgery in a hole under the center arch of her right foot that went all the way up into the top of the foot itself, and she faced the emotional adjustment of returning to a life with nerve damage and constant pain. But she was alive and she was home.

Toward the end of my third week in the hospital, I was getting really sick. It was tough lying in bed all that time, enduring the pain, even with all my friends and family visiting. People were always coming and going, I had books, TV, and music, and letters were arriving by the bushel, but I couldn't answer any of them. In fact, it had gotten to where I couldn't read or write at all, I was so overcome by discomfort.

At this point, most of the doctors had stopped coming to see me, because there was nothing they could do. The exception was Dr. Mel Bottner, a general practitioner who began and ended every day in my hospital room. Before he started his rounds, there he was, no matter what mood I was in, talking to me and my parents. They still remember him as the only man in the whole world who could make them laugh during the horror of those times. He was just that kind of a guy—he was everyone's saving grace with his gift for humor mixed with supreme sensitivity. In fact, my father still uses him as his GP, still thankful for how he was able to join us in the darkness that hung overhead, even breaking through it once in a while with his ready smile and words of encouragement.

My family really needed this kindness because they weren't getting anything positive from me. I was extremely self-centered, mostly oblivious to everyone around me. It's understandable; my feet were turning black from gangrene, and they hurt so badly, a feather brushing against them was unbearable. A hospital technician built a metal cage at the end of my bed like I'd had in ICU, a wire-framed arched tent that rose upward from the sides of the bed and met in the middle. They could place the sheet over the top and it wouldn't touch my feet. I couldn't turn over anymore, I had to lie on my back all the time, and I insisted on changing my own bandages and dressings. I couldn't bear for anyone else to do it because I needed to be in control of how much pain I was willing to inflict upon myself.

It was getting pretty obvious we had reached an impasse. My mother was exhausted from watching me suffer, and so was everyone else. A meeting was called between my parents and my team of doctors, headed by a staff surgeon, to discuss amputation. My mother's reaction was extraordinary. After they explained that amputation was the only way to save my life, she asked, "Can't you take my feet off and graft them onto Jami's legs?" She thought that was a viable option and she was willing to go straight into surgery beside me and do it, right away. What did she need her feet for? she said. She had a husband, a great family, and a great life. I was just beginning mine. She figured she could adjust more easily to prosthetics than I could. Her offer left everyone breathless; I don't think they'd ever heard such a selfless suggestion. They quickly informed her, however, that it couldn't be done, it was out of the question, and that she and my father should get some second opinions outside of the hospital to confirm my diagnosis. And they should do it immediately, as my health was deteriorating daily.

When my parents told me about the decision, I cried. Everybody did. We were stunned that our greatest fear was about to become a reality, but then, I was not exactly having a love affair with my feet. There was a part of me that wanted them to go away, they were causing me so much misery. I wonder if I really comprehended what was happening at that moment, or what I would be facing for the rest of my life. Probably not. None of us did. But we could all see that I was emaciated, as skinny as I had been when I was found, if not skinnier. It's not that I wasn't trying to gain weight, but eating had become a lost cause, especially hospital food. When they brought it to me, I burst into tears at the smell and the frustration of not being able to eat.

The truth was that if they'd flown in Beluga caviar from Russia and followed it up with lobster and rare filet mignon, I couldn't have eaten that either, because the infection was eating me. I was slowly disappearing, and in order to save my life, my feet would have to go. They promised me that as soon as they were gone, I would feel better and they could give me a discharge date from the hospital. That made this impossibly tough choice easier, while my mother called around and spoke with several doctors. The first two agreed with the diagnosis, but couldn't get to Scottsdale to examine me. Clearly we would have to go forward with the operation, but we were uncomfortable with the surgeon who was supposed to do the amputation. He specialized in hands, not feet, and when we asked him for a game plan for my future, we were not impressed. He said that following a three-to-four-hour double foot surgery, I would recover in the hospital for three weeks, at which time they would ship me off to California for rehab and fittings for prosthetics. Then I'd be on my own, just like that. As far as any of us were concerned, that was not an acceptable game plan.

We were despondent, wondering where we would ever find the confidence to move forward with this devastating plan of action, when a thread of hope arrived. It was Dr. James Malone, a vascular surgeon from Maricopa County Hospital in Phoenix, the silver lining around the dark cloud that was hovering over our lives. Dr. Malone had just relocated from Tucson when we found him, so he wasn't too backed up with work as yet. He came right over to the hospital to meet me and my parents and get a firsthand understanding of my case. It was love at first sight in all directions. From the moment we met him, it was clear that this man who specialized in foot and leg amputations had to be my doctor.

Dr. Malone had a terrific game plan. He began by telling us that my left foot had a small degree of life from the ankle down. The other one was in much worse shape. He agreed that amputation was our only choice, but there were two available types. The first possibility was to do a full amputation on one foot and a partial on the other, which would leave me with a club foot. I would have to wear a thick, heavy shoe and I would always limp, which would eliminate most physical activities in my future. The other alternative, which in his opinion was the right way to go, was to do full amputations on both legs, five inches below the knee. If we chose this plan of action, Dr. Malone knew a prosthetist who would be in the operating room at the time of the operation, guiding the doctor on exactly where to cut, so the prosthetics could fit perfectly. They would place temporary prosthetics on my legs right in the operating room, and when I awakened in bed later that day, I would see what appeared to be legs and feet under the sheets. Psychologically, this sounded right, and as it turned out, it was.

"If you take this route, I promise you Jami will walk out of here in three more weeks," he assured my parents, "on her own two feet. And she'll live a full life, able to do anything she pleases." That sounded perfect, but there was a setback. Dr. Malone was not on staff at Scottsdale Memorial, so someone else would have to do the surgery. My mother wouldn't hear of it; she told Dr. Malone that he was the one. When he explained it was against policy for a doctor to work in a hospital where he was not on the board, she retorted, "Fuck policy!"

She informed the staff of Scottsdale Memorial that they would either allow Dr. Malone to perform the surgery or she would pull me out immediately and send me to Maricopa County Hospital. They came back with a compromise. Dr. Malone could do the surgery on one of my legs with his prosthetist right there, if we would allow their surgeon to do the other leg, under Dr. Malone's supervision. Dr. Malone agreed, saying that if they worked at the same time, I would be under anesthesia for only half the time. Considering the delicacy of my physical condition, that was a plus. Bolstered by his assurances that he and his prosthetist would watch over the entire procedure, the surgery was set for January 24. That would give us three days to get blood from a family member and have it processed in case I needed it. Considering how weak I was and my inability to eat, it was almost certain that I would.

My mother and Poppy shared my blood type. Poppy was adamant that he would be the one to give blood, but when he went to do so, they refused to take it. He was seventy-five, the nurses said, too old to give blood. He would not accept that—this was the first real thing he could do to help—so he had his doctor in Chicago assure the hospital staff that he was in good enough health. He gave blood and so did my mother.

The days between the decision and the operation were much more difficult for everyone than I knew. My aunt Tona was finishing a plate of spaghetti she had just cooked when she got the call. When she heard about my upcoming operation, even though she knew it was the right thing to do, she went into the bathroom and threw up her entire dinner. When I called Lisa to tell her what was about to happen to me, she cried hysterically. She never had believed it would come to this. She'd left the hospital, certain that I would be close behind her. Now she was desperately disappointed and sad.

I heard later that Mike was so miserable when he got the news, he sat on a chair outside my hospital room and cried bitterly. Apparently, Poppy found him there and admonished him. "Mike," he said, "you can't react this way. She's alive and that's enough. Now pull yourself together." Poppy never minced words and he wasn't about to start now. He simply would not allow people to fall apart in the hospital. If they needed to do it on their own time, so be it, but he didn't want anyone influencing the rest of the family. He knew the importance of staying strong collectively, with everyone leaning on each other. That was Poppy's gift—his ability to rise above a situation and draw everyone else up there with him.

I was scared, sick, confused, and horribly disappointed during those days of preparation. At the same time, I was so tired of the pain in my feet, a part of me wanted those things off the end of my legs so I could get on with my life. I remember my dad, stifling his tears, telling me as calmly as possible that life would soon be back to normal. "The only difference," he said, "is that we'll be getting up in the morning and putting on our shoes and socks, and you'll be getting up and putting on your legs." I nodded and imagined being pain-free. It had been an awfully long time.

When I get frustrated, sometimes I get mean, and Joe Leal, the most wonderful prosthetist in the world, got quite a dose the day before the operation. When he came to talk to me, I was angry, frightened, uncommunicative, and filled with attitude. I was not nice to him. All the while he was explaining things to me, I didn't listen because I didn't care. All I knew was I had survived one nightmare and I was about to live through another one. I remember crying to my mother on the phone at three in the morning the day of the operation. They were giving me a blood transfusion because I was anemic and they wanted me to be as strong as possible for the surgery. "It hurts," I moaned to her. "It's cold and I'm scared. I hate this."

I know my mother understood my terror, but it must have

been awful to hear me sobbing in the middle of the night. She was suffering as much as I, on a different level perhaps, and I know that every time she left the hospital, she cried all the way home. She was glad I was alive, everyone was, but nobody could understand why I had to go through so much misery—or why any of us did.

12

The Parallel Bars

W HAT DID THEY DO WITH YOUR REAL FEET? DID THEY BURN them?"

Children ask the direct questions that grown-ups wouldn't dare to broach. I speak at their schools and I'm glad they're uninhibited enough to ask such things, but I don't have the answers. I guess that was more information than I needed to know, so I never asked. I also didn't ask how they removed my legs. I suppose they used some sort of a saw, but I never bothered to find out. All I know is that I was wheeled into surgery at 5 P.M. on January 24th, I went under anesthesia, and an hour and a half later I was wheeled back out without my legs. That was plenty of information for me to digest.

It all went down exactly like Dr. Malone had promised. Four doctors attended me, two of them cutting, two assisting, while the prosthetist watched carefully, guiding the surgeons as to where the cuts should be made so the prosthetics would fit perfectly. Unfortunately, the left side has given me a great deal of problems, while Dr. Malone's work on the right side has been perfect. Today, you can see that my two limbs are different shapes; the right is a clean cut, slightly longer than the other, while the nerves and tissues on the left limb are not attached as well as they are on the right. When the operation was done, the hand surgeon remained virtually uninvolved with the hard adjustment phase that followed and I felt badly about that, too. I can only say that what's done is done, and if this doctor hadn't been part of the surgery, it would have been complicated for the hospital and I would have been under anesthesia a lot longer. And yet, you have only to see my limbs to recognize Dr. Malone's superior technique and experience.

I was back in my hospital bed, my parents and my grandmother by my side, when I awakened from the operation. My grandfather had gone out to buy me tennis shoes; the doctors told him I would need them right away and he wanted to keep busy to deal with his anxiety. Still groggy from the anesthesia, I looked down at the end of the bed. Instead of me seeing a flat sheet, a pair of legs and feet appeared to bulge upward from under the covers. This was a terrific psychological boost for all of us, a gift that Dr. Malone and the prosthetist arranged when they attached casts on my legs a few inches below each knee while I was still in the operating room. A temporary pole-like structure jutted out of each cast with a prosthetic foot screwed on at the end. These feet were not made for walking more than a few steps at a time but they were weight-bearing so I could learn to stand on them, the next order of business.

In a perfect world, we would all be pain-free, but as we all know, this world is far from perfect. After the surgery, my amputated legs and feet still hurt, something they had warned me about, but it was a freaky thing to get used to. It's called "phantom pain" or "ghost pain," and although my feet don't hurt anymore, I still feel as if I can wiggle my toes, even though I don't have any. Over time, I learned to control the pain and the strange itching sensations by working with my mind to make them go away. At first, though, it was another item on the long list of things that didn't seem fair. If I had no legs, why should I have to suffer them hurting me?

I cried when my mother said she was about to leave for the night while I slept. I couldn't turn over by myself or move at all after the surgery. I felt terribly vulnerable and I wanted her there with me. She stayed that night—I'm sure she didn't sleep a wink—and my father stayed with me for the next two nights. They didn't want to leave me alone to face the next set of daunting challenges.

My physical therapy started less than forty-eight hours after the operation, which was a good thing, because it hardly gave me time to realize that I had no feet. Before I could integrate exactly what had happened to me, I was being strapped onto an electronic "tilt table" and being lifted to nearly an upright position, learning to bear my weight on the end of a sawed-off limb that was still healing from surgery. Good-bye, hyperbaric chamber. Hello, tilt table.

When a baby manages to stand up by herself and take her first steps, she doesn't necessarily feel a sense of achievement or the thrill of overcoming adversity. She just wants to get somewhere and learning to walk is the only way to do it. When I took my first steps along the parallel bars, however, it felt like a tremendous achievement, something I'd feared would never happen, so I reveled in it. Powered by a remote control, this flat electronic tilt table is still used in physical therapy today. They buckle you in with leather straps, and the patient controls the remote, which determines the angle of the tilt, as your upper body rises and your legs eventually touch the ground. That way, you can position yourself and determine how much weight you can bear, according to how much pain you're in and how strong you are that day. It's a secure feeling being strapped to the table and knowing you can back off whenever you want. When you're finally standing upright, you can release the straps, grab on to the parallel hand bars, and begin to walk away from the table, bearing most of the weight on your arms. That means you need to have adequate strength in your arm muscles to hold yourself up. At that point, I didn't.

At least I had stopped losing my temper. When my feet were diseased with gangrene, I was slowly being poisoned and it was showing in my attitudes. Once the disease was removed, I didn't yell anymore, but I did get pretty frustrated. Just imagine the burden on a newly severed patch of skin that was not meant to hold the weight of an entire body. I had to practice with the tilt table every day, grabbing the parallel bars and trying to walk, wearing the pair of tennis shoes my grandfather had bought me. My mother was by my side for most of my rehab; so was my grand-mother. My father came in and out, and Poppy was chief overseer. As usual.

It was such hard work and I was so resistant at first, I was ex-hausted at the end of a day. You see, exercise of any sort was alien to me. I just wasn't interested, I never had been and the idea of strengthening my body never had occurred to me. What for? It was strong enough to do everything I needed—until the opera-tion. Less than twenty-four hours after my surgery, a physical ther-apist came in to see me.

"Do you know what exercise is?" she asked.

"Yes," I said. That's a pretty dumb question, I thought, naively disconnected from the fact that it had anything to do with me.

"Do you *do* any exercise?" she asked.

"No," I said with absolutely no guilt. I had never seen the point of wasting afternoons in the gym, working on flexibility and building muscles. That was for other people who enjoyed that sort of thing—but it was about to change.

She patiently explained to me that since twenty-five percent of my body mass was gone, I had to make the rest of my body strong enough to compensate. When an able-bodied person gets up out of a chair, for example, she naturally uses her leg muscles to help her stand. I would have to use my hands, arms, and hips, I would have to make them strong, and she would be arriving the very next morning to start my resistance training on a pulley ma-chine with a hand grip.

I knew I had to do it, but I didn't have to like it. I greeted this "patient as a saint" therapist each morning with clenched teeth, hating every second of our work together, but I did it anyway, bol-stered by encouragement from my family and urged, not so gently, by Poppy. He acted exactly like a coach, pushing me, shaming me, doing anything he could to get me to cooperate with my therapist because he knew how important it was. I was one tough customer—I hated doing anything that made me sweat—and although Poppy and I were at each other's throats, he never backed down. Today, I know he is largely responsible for my determination, my stamina, and the aggressive nature that has helped me enjoy a great life, and I love him for it. At the time, though, I fought him hard. I didn't want to become an athletic person. But I *did* want to become an independent person, and I quickly realized that making my body strong was the only way to get there.

On February 1, eight days after the amputation, they changed my original casts and I saw my severed limbs for the first time. I wasn't aware how they removed casts—I'd never broken a bone before—so when Dr. Malone, with Joe Leal at his side, picked up a saw and moved toward me, I stopped him. They had to assure me that he was going to saw through the cast, not through me, before I let him continue. When the casts were gone and I studied my naked limbs, still irritated and healing from surgery, it was very emotional for me. I remember saying tearfully to these two men who went through so much with me, "You took off more than I thought you would." Some part of me felt betrayed, even though they did exactly what we had discussed. This was not the first time a patient had reacted that way, and Joe Leal patiently explained to me, yet again, where he had ordered the cuts and why. The reality is that today, the technology of prosthetics is so far advanced, they might have been able to leave on more of my legs. Maybe. But the question is moot now, the past is over and the present is all that is worth considering.

Joe worked tirelessly with me throughout my rehab, assuring me that the length of my limbs absolutely supported my desire to return to school and have a normal life. With the custom prosthetics I would get after I left the hospital, I would be able to do anything I wanted. I focused on that. I was a college sophomore and I was determined not to miss more than one semester. If I got strong, applied myself to the therapy, and overcame some pretty intense obstacles, I could accomplish my goal. I began to access a determined part of me that must have always been in there but had no reason to surface until that time.

The phantom pain was a major problem at first, but Joe and Dr. Malone helped me learn to rise above it. The human body is such an enigma. I remember having strange sensations like twinges and itches in my feet that obviously were not physical, so

how could I scratch them? I've since learned that pain and irrita-
tion are mental as well as physical, and so they can be dealt with
mentally. I perfected the important lesson of relieving an itch on
my nonexistent foot by thinking about scratching it. I did the
same with the pain and eventually it stopped taunting me.

Joe continued to assure me that the strange casts and poles I
was wearing were nothing like the legs I would be fitted for. I
would have several different pairs, he said, which I would be able
to change quickly and easily, to fit whatever activity I wanted to
do. One pair would allow me to wear a high-heeled shoe for
dress-up (with an Allen wrench, you could crank a metal peg to
adjust the angle for a high-heeled shoe), another would be for
everyday walking. It was hard to imagine, it was painful just
pulling socks up over the new casts, but I continued to move forward. There really was no alternative, and I owe a great deal to my
loyal friends, who reminded me that there was life outside the
hospital and my daily rehab sessions.

Lisa came to visit me sometimes; her boyfriend rolled her into
my room in a wheelchair, because she still couldn't walk. I loved
seeing her and I felt courage when she came to visit. We had gone
through this whole thing together, she was back home, and soon I
would be following her. Other friends came to fill me in on the
school gossip. One day, my parents wrapped my little dog, Precious, in a coat and snuck her into my hospital room. I was really
happy to see her but when they let her out, she ran around the
room like a maniac. After five minutes, they had to sneak her
back out. We had some good laughs but they never did that again.

Mail bags arrived at the hospital every day with tons of letters
from children in local schools. In preparation for writing this
book, I went through a box filled to the brim with letters, notes,
pictures from 1987; there were even a few of our MISSING posters.
The family gathered in the living room to scan through it, and
amid lots of tears and tough memories, I read all of these notes,
some of which I'd been too sick to read back then. They were
mostly from children who told me a few things about themselves
and drew me pictures, with sparkles and sequins pasted on that
fell off all over the living-room floor. There had been too many

letters to answer back then, but now they warmed my heart so much. A second grader gave me quite a chuckle when she described herself:

I have brown hair, green eyes and a good sinus of humor.

Letters also arrived from adults who had been following my story, telling me I was in their prayers and talking about their own experiences. I was surprised at how many people knew amputees or were amputees, themselves. The following is an excerpt of a letter from a rock climber named Nancy:

Dear Jami,

I taped a TV segment on a man named Hugh Herr, on "National Geographic Explorer." He was climbing Mt. Washington when he was caught in a severe snowstorm. He had amputations of his feet and legs due to frostbite, and he continues to climb some of the hardest, toughest routes in America.

She gave me her phone number in case I wanted to see the footage, or just talk.

Another woman named Carolyn sent me one of the more personal letters I received:

Dear Jami,

I know how devastated you must feel. I think you should give full vent to your feelings of anger and grief. Don't just cry. Arrange some total privacy for yourself—then open your mouth very wide and WAIL! Do this as often as you feel the urge. It will do wonders for you.

By the way, an amputee friend of mine, although she is no devastating beauty, has been married four times to extremely attractive men. I knew two of her husbands. They were considered great "catches." So I send you the conviction that your life can still be wonderful. Here's to a long healthy life full of love, joy, and dancing.

The idea that so many people wrote me notes and, in some cases, three-page letters, was overwhelming. Now I *had* to get better, not only for myself, but for all of these well-wishers who didn't know me but had taken time out of their busy lives to assure me that I was not alone.

And then there was Mike. I've never been one to follow rules; that was evident from my teenage years when I drove my parents to distraction. When I started feeling better and I had some private time with Mike in the hospital, we threw a washcloth over the video camera (video is standard equipment in the children's ward), he climbed up on the bed with me, and you can guess the rest. We did that on two separate occasions and I have to say, it did my self-esteem a world of good. Mike and I were not destined to stay together all that long but I was lucky to have him during this part of the ordeal, because I didn't have a chance to wonder if I was still attractive to men. I learned right away that I could be loved and wanted as a whole woman, even without my legs and feet. It was also good for my psyche to be defying authority by breaking the hospital rules. It was a little bit of the old Jami resurfacing and I liked meeting up with her again.

Nobody knew the old Jami better than my brother Jason. Today, we have a very close bond, but when I was teenager, I was a tough older sister. Jason is two and a half years younger than I, and even though I was loyal to him when he needed me, I knew exactly how to push his buttons and humiliate him. Of course he adored his older sister, but I only let him play with me if he pretended to be a girl. I did all the standard sibling-rivalry stuff: When we rode in the backseat of the car together, I used to draw an imaginary line and force him to keep his arms on his own side. I even remember complaining to my mother, "Jason's breathing my air. Make him stop." I had him so terrorized that once when he lost his house key, he and his friends waited outside in the winter cold rather than taking the risk of waking me from a nap. I used to make Jason pay me for gas when he needed a ride somewhere, and sometimes I woke him up in the middle of the night to help me push our parents' car out of the garage so I could steal it for a joy ride. When I got caught and my parents had to bail me out of jail one time, Jason kept his mouth shut. He was that scared of his tough older sister.

When I was learning to walk again, I called on the toughness of the old Jami to get me through it. I had enough of myself and my iron will to avoid seeing a therapist or social worker, but my family probably could have used some help while they witnessed my struggle to get my legs back underneath me. My mother got the worst of it but she kept herself together by remembering, "She's alive, she's alive." That was the mantra that got her through my recovery process. It got me through, too, while I learned how to change my own bandages, deal with rashes and irritations on my limbs, and work on the parallel bars. I walked longer and longer distances on my own and I continued to strengthen my upper body. Nothing could deter me from working toward my goal: going home.

13

Breakdown

O N THE AFTERNOON OF FEBRUARY 19, 1988, I WALKED OUT OF Scottsdale Memorial Hospital on my own steam. They had arranged a press conference in the patio of the hospital cafeteria when I was discharged. Hundreds of people were waiting to see my triumphant steps to the podium, but what if I couldn't pull it off? I hadn't walked long distances yet and I had never been the focus of a press conference. It was intimidating, and yet, I'd had to face so many new and disturbing challenges lately, in a certain way I was prepared.

On that fateful day, I did my physical therapy early in the morning as usual. Then I showered, washed my own hair, and got dressed by myself. After forty-nine days, I was getting out of the hospital. I still remember the pink outfit I chose, flowing pants and a top which fit loosely over my skinny body. I still had very little appetite, it was something I would have to work on consciously, and although it would take a good year for it to return fully, I knew it would be easier to eat once I got home.

I was wheeled into the elevator and down to the first floor next to the cafeteria, where my dad and Dr. Malone were waiting for me. My father stood beside my wheelchair, holding my walker, and I could barely get out the words that I whispered to Dr. Malone: "I don't know if I can do this."

"Jami," he said, "I know you can. You told everyone you would walk out of here, you've done the work, and now it's time to show them."

I stood up, grabbed on to my walker, and steadied myself. Then, with my family and my doctors behind me and Lisa by my side (she arrived that morning to walk out with me), we slowly walked into the cafeteria, where a huge crowd was waiting. I heard gasps as I carefully made my way across the front of the room to take a seat behind the microphone. I felt proud. In that thrilling moment, I carried with me a newfound sense of joy, independence, and security in myself and my doctors. Everything they had promised had come true, both good and bad. They said I would live and I was alive. They said I would need amputation and I did. They also said I would walk and I was walking. Now I had every reason to believe that the next phase also would unfold as they had predicted.

I looked out at the smiling faces and I smiled back. The last months flashed before me. I had done it, I had survived being lost and stranded, I had made it through the whirlpool bath, the hyperbaric chamber, having my legs removed, the tilt table, and now I was standing here to tell my story. Granted, there was a lot of hard work ahead of me, but I had been given a second chance at life and all these people wanted me to succeed. A sudden calm came over me. The worst was over. If I could live through the last two months, I could live through anything. Even a press conference. With Lisa sitting on a chair beside me, I read a statement that I had prepared with help from my parents and my wonderful lawyer, Richard Plattner:

> I want to thank my family for their ceaseless efforts to find me when I was lost and their steady, cheerful support since I was found. They've put up with a lot from me for the last two months and I love them more than I can ever say.

I thanked the doctors, the nurses, and the entire hospital staff. When I explained a little bit about how we got lost, Lisa and I both giggled when we told everyone how we passed the time,

waiting and playing with Jason's baseball cards. The press conference was the first time Jason really understood how far-reaching
my disappearance had been. Lost in his teenage world, he had
been somewhat oblivious (that's the privilege of being a
teenager), but as he witnessed the enormous crowd gathered two
months after the fact to support me and see me walk, he became
aware of how many people had been touched by my ordeal. I
smiled at him. Our relationship would never be the same and
that was a good thing. Then, I thanked all the people who had
written and sent cards, telling them that although I would not be
able to answer them, they all meant so much to me. I finished by
saying:

> Most of all, I'm looking forward to getting back to a normal life. I
> want to work hard to learn the new skills I'll need to take care of myself.
> I guess you'd have to say that I need to get my feet back underneath me.

I buried my head in Lisa's shoulder to hide my tears of relief.
When Dr. Malone took a seat to answer medical questions from
the press, I stood up, grabbed on to the walker, and walked on
out of there. I placed one foot in front of the other all the way
through the lobby and finally outdoors, blinded by flashbulbs on
all sides. I ignored them; I was too busy enjoying my freedom. I
smiled at my one-year-old nephew Jonathan, whom I'd placed on
my lap and given wheelchair rides down the hospital corridors.
I'd been deprived of too much family time; I was not about to
miss any more. I walked to the waiting car and got in. I was ready
to go home.

The hospital staff were very emotional, we had gotten so
close. My parents had become close to them, too; there were tearful good-byes, and my mother would miss them, but not too
much. I remember her saying, "When you know the entire staff
on a first-name basis, not just on your floor but throughout the
whole facility, and you're in the habit of saying good night to each
of them individually, you've been in the hospital a long time."
Too long.

It was delicious to sleep in my own bed that night, even

though I woke up a lot. Both Lisa and I twitched in our sleep for the next two years—there must have been internal organ damage from the dehydration—but being home was the greatest feeling in the world. It was so good, I went to bed after a celebratory family dinner and I didn't get up until 1:30 the next afternoon. Some of my friends arrived later that day to spend time with me. I loved that, but I was in a lot of pain, which increased as the day progressed. I went to sleep that night, got up the next day, had a manicure just because I could, and left for Tucson, the next leg of my uphill journey to independence.

My mother, my grandmother, and I checked into a motel there, near the clinic where we would be spending the next four days while I got fitted for my first pair of custom prosthetics. They would need me at the clinic each day for many hours to take casts of my legs and to try out different kinds of feet. When we were checking in at the motel, we needed to make sure our room had wheelchair access, yet another rude awakening as to my condition. At times it all seemed insurmountable—these were stressful days, to say the least—but Joe Leal's clinic was as warm and friendly as it could possibly be.

I was happy to see him again but I was devastated when he removed my temporary prosthetics, rendering me unable to walk. While the technicians spent the afternoon shaping the cast of my new prosthetics, they didn't need me there so I had the afternoon off. My mother saw how distressed I was, being confined to my wheelchair, but none of us knew what to do with ourselves or how to act. The motel room was pretty dismal but maybe a trip to the mall would be a good distraction, my mother thought. The three of us headed to a nearby mall but once we got there, nobody felt like shopping, and since I'd never been in a public place without legs, I felt terrible. I was suddenly aware of people staring at me; I felt like a freak and I began to cry. My grandmother tried some tough love to snap me out of it.

"Stop it right now," she hollered at me. "You're here! Isn't that enough?" She modulated her voice a little as she continued, "Everything will be all right. Now pull yourself together!"

That was the only time I ever remember her raising her voice at me. She must have been pretty desperate, but I couldn't stop crying. It was as if all the tears I'd saved up during the last two months poured out and there was nothing anybody could do to stop it. My mother wheeled me out to the car. As she was helping me into the seat, I wailed, "Why did this have to happen to me? I want my legs back. I can't do this anymore."

That was the first and the last public breakdown I ever had, and I have to say, it was long overdue. I'd been so damned strong for so long, and while it might have helped other people to see me that way, I needed to be human, both for me and for my mother and my grandmother. I really think my breakdown helped them accept their own all-too-human feelings, which they were struggling with so much of the time. All three of us had a lot to get out of our systems, and I think when they finally saw me losing it, something in them let go a little bit too.

By the time we got back to the motel, I'd calmed down enough to take a short nap. We all relaxed for a few hours; then we returned to the clinic to meet and greet my new feet and sockets. I felt better when they attached them onto my legs, and I managed to eat some dinner that night, but by the next morning I wasn't doing so well. The sockets were too small and I had a terrific migraine that lasted all day. Joe Leal spent the next several days adjusting my new legs. It was a grueling process, but he was the best in the business. I headed back home on Thursday with a brand-new pair of prosthetics that felt pretty good and worked much better than the old ones.

I started out with a stiffer type of foot because it felt best. Joe told me that would change over time, that my body would keep shifting throughout the next few years. He explained that immediately following the surgery, there's a lot of water retention and my limbs were still swollen. As the flesh healed and the swelling went down, the actual shape of my limbs would shrink. The first two years were expected to be the most difficult, and nothing would be stable, but I could return to Tucson whenever I needed my sockets or feet adjusted. I was overwhelmed when I thought about it, but as I began to use my walker again, it was amazing how much easier it was with the new feet. In the end, my time in

Tucson had provided me with a lot of healing and hope for the future. I was making progress—not yet moving fast forward, but definitely a step farther on the long road ahead.

While I was in the hospital, my parents had moved my things out of my apartment in Tempe and into their home. I was back in my old bedroom, with a wheelchair and also a walker, which I greatly preferred, but I couldn't walk long distances yet; I wasn't strong enough. And doing things with a walker was awkward. I sometimes awakened in the late mornings, since I slept poorly most nights, and my parents already would be at work. I didn't mind being alone, and I would take the walker into the kitchen to fix some breakfast, but I had to eat it right there because I needed both hands to walk. I had quite a love/hate relationship with that walker. I loved it because it helped me get around. At the same time, I hated it because I *needed* it to get around. This dependency motivated me all the more to strengthen my body, with the goal of leaving the walker behind.

At this stage, my primary therapy was swimming, or should I say, walking across the bottom of a swimming pool. My aunt Vicki and uncle Les lived in an apartment complex that had a shallow heated pool and no one else in the complex ever used it. It was a short distance from my parents' house and I had to go there every day, doctor's orders. Enter Poppy, the formidable coach. Each morning without fail, he showed up and drove me to my aunt's house. I would use my walker to get to the edge of the pool and then I'd grab the rail and walk into the pool. It was hard work and I tried to play hooky from time to time but Poppy would have none of that. He was a tough taskmaster, unwilling to listen to any of my feeble excuses. Come rain or shine, he was at the house, pushing, prodding, and getting me to therapy.

When I got in the water, the buoyancy took over and I was as light as air, remembering what freedom felt like. Floating back and forth across the pool with my feet barely touching the ground improved my gait and helped me with my balance. Then came the best part, when I would take off my legs and just swim. It felt great, and kicking my limbs helped to strengthen my hips. When I was done, I would grab the rail, swing my butt onto the stairs, and pull myself up the steps to where Poppy was waiting with the towel. I'd put my legs back on and use my walker to get me back to the car. Then I'd collapse in bed and doze.

I was determined to miss only one semester at Arizona State University (ASU), which meant I had my sights set on returning to school in the fall of 1988. Mike and I were still together, although he was in New Mexico and I was in Scottsdale. We didn't see a lot of each other but it was enough to take my mind off my rehabilitation and have some fun. I think if I were honest with myself, I would admit that our problems had started at the end of the year, before Christmas, and a breakup was inevitable. It seems that the accident had postponed it and, selfishly, I was glad. Having him there when I was recovering was really good for me, but as time progressed, our relationship deteriorated and we split up. It was inevitable; we were both young, we didn't live in the same city, and we didn't have all that much in common anymore. It wasn't pleasant—breaking up never is—but it wasn't too bad either.

Soon afterward, I found a new love brewing with an old friend. His name was Darren. We'd dated briefly when I was sixteen; it was one of those three-month deals. He had just separated from his girlfriend, I had just split with Mike, and we came together naturally. In fact, my friends showed up for me in the most unbelievable way when I was recovering. I knew they would, I knew how loyal they were, but it really surprised my mother. She hadn't been crazy about my group of friends but she quickly saw how mistaken she'd been. Suddenly they had a friend with no legs and they stood by me without skipping a beat, carrying me around, showing up for me on a moment's notice, and doing whatever I needed.

On Memorial Day weekend, they were all home from school and they picked me up one day and took me away with them. My mother was scared—I hadn't been away from her since the surgery—but Darren and my friends had rented an apartment in San Diego and I wanted to be with them. It turned out to be the best therapy of all, because we had so much fun. I needed some of that, and my friends took great care of me. Several times every day, one of the guys carried me up and down the stairs. I will never be able to let them know what their loving care did for me.

During that weekend, my girlfriend Jae wheeled me to the beach one afternoon so we could catch some rays. The minute the wheelchair hit the sand, I went flying through the air and landed on my butt. Thank God it was sand. I wasn't hurt and I took it pretty well, but I think Jae felt worse about it than I did. Laughing, I pulled myself back up into my chair, but wheeling me across the sand was no longer a viable plan. I waited while Jae ran the hundred or so yards to the apartment to get Darren to carry me to a nice spot on the beach. When I told my parents about my fall later, it upset them, but I took it in stride. I was thrilled I could go to the beach at all, so if a few falls and bumps went with the territory, so be it.

Throughout my rehabilitation, I had good days and bad days, depending upon the weather and my pain quotient. I guess I was like an old sailor who could predict rain from feeling his joints ache. On the days when my limbs didn't hurt, I was usually in a good mood. If they did hurt, I felt depressed and hopeless, wondering when it would all stop and life would feel good again. Luckily, I lived in the desert, so rain was infrequent, but other things got in my way. The inside tissue between the bone and the ends of my limbs had become so badly bruised, my walking was limited, which always put me in a bad mood. Dr. Malone assured me this was par for the course. It was constantly two steps forward, one step back, and sometimes, no steps at all.

Despite my bad days, though, I was making remarkable progress. I enjoyed driving a car; I could do it early on with my casts, so I never needed hand controls. I just skipped right over that one. Sometimes I got in the car, left the walker sitting in the driveway, and took myself to a drive-through fast-food restaurant. I have a vivid memory of seeing the walker standing there idle as I drove away, wondering what people would think, seeing it there in the driveway. It was just a strange-looking thing, seemingly out of place wherever it was. I was determined to make it obsolete.

14

Back to School

Each time I went to Tucson to have my feet or sockets adjusted, I got depressed. Even though I liked seeing Joe and I always left feeling better physically, I felt my loss acutely during those trips to the clinic. I also felt my loss whenever I met with Richard Plattner, as we were busy preparing a case against the state for negligence. And then there was the pain that was never far away.

The doctor took routine X-rays, particularly because I complained of pain so much. Bone spurs were apparently common in cases such as mine, but my X-rays revealed no bone spurs, which was what the doctors had feared. That was the good news, but the bruised tissue had become so oversensitized, a mere touch sent me through the roof. Until this condition repaired itself, I was directed to stay off my feet as much as possible, which meant I had to be in the wheelchair. This did not go over very well with me; the chair meant a loss of freedom, but then, *no* chair meant too much pain. It was a vicious cycle, escalated by sudden crises, which seemed to occur at every turn.

One Saturday morning when I was hurting too much to walk, my mother wheeled me next door to my aunt Tona and my uncle Mark's house to see my grandparents. I got tired and my uncle offered to wheel me back home so I could take a nap. The driveway was gravel and he must have wheeled over a large piece, because

without warning I found myself lurching out of the chair and flying through the air once again. I landed on the base of my right
limb, which was already hurting too much to bear any weight.
The pain was indescribable; suffice it to say that you could hear
my screams for blocks. Everyone came charging out of the house
to pick me up. My uncle was so upset he could barely stand it, and
I had no energy to make him feel any better. I iced my limb all
day and into the evening, but it took a full three days before it returned to normal. Pain had become a daily challenge for me and
I never knew when bad would turn to worse.

A pattern was emerging: each difficult phase provided me
with lifelong lessons and rewards. When I realized that my only
hope for relief was to change my frame of mind, I started viewing
pain as an annoyance that I could work with. During the two years
following my surgery, pain constantly lurked in the shadows, as if
it were biding its time, waiting to strike when I least expected it.
This required me to be on constant medication, which I hated because it made me feel disoriented and fuzzy. Between the muscle
cramps, irritations on the ends of my limbs, headaches, and stomach pain, I had a great excuse to sit around, do nothing, and feel
sorry for myself, but that kind of behavior was against my nature.
I was built to keep moving forward and I did, even though it was a
constant test to rise above the pain of the day.

Few of us realize how powerful the mind is, that when you
gain control of your mind, you can also gain control of your body.
I was determined to transform my situation, and I made great
strides in placing mind over matter and making my body and my
life a happy place to be. Again, it was the old, "I'm alive, I'm
alive," that kept me going, and I actually got to the point where I
could perceive any unexpected phantom pain as a symbol of security, a comforting memory of the feet I once had. I learned to
derive satisfaction from successfully itching or wiggling an invisible toe, as I programmed myself to know that I could walk as if my
feet were still there. I'm not saying it was easy. It took a long time
to accomplish and I still work with it to this day. But I can do it
when I need to.

I've learned that passing the big tests in life tends to make the small ones seem insignificant. And so, although heading back to school was not without its challenges, finding an apartment and moving away from home felt like a snap, compared with the last several months. Not for my parents, though. As much as they wanted me to be on my own, they were afraid for me. To make matters worse, I had insisted on apartment-hunting without them and I eventually put down a deposit on a basement unit that was accessed by a few stairs.

"Wasn't there a ground-floor apartment available?" my father wanted to know.

"Yes, there was," I told him.

"Why didn't you take it? Then you wouldn't have stairs."

"I liked the basement one better. Besides, what's wrong with stairs?"

End of conversation. My attitude came directly from Poppy; I had inherited his fierce determination and no one argued with me. I needed to keep on moving, but I felt for my father. He had seen more than a father should see, like the times I crawled around on the floor like a baby when my legs were off. Of course my mother agreed with my dad that I should find a place to live without stairs, but she didn't try to talk me out of it. I was an adult and I demanded to be treated like one. My mother bit her lip, repeated her mantra, "She's alive, she's alive," and let me go about my business. My girl-friend Jae, who also was attending ASU, agreed to be my roommate and soon afterward, my parents drove me, my wheelchair, and my walker to Tempe. I was ready to start school.

My new relationship with Darren was part of the reason I never felt sorry for myself or worried if I looked all right when I started back to school. I was never all that focused on body image anyway, maybe because there was such support in my family for just being me. I was not under any illusions; I always knew I was not model material, that I was average-looking with an average body. I didn't make the audition in seventh grade to be a cheer-leader, I just wasn't that kind of girl, and I really didn't mind. I had friends, even in junior high school, who refused to leave the house without mascara and lipstick, but I never cared enough or had the patience for that. I didn't strive to fit into society's image of what was considered beautiful, I was usually five to ten pounds overweight, and still, I had no interest in exercise. I knew I could take the weight off if I applied myself but I didn't care, and it never stopped me from dating a guy I liked. I guess I was disgustingly well adjusted, even when I was young, and I thank my parents for giving me a solid sense of self. I simply accepted myself, exactly as I was—with one major exception.

At fourteen years old, I stood five feet, one-half inch tall, and my breasts were 36 double D. Get the picture? I hid my body in sweats and oversized T-shirts in the heat of the Arizona desert, and all I could think about was getting a breast reduction so I could feel more comfortable. My mother was sympathetic. When I was fifteen, she took me to the doctor, who said I had reached my full height. We discussed a breast reduction with him and he was not opposed. The rest of my family was, though, telling my mother that she was crazy to think about giving me this operation at such a young age.

"Wait," they all advised her. "She's too young. When she reaches her twenties, she might not care anymore."

"But she's got a bad body image *now*," my mother retorted. She figured by the time I was twenty, one of two things would have happened. I would either have outgrown the problem and wouldn't care anymore, or the damage would be done. When the insurance company, predicting future back problems, agreed to cover the entire cost of the operation, that clinched it for us. We decided to go for it, against everybody else's wishes. I was really excited about it—until the night before the surgery. I got nervous and lost my patience, so after I finished a snippy conversation with the doctor, he called my mother. "I don't know if we should go through with this," he told her. "I'm not sure she's ready."

My mother knew my pattern of getting defensive and angry when I was scared. We talked for a while, and she was more than ready to let me wait, but I decided to go ahead. When I arrived for surgery the next morning, I gave the doctor a kiss on the cheek while I was being prepped. "I'm fine now," I told him. And I was. The surgery was a success, my breasts were reduced to a 34C, I healed quickly, and I had no more body-image problems.

As I reentered college after the accident, I still had no body-image problems, even with a new pair of legs. Darren and I got close really fast, probably because we had known each other before and we already had a sexual history. Even though many things about me were different from the girl he'd known in the past, he welcomed me with open arms. It helped so much to have a boyfriend who loved and cared for me, so I didn't have to wonder if I was still attractive to men. My family, as always, provided the stability I needed to fit myself back into society, and my life during that year was filled with many different kinds of emotions. I suppose everyone's is, but my highs and lows were pretty dramatic. While my parents adjusted to not seeing me every day, I had the joy of dating a man I cared for (of course, we had some fights, too), and of being a normal schoolgirl, hanging out with my friends after I nearly had died. On the more difficult side, I had the misery of endless visits to Joe, my prosthetist in Tucson, and excruciating epidural injections in the ends of my limbs to try to stop the pain.

It was still two steps forward, one step back. I went to the gym each day, working to strengthen my upper body and stay as flexible as possible, but I was soon faced with a new and serious problem. Shortly after the spring semester began, I found myself in the hospital again, for surgery. This time, X-rays exposed the anticipated and highly dreaded bone spurs; my young bones thought they were supposed to keep growing and so they did. It was no wonder my legs were hurting so badly—I was walking around on raw bone. Surgery was the only answer. The operation went fine but it was a huge setback as it landed me in the old wheelchair again. Once again, I was dependent upon family and friends to help me get around. I couldn't wear one of my legs while my limb healed, so my father arrived at my apartment in the mornings, put me in the car, drove me to the campus, and put me in the wheelchair so I could get to my classes. I hated it, but my choices were either to sit in the chair or miss more school. To me, that was no choice at all.

Luckily, my youth was a plus, I healed quickly, and before too long I was walking again. That was when I moved in with Darren.

He was a man whom I thought I would marry, which was why I moved in with him so soon after we started dating seriously. My parents were supportive, partly because I would be living on ground level, partly because they knew Darren would take care of me. The thought of me living alone, with the potential of so many unpredictable physical problems, was upsetting to them. Especially since things kept happening, which I had no control over.

For example, I took baths rather than showers because it was easier. Thank goodness I was a "telephone person"—I always had a cordless phone close by me wherever I was in the house, and I brought it into the bathroom with me one day while I took my bath. I had a deep tub, and when the bath was over, I put the ends of my short limbs along the edge of the bathtub and got ready to push off with my arms. Unfortunately, my right arm slipped beneath me and my shoulder popped out of its socket. It was unbelievably painful, so I stayed where I was and grabbed the phone with my other arm. I called around and contacted Darren's mom, who drove right over to help. She managed to cover my naked body with a towel before my dad and the paramedics arrived. They took me to the emergency room, where they discovered I had dislocated my shoulder. I was pretty shook up, especially when I thought about what might have happened if I hadn't had a phone nearby. I arrived back home with a sling on my arm, which made getting around even more difficult. I was able to get rid of the sling in record time, but my shoulder was sensitive from that day on.

Then there was the ongoing difficulty of finding a place to park on campus. I had disabled privileges, and I could use my disabled placard whenever I needed it, but I was stubborn and I tried to avoid it whenever possible. The trouble was that the campus lots were usually full. One day when my legs were bothering me, I decided to use one of the twenty disabled spots that were right beside the entrance. I parked, put the placard on my rearview mirror, and got out of the car. I guess I was moving quickly—I was running late—when two students who didn't know me started harassing me. My long pants and my ease with my prosthetics, even when I was in pain, worked against me that day.

"You can't park there," they said. "Those spots are for handi-capped people."

"Would you like to see my legs?" I asked them, pretty ticked off. I lifted my pant legs and showed them my prosthetics.

They didn't back off. "Looks like you're walking just fine," they said, continuing to taunt me as I walked away. I was furious but what was I supposed to do—start arguing with them? People can be so mean. I decided then and there that part of my future work would be to educate everyone about people with different abilities. For now, I was late to class.

15

Goldman v. Arizona

Richard Plattner filed a lawsuit, *Goldman v. Arizona*, in the spring. Lisa's lawyer, Ty Taber, filed *Barzano v. Arizona* at the same time. The judge decided to try the two cases together, since they were identical in nature, and Richard and Ty worked closely in tandem. They agreed there was no debate as to whether or not we should sue. Arizona had closed an open state highway after we turned onto it, never bothering to search for travelers in distress. When we were reported missing, neither the DPS, the Department of Transportation, nor the police had done anything for a week, despite our parents' cries for help. It had been all over the news, DPS reports said there were wheel marks in the snow, so there were plenty of facts to substantiate our allegations.

On top of that, Lisa's feet were still causing her severe problems. She was having surgery after surgery and no one knew whether she would heal completely. Losing my legs was clearly something I would have to deal with for the rest of my life. My family was burdened with the cost of surgeries, prosthetics, and continuing medical care, which was already off the charts. Who knew what kinds of expenses Lisa and I would incur over the remainder of our lives? Furthermore, what would happen when I was no longer eligible for insurance under my parents' current plan? If I was lucky enough to reach seventy or eighty years old, what if I had no one to take care of me? What if, for some unexpected reason, I no longer was able to use prosthetics? What if I was confined to a wheelchair and needed twenty-four-hour home care? Anything could happen.

I was twenty years old, I didn't want to think about such things, but I had no choice. I had to grow up fast, I had to fit back into society, and I needed some financial assistance to secure my questionable future. But how much? How do you put a price on what happened to me? We wanted to allow the jury to make that determination, but it wasn't an option. Arizona law demands that when you sue the state, you must first file a "notice of claim" in which you ask for a specific amount of money, which cannot be changed once the suit is in motion. If you fail to give them a number, the entire case can be thrown out. We chose a high number, ten million dollars, which we figured contained a great deal of wiggle room for the jury. If we got a fifth of that, we'd be happy.

It should have been a slam dunk. There's that "should" word again. No one was more surprised than I was on the first day of depositions. My father was obviously suffering from post-traumatic stress syndrome, a condition that was apparent in his emotional fragility, the way he cried at a moment's notice. Now he was being made to relive the biggest nightmare of his life while being insulted and accused. Statements like "C'mon, Mr. Goldman, we all know this case is about the money," and worse, were hurled at him. There was nothing he could do but try to deal with it without losing his cool. My mother was treated no better during her deposition, as she was placed on the defensive and shouted at by the other side. This was a brand of trouble none of us had imagined in our worst nightmares. Hadn't we already been through enough?

Apparently not. Until those depositions, I thought I was the luckiest girl in the world to have survived such an ordeal and still be here to talk about it. The trial hadn't even started yet, and for the first time since I was found, I felt like the luck of the draw had gone against me. From the moment I walked into a windowless room the size of a closet in the attorney general's office to give my deposition, before I even sat down, I could sense the bitterness to come.

These days, Arizona law dictates that a witness can be deposed for a maximum of four hours unless special permission is granted by the court. Back then, though, there were no limits on time. On three separate occasions, I was forced to endure some hellish days of accusatory depositions, the first two in January and May of 1989, and the last one on February 22, 1990. In the end, I was put through about nineteen hours of questions and answers, which printed out onto 620 pages.

It was hell: Lisa, my father, Richard, and Ty, Lisa's lawyer, were there all the time. So was one of the attorneys for the state, a plain-looking, rotund man with a mustache and a nasty demeanor, who started in on me first. He criticized me for not having a map in the car as well as not having blankets, water, sleeping bags, extra shoes, all the things he decided could have saved my legs.

You see, Arizona is a "comparative negligence state." That means that if the jury finds the state guilty, the same jurors must also determine if the plaintiffs (that would be Lisa and me) were guilty of negligence as well—hence the term "comparative negligence." If so, how guilty were we? Once they came up with a percentage, whatever we were awarded in damages would be reduced by that much. Until the depositions, I wasn't worried about it. Maybe I should have been better prepared for an emergency, but surely everyone would agree that it wasn't my fault the state closed the gate without searching for me. No one in his or her right mind could possibly consider me at fault, I reasoned. Boy, did I have a nasty surprise in store.

To my amazement, the state tried to determine that I always had been irresponsible, even as a teenager. That was laughable; I was a very responsible kid, but they asked me probing, irrelevant questions about my behavior as a fourteen-year-old. They wanted to know if I was a bad teenager. What was I like in high school? Did I ditch classes and come home late at night? Did I talk back to my parents?

I was shocked that such questions were allowed, but they

were. I tried to answer them truthfully and to the best of my ability. And yet, at the end of three days, I felt insulted, belittled, and invaded. Several years would pass before the actual trial, which I originally had anticipated as a way to feel better about everything. I thought it would result in justice and it would offer me some sense of redemption, so I wanted it to happen as soon as possible. Now, with the terrible depositions behind me, I faced the upcoming trial with dread, seeing that in order to stand up for myself I would be put through a great deal of humiliation. I can only imagine what a rape victim goes through when she finds the courage to come forward and accuse her rapist and then gets shot down for "asking for it." No wonder so many women choose to keep their mouths shut.

Richard felt so badly about the way I'd been treated, he vowed to do everything he could to eliminate such abuse in the future. In 1993, well after our trial was over, he filed a petition with the Arizona Supreme Court to change the state ethics rules and deem "cruel" behavior against a plaintiff to be inappropriate and unlawful. Thanks to Richard, the task of establishing a committee on ethics reform was placed on the Supreme Court's agenda. It sounded hopeful, but to this day it still sits on the agenda, waiting to be reviewed. They haven't yet appointed one committee member, so I guess it won't be happening anytime soon.

When the depositions began, I was living with Darren. I've been fortunate to have men who cared for me during challenging times in my life. It all started with Poppy, who gave me a strong sense of self-esteem. Then there's my dad, who is responsible for my sense of humor. He can be very funny, bordering on obnoxious, which is the best medicine when I get too serious. He's a mush ball of love, he has a terrific sense of who he is, and he stayed by my side during every moment of those depositions, offering me strength. Mike, my first real boyfriend, had been great for my self-esteem in the hospital and now Darren was there for me during the depositions and my readjustment to life at school as I faced the all-important question: What did I want to be when I grew up?

My high-school years had been pretty normal; I was a decent

student, but I hadn't excelled at anything in particular, mainly because nothing had ignited my passion. When it was time to apply to college, I'd taken an aptitude test that was supposed to point me in the right direction. My results had given me no direction at all; I only knew I would graduate high school, get a degree in college, get married, and have a child by the time I was thirty. And so I had enrolled in ASU, because it was a forty-minute drive from home and I could see my family whenever I wanted. Just before the accident, I'd transferred from a liberal-arts to a business program. I suppose if life had gone on as it was, I might have worked in the family commercial photo lab and stuck close to home.

Now everything looked different. I had no idea about kids or marriage and I was still living with Darren when yet another change was on the horizon. This time it was something I really wanted, something that never could have happened if I hadn't had prosthetics. I was at Joe Leal's clinic having a fitting for a new pair of legs when he said, "Hey Jami, how would you like to be taller?"

"You're kidding, right?" I asked him.

"Nope. If you want to be taller, I can do that for you."

I was thrilled. What woman doesn't want a little extra height, especially when she cranes her neck, stretches her spine, and still measures in at five feet, one-half inch? I gave the nod to adding two inches to my height and went back to Darren, completely excited. I could hardly wait to tell him but I was surprised to find out that he did not share my enthusiasm.

"It'll make you look out of proportion," he warned me.

"It won't," I said, disappointed at his reaction. "It'll look great. Just wait and see."

My mother wasn't crazy about the idea either, but she didn't care as much as Darren did. I guess he liked me the way I was, but I'd never liked being short. If I hadn't been concerned about upsetting Darren, I probably would have told them to make me five foot six right away. That's my height today, it's been my height for the last seven years, but I took the height gain slowly, an inch or two at a time as I got new legs, trying not to upset the people around me. When I realize that I went from being a busty short girl with a few extra pounds to a slim, athletic tall girl who carefully measures her body fat, I realize how much I've changed physically. I can understand it would be hard for people around me to accept, but I also can see that Darren's lack of support was a sign of tough times to come in our relationship.

16

Trial by Fire

O<small>N APRIL 29, 1990, THE FOLLOWING LETTER TO THE EDITOR</small> appeared in the *Arizona Republic:*

PAYING FOR GREED

Editor:

Has our society sunk to a level so low that it will allow greed to be the ultimate driving force behind human action? If Jami Goldman's lawsuit against the state succeeds, will this establish a precedent releasing people from the responsibility of their own actions? Is the state going to end up paying for Miss Goldman's poor judgment? Perhaps Miss Goldman should sue her companion?

Phoenix

Here is a segment of the rebuttal to that letter which appeared in May:

MOTIVATION NOT GREED

Editor:

. . . greed is not the motivating factor. Righting the wrong done by government agencies is. It may be that the search for the missing women was carried out with reasonable care. At first it was not known which state the women were in, let alone what road they were on. But there is no question that closing a road during a severe snowstorm, without prior warning and then not checking the closed road by snowmobile or plane is greatly negligent.

Maybe the loss of $10 million will get some government department heads thinking. Perhaps some changes will be made to prevent this from happening to me, my mother or my visiting cousin next year.

Mesa

This rebuttal was an eye-opener. Everyone was following our story, but mostly it was from afar. Few people had the courage to identify with me or to admit that it could have been a family member or themselves, trapped in my situation. It made them feel much too vulnerable, even though the above letter proved to be prophetic. A year after our trial was over, an English couple looking to chop down a Christmas tree got stuck in almost the identical spot. It was a far less dramatic sequence of events—they got away quickly and with no injuries—but videotape from their rescue vehicle revealed some of the same confusing conditions that we had faced after the actual storm had stopped: The sky was blue up above while the wind at ground level was blowing so hard, there was a horizontal blizzard and a whiteout. It was so bad, you couldn't see the end of the hood of the vehicle from which they were filming.

Since my case had been heavily publicized and we had been publicly criticized for causing our own problems by failing to have the necessary survival equipment with us, the jury pool had to be seriously tainted. As we faced jury selection with the trial so close—it was stepping on our heels—Richard felt we needed to do something to counteract public opinion. His idea was to shoot a "day in the life" sort of home movie, showing prospective jurors my average day. It would show the bruises on my limbs from crawling around on the floor as I got up, pulled myself to the sink to brush my teeth, scooted to the toilet on my knees, put on my prosthetics, all the ways in which I had been forced to restructure my life since the accident. I wasn't thrilled about doing it; it sounded like the most vulnerable thing in the world, extremely intimate and invasive. But if I wanted to win the case and secure some money for my future, it was necessary. I did everything Richard suggested, crawling, scooting, and all the rest of it, and I know it was important, but it was absolutely devastating. In fact, you can see the humiliation written all over my face in that film, but only *I* knew that an additional source of my upset came from my difficulties with Darren.

Passionate relationships are often filled with friction and arguments. That was certainly the case with Darren and me. On the Saturday morning we'd set aside to shoot the film, Darren awakened pissed off that he had to get up early on his day off. He'd promised his full support during the filming, but after arguing with me for a few minutes, he left in a huff and didn't return until much later in the day. He must have had his personal reasons but his attitude made a difficult situation worse. I felt and looked pretty miserable for the next several hours while we did the film. One of the "highlights" was the frustrated look on my face when I was having trouble with the Allen wrench, as I tried to change the angle of the heel on my old prosthetics. It worked for our purposes, though. I looked fully miserable because I was, so I suppose I can thank Darren indirectly for the extent of the misery I displayed in that home movie.

It was no surprise that he and I split up. It had been coming for a while, but I hadn't wanted to acknowledge it. After being with him for close to two years, I moved out of his place and got an apartment of my own in South Scottsdale, before the trial started. Darren and I still really cared about each other but it wasn't working out. Although it was a lonely and debilitating time, it was better that I was alone during the trial. I didn't need to add domestic squabbles to my overloaded plate of distasteful surprises that emerged most days in that courtroom.

The trial date was extended to September 1990. The truth is that I would have skipped the trial altogether and settled out of court if I'd been given the opportunity. It was a unique case, and we had no idea how much money I could get, so I would have taken anything reasonable to avoid the trauma. But I was never offered that option, not before, or at any point during the proceedings. Why they never offered to settle was an enigma, until we began to suspect that the defendants' representatives were hungry for publicity. We were pretty suspicious when, in December of 1989, the state's attorney left the employment of the state and moved to a private defense firm, taking his high-profile cases with him. Of course, mine was at the top of his list. Now he was a partner in a private law firm, he had a career-making case that was being covered continuously by the press, and he was billing the state by the hour. This change, which appeared self-serving, did not bode well for the outcome of my case.

On the first day of voir dire, the jury selection process, Richard warned prospective jurors that there would be graphic medical evidence, such as photos of my frostbitten feet and my severed limbs, as well as lengthy testimony about some gritty medical procedures. When he started explaining the epidural, the insertion of a long needle between the vertebrae of the spine, a cowboy-type juror-to-be passed out and fell off his chair. He was revived and the judge had a meeting in his chambers with this prospective juror and the lawyers.

"Can you go on?" the judge asked the cowboy.

"I'm fine now," he said, acting macho to cover his embarrassment. "I just wasn't expecting to hear about needles. I have a thing about needles. But I can go on. I promise, it won't bother me again."

This man had been so humiliated at passing out in public, he would hold it against us during the trial, but we didn't know that. He was chosen for the jury. So was a nineteen-year-old young mom from Phoenix who was sympathetic to our cause, and an engineer who *appeared* to be neutral. Our final twelve jurors included one nineteen-year-old, with ages ascending from there to mid-fifties—hardly a jury of my peers. But we did the best we could with what we had.

During the first week of the trial, Richard asked my father to leave the courtroom and not to return. He did not do this out of meanness; Dad had been my solid and unwavering advocate in the many months preceding the trial, but when it started, something crumbled inside of him. He had become the poster child for post-traumatic stress syndrome as he began to cry during opening statements and he couldn't stop. Richard was afraid the jury would view his never-ending pool of tears as a sympathy play, and the idea of listening to him sob and sniffle throughout the entire testimony was not a welcome thought, as it would not further our cause. My father reluctantly agreed to stay away, taking over the lab and keeping the business running, allowing my mother to be in court every day.

My grandparents were back in Chicago. They already had been through a great deal, and unbeknownst to any of us, my grandfather was suffering from a serious blood disorder. It was better that they were away, because the last thing he needed was more stress. My mother, on the other hand, was always there; she approached it like a job, and I can only imagine what it took out of her to suffer the viciousness of seeing her daughter being accused of irresponsibility. Especially after all that I was going through with my legs on a daily basis. Over the next two and a half months, at the end of a day in court, my mother often cried in her car. When she got home, she turned on the television and stared blankly into the screen, preparing to get up the next day and do it all over again.

I was still in college, which was a good thing for me, because I spent part of each day doing business as usual. After a day of classes in Tempe, I'd drive to the courthouse to meet my mother and listen to the fabrications of the state's experts and witnesses who were recounting bad information to the jury. It was frustrating to hear lies being tossed around, when all I could do was lean over to Richard and whisper in his ear. He had impressed upon me the influence of my nonverbal communication on the jury, so I had to watch my demeanor and dress conservatively—no V-necks or sleeveless tops. I wore mostly pants with dress shoes, no tennis shoes, and at strategic times, I wore skirts to bring the jury's attention to my loss.

I'd been raised to believe that telling the truth would benefit me in the end, and I arrived at court with pride that I'd managed to save my life under terrifically adverse circumstances. Now, two and a half years and a double amputation later, as the proceedings got under way, things were not going as I had expected. I awakened each day with dread; it was hideously unfair that Lisa and I should be accused of cruising around back roads in bad weather on a lark, not taking care of ourselves, not caring that we were lost—or if we ever got found. That was so far from the truth, it was ridiculous.

I was stunned when so-called weather experts took the stand and lied, telling the jury that it didn't snow all that hard, proving their point with falsified charts and graphs. Some people will do anything for money. State witnesses swore they had seen us in places we'd never been, it was like a déjà vu from the time we were missing, as people claimed to have seen us in convenience stores fifty or sixty miles from where we were stranded. They held on to their lies like some kind of precious treasure. A man who owned one of these convenience stores had remarked to his wife when he saw us on TV, "I reco'nize them girls. They bought the peanuts right here."

That was impossible; we'd discovered the peanuts several days before we were found and they actually had been in the car for two weeks. The state's attorney subpoenaed the man, but he had passed away. The wife was willing to testify in place of him, and the state's attorney thought that was a great idea. She wanted to corroborate her dead husband's false testimony, but her testimony was thrown out because it was hearsay.

One day, a world-famous mountain climber, a witness for the state named Lute Jerstad, who had scaled Mt. Everest, testified that we should have hiked the sixteen miles in our ski boots through the blizzard. Never mind that the snow came up to our thighs, that we couldn't walk in ski boots, and that we hadn't eaten or drunk much in three days. He insisted there was no reason why we couldn't have made it. He seemed to overlook the fact that Lisa was coughing up blood and that the wind was blowing so hard, there was a horizontal whiteout blizzard at ground level.

The next witness the state called, a supposed engineer "expert," expanded upon some nonsense theory of how we got stuck, agreeing with the mountain climber that we should have walked out of the area during the blizzard. Incensed, Richard ordered the Blazer driven into the garage in the basement of the courthouse, where he had it jacked up. With the judge's permission, he took the jury down there to demonstrate that everything had happened exactly as we said it did. Amid loud revving of the engine, he explained how my decision to save gas in case we could drive out of there was sound, but that it had backfired. I was hardly a car mechanic. How was I to know that when a car idles, the battery will not recharge unless you allow the engine to reach a certain level of RPMs? The few times we turned the car on for heat and turned it right off again, we thought we were saving the battery, but in effect, we were using it up. Didn't that sound like an honest mistake?

Over the difficult days to follow, Mike, Adam, my brother, my parents, and Lisa's parents, as well as our various experts, testified on our behalf. We found the couple who were at the gas station the day we got lost; I remembered their personalized license plate, REINEY 1, and they were easy to locate. They testified that we had been alert and serious when they met us, anxious to get back home as quickly as possible. They recalled giving us directions, confirmed our testimony that there were no maps for sale, and understood how we must have gotten confused on the roads. Our frostbite expert explained that when the sun came out, it was logical to try to leave the car, but we had no idea that it was the coldest morning of the year. Add to that the ski boots, our weakened condition from hunger and thirst, and the length of time we were in the snow, and frostbite was inevitable.

In the state's opening statement, they had referred to our highway maintenance expert witness as a "hired gun" from out of state. When I took the stand and refuted the state's allegations that our man was a "hired gun," the attorneys from the other side objected violently, insisting they had never said that. The judge called a recess, ordered the lawyers into his chambers, and had the court reporter check his transcripts for the exact wording.

The bumbling court reporter couldn't find it. Richard had copied the words down verbatim, as had Ty, during opening statements and insisted that the reporter keep looking. He eventually found the transcript but he had erred, typing the words "hired guy" instead of "hired gun." In the end, without a clear record, the judge was powerless to admonish the jury to strike the statement from their consideration.

It was a dramatic moment when Richard showed our "day in the life" video. The jury felt the full impact as they watched me crawling along the floor to do the simple rituals that everyone performed when they got up in the morning. Then they watched me walk to the stand with my prosthetics, which brought the point even closer to home. Richard had gotten their full attention; they listened carefully when I spoke about how Lisa and I had battled the cold and the winds to get out of the car and wipe off the hood, even in the blizzard, to assure our rescue. I explained our survival techniques, how we had tried to walk out as soon as the sun came out and how Lisa had collapsed. As Richard masterfully presented an emotionally powerful picture of our eleven days in the car and the negligence that the state displayed by refusing to search for us, there was no doubt that the state was guilty. We knew the jury would rule in our favor, but we feared that the comparative negligence issue was threatening our chances for a good settlement.

My cross-examination was brutal. In an attempt to depict me as a bad girl with a bad upbringing, the state treated me like a hostile witness, cutting me off any time I tried to expand on an answer. The worst part was being criticized for staying in the car, the very thing that saved my life, and for not trying to cross-country ski out of there. No matter that neither of us knew how to cross-country ski or that we had no cross-country skis with us. It was deeply emotional for me and I have to say that I was worn down. I tried to hide how hurt I was, but it was difficult to control myself as I cried bitterly, despite my best efforts to hold back my tears.

In a last-ditch effort to impress the court as to how desperate our situation had been, Richard came up with a plan. If the jury could see the actual place where we had been lost, if they could feel the isolation and abandonment we underwent in a three-dimensional way, he was sure the tables would turn in our favor. He approached the judge with a request: If he chartered buses at his own expense, could he please take the jury to the White Mountains where we were stranded? He felt it was crucial to our case and would definitely affect the outcome.

Amid much protesting and gnashing of teeth from the other side, the judge frowned and let Richard know that he was not inclined to grant such a request. It was much too complicated, it would take too long, and he wasn't certain it was relevant. Richard argued that two-dimensional photos and videos were inadequate to transmit a true sense of what had happened. If he chartered a small plane and took the judge there first to see for himself, perhaps His Honor could make a better-informed decision on this matter.

"All right, Counsel," the judge said, "but can I bring my bailiff?"

He was referring to Ben the bailiff, who went on to become attorney general on the remote island of Yap somewhere in the South Pacific. I kid you not—the cast of characters was worthy of the best fiction, but they were real. Richard agreed immediately; the judge could have brought a dozen midgets and dancing girls if it would get him to the accident site. It was a small victory when, the next morning, His Honor, Ben the bailiff, Richard, Ty, and the state's attorney boarded a private plane that Richard had chartered. When the pilot lifted the small twin-engine aircraft into the sky with five men in suits facing each other on two seats, Richard could only have been closer to the judge if he were sitting on his lap. In fact, Richard's and His Honor's knees were practically interlocked, Ben's and the state's attorney's knees were in the exact same posture, and everyone was relieved when the plane touched down at a private airport close to the notorious closed gate. The odd group of five piled into a waiting four-wheel drive, which Richard drove the eight miles up to the gate, and another eight through the snow (it was late November) and along the road, stopping at the site where we had been stranded.

The judge got out of the car and stood there, taking it all in. Words weren't necessary; the light was starting to dawn in his eyes as to how desolate the area was. Richard spoke very little, hopeful he had made his point. A few minutes later, they got back in the car. They stopped at a Mexican restaurant in Eager, Arizona, en route to the airport. After they devoured a hearty mid-morning meal of spicy Mexican food, Richard paid the bill and they were back at the airport, ready to leave for Phoenix. But there was a problem: The pilot was having trouble starting one of the engines. Standing outside the plane in the cold, the judge looked nervously at Richard, as if it were his fault, while the pilot cranked the stubborn engine over and over.

"What's happening here?" His Honor wanted to know in his best courtroom voice.

"Oh, nothing to worry about, folks," the pilot said. "It's the altitude. Probably some condensation in the fuel line. I just gotta get it going and it'll blow itself out. No biggie. We'll be on our way in a couple of minutes."

Ben the bailiff turned to His Honor, nodded his head, and stated in a somewhat supercilious manner, "That's plausible."

Richard looked from Ben to the judge to Ty. Why did this have to happen now, when things were going so well? After twenty minutes had passed, Richard and Ty noticed that His Honor's face was turning a sickly shade of green. Was it fear? they wondered. They didn't have time to find out, because the engine turned over and the pilot motioned for everyone to board the aircraft. Finally. Once they were buckled into the same overly cozy positions, with Richard's legs practically wrapped up with those of His Honor, the two men staring into each other's faces, they lifted off.

On their way out of the area, Richard had directed the pilot to pass straight over the spot where we had been stuck. "See, Your Honor?" Richard said, pointing out the window. "The girls were stranded right there." But His Honor was paying no attention as his greenish face was taking on shades of white, and beads of sweat were popping up all over his forehead, on his neck, and under his lip. The judge groped around for an airsickness bag and in the next moment, he was vomiting ferociously. When they landed, safe and sound, His Honor was carrying two airsickness bags filled to the brim with undigested Mexican food. The next day, he denied Richard's request to take the jury to the scene of the accident, deeming it irrelevant to the outcome of the trial. Bad luck for the good guys.

In the end, the state, armed with whatever fiction they could conjure, had painted a false picture of two bratty young well-to-do girls from Scottsdale. In closing arguments, they told the jury that while we were looking for a place to party, we got stuck in a snowstorm with no map, blankets, food, water, sleeping bags, or sensible shoes. If only we had been better prepared, they declared, we could have fared much better than we did.

Only Lisa and I knew the truth about what it had taken to survive our stint in purgatory. Now it seemed like it would remain our little secret, no matter how graphically and honestly we described it. When I realized I would have to accept responsibility for something I had not caused and learn to live with it, I felt horribly betrayed, but that was the hand that life had dealt me. This trial by fire was causing me to grow up faster than I wanted to, but then, from the day we got lost, events seemed to be conspiring to end my childhood forever. I would come out of this as an adult with adult concerns, temporarily soured toward the judicial system, filled with disappointment that telling the truth, something I thought would bring me freedom, had only brought me more suffering.

17

The Verdict

THE JURY BEGAN DELIBERATIONS ON DECEMBER 1, 1990. ACCORDING to after-the-fact reports by several jurors, they had ruled in favor of us, the plaintiffs, by midafternoon of the first day. They had even awarded sizable amounts of money (nothing like what we asked for, though) to both Lisa and me, absolutely agreeing that the state had placed our lives at risk and we deserved to be compensated for damages. So why were they out for three more days, an uncommonly long time for such a trial? It was largely due to two jurors, the nineteen-year-old mom and the engineer. She considered us completely innocent of negligence, while he considered us completely guilty. As they each stood firm in their beliefs and refused to compromise, they were instrumental in getting our award amounts diminished considerably. I know this woman must have felt terrible about that, but that was what happened.

All twelve jurors had agreed upon the initial numbers, awarding me a little bit more than Lisa because of the amputations I had endured. It was a good deal of money, about what we had figured with the jury's wiggle room. Although no amount could ever compensate me for my loss (it's impossible to put a price on your legs and feet), it would reduce the stress of paying for my prosthetics and medical bills, while providing a reasonable nest egg for my future. If that was all the jury had been required to do, we would have been finished that first night and I would have felt like justice had been served. But the jury was also responsible for deciding the comparative negligence issue, which was much more complicated.

They deliberated with "dynamite" instructions from the judge, which basically translated into: Don't abandon your principles or do anything you think is wrong. At the same time, it's okay to compromise.

What did that mean? When they first voted, the entire jury, even the ones who were against us, had been willing to consider us twenty percent guilty and leave it at that. I would have accepted twenty percent responsibility—I admit I could have been better prepared—but the young mom and the engineer dug in their heels. And so, the debate was on between this woman who considered us one hundred percent innocent and the engineer who thought we were one hundred percent at fault.

I learned later that as the jury turned their attention to dividing up the fault, voices got raised, insults were brandished, emotions flew out of control. The engineer stuck with his decision. To make matters worse, while he was busy blaming us with such vehemence, the cowboy, perhaps still licking his ego wounds from having fainted, sided with the engineer.

On December 4, the fourth and final day of deliberations, we got a call from Richard at about 5:30 P.M.. The judge had asked the jury if they wanted to go home at five, their usual time, since it appeared they had not yet come to a verdict They sent a message, via Ben the bailiff, saying they were almost there and could they please stay? Of course, said the judge, more than willing to work into the evening to have it done. At 9:40 that night, Richard called us back to court. The jury had a verdict and as soon as the principals were gathered in the courtroom, they were prepared to read it.

If you've ever awaited a jury verdict, you're familiar with the heart-stopping minutes that feel like hours while the bailiff shuffles back and forth between the jury foreman and the judge. It seems like so much unnecessary red tape as the foreman hands over the verdict, the bailiff delivers it to the judge, the judge reads it and hands it back to the bailiff. Once he returns the paper to the foreman, the foreman prepares to read it while your heart feels like it's going to leap out right through your ribs. Torture of the first order.

At 10:10 P.M., we all stood. Richard and Ty were at the attorneys' table, the state's attorneys were at their own table, and my mother, my father, and I were directly behind Richard, with Lisa and her mom beside us. The foreman, who incidentally happened to be the engineer, said something like: "The jury finds in favor of the plaintiff, Jami Goldman," and he announced the amount of the award. He repeated the same verdict for Lisa. That was very nice; the state had presented such a virulent case, they could have caused a shutout.

The foreman went on: "We assess the fault at forty-two, fifty-eight percent, in favor of the plaintiff."

That was not so nice. Our money would be reduced by forty-two percent. A moment passed while we tried to do the math. We really hadn't expected that kind of a split; we thought it would be all or nothing.

I burst into tears, burying my head in my father's chest and sobbing with no self-consciousness whatsoever. I had been left with a lot of money, and although it was a far cry from the original amount, maybe a tenth of what we'd asked for (we never thought for a minute we'd get our original number), I would have happily taken less if they had offered to settle at the beginning. The money was not the issue. Being blamed, however, was. Knowing that the jury considered me forty-two percent responsible for what happened to me was more than I could bear. Just because I had no blankets, sleeping bags, or map, I had done nearly half of this damage to myself? Did that mean that losing one leg was the state's fault, and losing the other was mine? I didn't believe that for a second.

"What did I do wrong? Tell me what I did wrong," I moaned out loud, unable to control myself, no longer caring about appearances. Lisa was crying, too.

It was about 10:30 P.M. when the reporters began to swarm

around us. I got hustled toward the back elevator to avoid the press while Richard stayed behind to deal with them. I was inconsolable as I made my way to the car. I had done everything in my power to sustain my life but it wasn't good enough for this jury. And since when was it considered negligent to take a wrong road and get lost? It felt like such a massive betrayal, all I could think about was getting back at the state by appealing the case. How could we possibly leave things as they were? Wouldn't that be like betraying myself?

We drove to a nearby restaurant called Fat Tuesday's to try to settle down after the commotion. Richard promised to meet us there after he'd dealt with the press and talked to some of the jurors who were willing to stay behind. The cowboy and the engineer took off immediately—they had no interest in giving us another moment of their time—but the young mom waited. She was in tears just like I was; she felt betrayed too, and furious with her fellow jurors for being so hard-nosed. I appreciated her sentiment and her desire to stand firm. Those are admirable qualities, her heart was in the right place, but it just didn't end up like she'd planned. Richard spoke with her awhile, thanking her for her support and trying to calm her down. When the press approached him with the inevitable question "Do you plan to appeal?" he told them, "That's something my client and I will be seriously considering."

Conversation about retribution started as soon as Richard arrived at the restaurant. I was so worked up, I was ready to file the appeal right then and there. I believe in taking responsibility in this life, but injustice always has infuriated me, whether it's against me or anybody else I care about. I remember when Jason was in the fourth grade and some sixth-grade girls tried to keep him in school for recess for no good reason. I yelled at them, and I must have been pretty fierce, because they immediately let him go outside where he belonged. I simply cannot tolerate injustice, and this division of guilt was absolutely unjust.

Richard said he believed he could win an appeal and maybe come out with a better division of money, but it was a risk. What if we did worse? I was a student in college, and the trial, so time-consuming and emotionally draining, had gotten in the way of my concentrating on my studies. Did I want to allow an appeal to take up all of my time and energy again? What about my family? They practically had stopped their lives to be there for me during the last three months. Was I prepared to put them through this thing all over again? Did my dad have enough tears left?

My mom assured me that ultimately it was my decision and they would support me. At the same time, I needed to understand that she could not be there every day like the first time. She feared that my grandparents would be more involved the second time around; they might be in Arizona, and she was concerned what the stress might do to them—or was already doing to them. There was also a new jury to consider, which might not be any better than the one we just had. Although it was hard to imagine, it also might be worse.

I had a lot to think about and I vacillated a great deal over the next few days. Did letting go of an appeal mean I was accepting fault? I didn't think so. Would appealing ensure a different or a better experience? Not necessarily. Richard cautioned me that it would take about a minimum of three years for the Court of Appeals to come up with a decision whether or not to allow the case. During that time, no money would pass hands, and then it would take longer if either side asked for reviews at the state Supreme Court, something the state would undoubtedly do, if only to prolong the agony. Any way you looked at it, an appeal was a huge risk. With what we'd already been awarded, I'd end up clearing a good amount of money after the fees and court costs were subtracted. Wouldn't it be better to call it quits, invest the money wisely, and walk away with some security for my future? That had been our original reason for suing. What if I ended up with a lot less? Or with nothing?

Nobody in my family was leaning toward the appeal, but they left the decision up to me. They understood how justifiably angry I was and they knew if they tried to sway me, I would become resentful. After I took some time to think it through, I decided to let go, to take the money and start my life anew, a decision that worked immediately in my favor. Since talk of an appeal was troubling the state, they decided to pay me quickly to avoid finding themselves in even worse shape than they already were. And so, on December 28, 1990, we had the money in hand (I'm not at liberty to disclose the exact amount but it was around a million dollars) and I was ready to get on with my life. At least the jury had found the state more negligent than Lisa and I. That would have to be enough.

A post-verdict jury survey that Richard ordered also helped me to get some closure. Only four jury members agreed to take part in it, but it clarified some of my questions and it helped me better understand how it had unfolded. Richard had made a positive impression on most of the jurors. They considered him professional, well prepared, and protective of his clients. They found his opening statements well thought out, his closing the same, and all in all, they thought he had done a good job. They liked Lisa's lawyer, Ty Taber, a great deal as well; they found him friendly, well prepared, and knowledgeable.

The state, on the other hand, had left a negative impression. Although most of the jurors felt in their hearts that we should have been better prepared to travel through the snow and so we were partially responsible for our fate, they also thought that the state had been unnecessarily cruel and insensitive. Of course, the survey made no difference in the outcome of the case, but at least I wasn't the only one who'd been offended, which helped me feel less alone and misunderstood.

In the end, I'm happy to report that immediately following the trial, Richard was elected president of the Arizona Trial Lawyer's Association. He deserved that and he continues to conduct his life with great dignity and professionalism. My life is as great as I could ever imagine it to be, my parents are thriving, and love won out, just as I had hoped it would. I also learned that growing up is about accepting life exactly as it is, and understanding that no matter what accusations people hurl at you, as long as you remain steadfast on the inside and know who you are, no one can touch your essence. I understand now that justice *does* exist, but like most things, it has its own timing and it usually looks a lot different than we might expect.

18

Finding My Way

I'VE HEARD IT SAID THAT IF YOU WANT TO GIVE THE GODS A GOOD laugh, tell them your plans. If that's true, I could be a one-woman comedy show, because nothing in my life has gone according to my plans. Perhaps the greatest skill I had to learn besides walking again was accepting what life had to offer, on its own terms. From the day I got stuck in the snow, it became clear that my terms had nothing to do with the way my life would unfold. I certainly hadn't counted on being single again. Until Darren and I split up, I believed he would be my husband and we would have a family together. I hadn't imagined it any other way, and yet here I was, living alone and facing the prospect of dating.

I don't ever remember saying, "I don't want to live like this." Even when I woke up in the morning and looked down at what life had dealt me, I never once wished I had perished in the snow. I never forgot that I'd been given a second chance. That eliminated feeling sorry for myself or getting into any lengthy "Why me?" attitudes. I had other priorities, like what did I want to do with the rest of my life? I was alive because I had been part of a miracle. I also had some financial security to make my life easier. I felt I owed it to myself to appreciate each day, to be strong and grateful and not to complain too much. To the people who had taken part in my healing with their thoughts and prayers, I felt I owed them (in an indirect sort of way) the privilege of watching me give something back to a life that nearly had escaped me.

Even though I'd moved out of Darren's house, I hoped he and I would get back together. I was trapped in the kind of thinking that's all too common among women—that I had done something wrong, that it was my fault things hadn't worked out between us. Now that the trial was over, I figured I'd be much easier to live with and maybe we could try again. I wasn't seeing the truth—that Darren and I were on different paths and separating was all for the best. Darren must have shared my illusions about getting back together—I guess we were pretty attached—because we saw each other on and off. We even had an affair for a short period of time when he was dating someone else. We knew it was wrong but it was tough to let go of each other. Luckily, we ended our third time around pretty quickly, admitting that we both needed to move on.

It was a scary prospect; this was the first time I'd been without a boyfriend since I'd lost my legs and I was pretty skittish about getting back out there. I'd gained a little weight when Darren and I separated, I didn't feel particularly attractive, and I stayed home a lot. I always had lots of friends, both men and women whom I hung out with, but the prospect of dating was daunting. I would have to deal with some sensitive issues for the first time: When I meet someone, do I tell him about my legs right away or do I wait until it looks like we might get intimate? If I tell him on the first date, will it push him away? If I wait, will he think I've lied to him? How long do I wait, what's too soon, and how long is too long?

The bottom line was that I was afraid no one would want me once they learned that I came with removable legs and feet. On top of that, I encountered sudden unexpected physical problems. One day when I was walking across the ASU campus with an armful of books, I tripped on a huge crack in the sidewalk. I fell, my books went flying, and when I put out my arms to catch myself, I dislocated my good shoulder. I was rushed to the hospital. Now both shoulders were damaged. With unavoidable accidents like these, who would be interested in me? Would anyone be able to view me as a whole woman? Maybe I was just too much trouble for a man.

I started out slowly, dating a little bit, and I found my way. I discovered no pat way to handle my dilemma; every situation was different, so I took each one as it arose. I always wore cosmetic legs back then, so I could go through an entire date, even get up on the dance floor and go out for drinks later, and the guy wouldn't know—unless I chose to tell him. As I dated a little bit more, I lost a few pounds, I gained confidence, and I'm happy to report that no one ever freaked out on me when they learned about my legs. I'm sure it must have put some people off; there were times when we exchanged phone numbers and I never heard from him again. But that happened to girlfriends of mine who had two healthy legs, it was all part of dating, so I did my best to keep trying.

It would be seven years before I met my husband—real love is hard to find—but I never gave up on the dream. I remember calling my mother in the middle of the night (thanks to me, she basically went through her life sleep-deprived) and moaning, "I haven't met a guy I've cared about in months. Am I ever going to find someone to love me? Will I ever have children?" She soothed me as best she could; she told me to be patient and I would get everything I wanted. I don't know if I believed her, but the truth is I had some growing up to do before I embarked on something as serious as marriage.

I've watched people get married and have children at the wrong time and for all the wrong reasons, like fear of being alone or thinking it was their duty to do what their parents did. The real question I should have been asking myself instead of "Will I ever get married?" was "Where does happiness come from?" Today I know that it comes from within, not necessarily from finding a husband or having children. These things certainly can be satisfying and fill you with joy, but true fulfillment doesn't come from the outside. If an unhappy woman gets married, no amount of children or a husband will fix that. She'll just be an unhappy woman who is married with kids. What kind of messages will she be passing on to her children?

My time alone, as much as I resisted it, taught me that until I could wake up happy with myself for no outside reasons, I could never be happy with someone else. It took a lot of focus and I've weathered plenty of disappointments along the way, but today I can say without reservation that I see my life as completely wonderful, pain and all. I loved my high-school and my college years, I've enjoyed accomplishing goals, both large and small, and most days, I wake up with a smile on my face. If I don't, I find one pretty fast—because I'm alive. I faced my death for many days, I struggled to stay alive, and I succeeded. When I remind myself that I could just as easily be dead, I can't possibly feel like life has let me down. I'm vital, I have a husband, I can love and be loved and I have the energy and the means to go after my goals and dreams. Does that sound unlucky to you?

And yet, there were times I was as confused as anyone else, gazing into the mirror, wondering if I was cool enough to meet a great guy. Happily, I caught on pretty quickly that a different body, fancy clothes, expensive cars, or even beautiful legs could not make me desirable. That had to come from the inside out. I've learned to find happiness from being with my family and my friends, from my day-to-day achievements, and I've learned to love myself, legs or no legs. That's what true love is all about, and until you have it for yourself, you can't expect anyone else to give it to you and you can't pass it on.

I learned from my beloved grandfather, Poppy, that when you don't get exactly what you want, you move on and go after something else you want. He believed that everything happens for a reason and as long as you work hard and don't give up, you'll find your way. After Darren and I broke up, Poppy took me to lunch. There he sat, powerfully centered in himself, tall and beautiful with his snow-white hair, a constant symbol of strength and comfort to me.

"It wasn't supposed to end like this," I told him, tearfully. "Darren and I were supposed to get married. I know he really loved me."

"I'm sure he did," he said, "but that's the way life is. You're a strong young woman, Jami, you can get over this. I promise you, you'll find someone else who really loves you in the way that Darren did, maybe more. And you'll be happy. For now, think about yourself, about investing your money wisely, about building a secure future. The rest will fall into place."

Poppy always told me the truth even when I didn't want to hear it, so I believed what he was saying to me. He taught me so much about life. A self-made millionaire, he began his career working for Mutual, a company that sold eighteen-wheeler truck parts. At thirty years old, he was drafted into the army, where he remained for two years. Within two months of completing his term of service, he joined forces with a friend to open Merit, a direct competitor to the company where he had worked as an employee. He never went to high school or college, but he managed to make good money when he and his friend started a mail-order business for truck parts. He was a great businessman with a tremendous work ethic and he was an example to everyone who knew him. He was also a regular guy who loved to play craps in Vegas and liked the horses, but he only gambled when he could afford to lose. He was just an all-around smart and loving person, and a great source of wisdom and common sense.

One of the first things I did to declare my independence was buy myself a house. Using some money from my settlement, I found a sweet little one-story, two-bedroom house (I called it a "starter house") in Scottsdale, with an attached garage so I felt safe going in and out. The upkeep was low, it had a lawn in the front and a gravel backyard, and it turned out to be a smart investment. I had several roommates who lived there with me, one at a time, while I finished school and thought about my future. I was about to graduate in June with a Bachelor of Science degree in Communication, and I had no idea where I was headed. I only knew I was destined to do something completely different than I'd imagined, but what would it be?

Left: Jami and Grandma (Shirley Cohen) in Israel, 1985—Courtesy of Robin Goldman

Below: Jami's future support team at Mark and Tona's wedding reception, 1981 *(clockwise from left:* Jami, dad Michael Goldman, Mark Cohen, Tona Cohen, Poppy Cohen, brother Jason, aunt Ellen Cohen, Grandma, mother Robin Goldman)—Courtesy of Robin Goldman

Jami and her hero, Poppy (Seymour Cohen), at her grandparents' fortieth wedding anniversary, 1983—Courtesy of Robin Goldman

Jami and Mike Barzano ("Look at my real legs!"), Halloween 1987—Courtesy of Robin Goldman

More real legs. Jami's junior year of high school, 1985—Courtesy of Robin Goldman

When hell froze over. Arizona, January 1988—Courtesy of Robin Goldman

Jami and Lisa in Puerto Vallarta, 1990—Courtesy of Brittney Sappington

Lisa's college graduation, 1998—Courtesy of Brittney Sappington

Jami and her beloved Poppy, 1993—Courtesy of Shirley Cohen

Jami and her family. Hawaii, 1995 (brother Jason, mother Robin,
Jami, and dad Michael)—Courtesy of Shirley Cohen

Jami and her best friend, Brittney, at
Jami's bridal shower, 2001—Courtesy of Jae Halland

Some of the Girly Girls, 1998 *(clockwise from upper left:* Tia Wise, Laurel Quarders,
Tanja Janfruechte, Jami, Wendy Brayer, Jae Halland, sister-in-law
Judi Goldman)—Courtesy of Jae Halland

Jami at the St. Mary's Child Care
Center, Long Beach, California,
1994—Courtesy of Jami Goldman

Jami and Savannah, Brittney's
daughter, 2001—Courtesy
of Brittney Sappington

Jami and cousin Mackenzie,
1999—Courtesy of Tona Cohen

Ready, set . . . Jami training at Huntington Beach High School, 1999—
Courtesy of Beau Marseilles

Jami's first race, Chula Vista, California, 1997—Courtesy of Mike Goldman

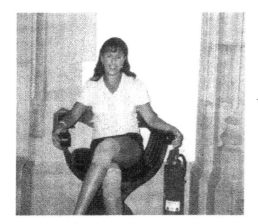

Jami before her first international
meet in Duderstadt, Germany,
1997—Courtesy of Robin Goldman

The British Track, Birmingham,
England, 1998—Courtesy of
Robin Goldman

Cheering baseball in Tokyo, Japan,
with Brian Frasure, 1999—Courtesy of
Robin Goldman

The jitters before Nationals, 1998, George Mason University,
Fairfax, Virginia—Courtesy of Sarah Reinertsen

Gold medal joy! Nationals, 1999,
George Mason University—Courtesy of Sarah Reinertsen

Sarah Reinertsen and Jami on the winners' podium, International Sports Organization for the Disabled (ISOD) World Championships, Spain, 1999—Courtesy of Lindsay Nielsen

Marion Jones and Jami, Olympic Trials, Sacramento, California,
July 2000—Courtesy of Jami Goldman

Paralympic exhibition runners (*from left:* Kelli Bruno, Mike Orlie, Sarah Reinertsen,
Joe Lemar, Jami, and Lindsay Nielsen), Olympic Trials, Sacramento, California,
July 2000—Courtesy of Jami Goldman

Left: Camp Dream Street, Jami's first summer as a camp counselor, 1997, Malibu, California— Courtesy of Zonnie Thierbach

Below: Jami flying through the trees at Dream Street— Courtesy of Zonnie Thierbach

Jami's first snowboard lesson. Breckenridge, Colorado, 1998— Courtesy of Tabi King

Getting engaged, 2001—Courtesy of Tom Jones

Beau Marseilles ("the love of my life") and Jami at brother Jason's wedding, 1998— Courtesy of Judi Goldman

A future Paralympian strikes a pose with Jami at the Disabled Sports USA National Track and Field Competition, 1999, George Mason University—Courtesy of Tabi King

Bryanna: A shining star, 1999—Courtesy of Veronica Copeland

Breakfast with California senator Barbara Boxer, Washington, D.C., 1999 (*from left:* Matt Smith, Jennifer Barrett, Senator Barbara Boxer, Jami, and Roderick Green)—Courtesy of Lindsay Nielsen

Supporting prosthetic research for the Department of Veterans Affairs. Washington, D.C., 1999—Courtesy of Mike Goldman

Jami, Pearl Jam's Jeff Ament, and Kristin Ortiz, Maui, 1998— Courtesy of Beau Marseilles

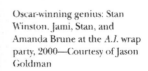

Oscar-winning genius: Stan Winston. Jami, Stan, and Amanda Brune at the *A.I.* wrap party, 2000—Courtesy of Jason Goldman

Jami roughing it at the Avon Walk. California, 2000—Courtesy of Jeanette Nicely

Jami and her walking partners, Jeanette and Traci—Courtesy of Jeanette Nicely

Wedding photo—Courtesy of Tom Jones

19

A Love of Children

WHAT I LIKE BEST ABOUT KIDS, AND WHY I'VE ALWAYS LOVED being around them, is their honesty. I've spoken in various classrooms across the country since my accident, educating kids not about their ABC's but about accepting people who are different. I try to impress upon them how important it is not to judge other people and to lead a healthy lifestyle by eating well and exercising, things I never thought about when I was a kid. It excites me to see a roomful of children, wide-eyed and filled with curiosity, and be able to teach them about kindness and compassion.

I always knew I would have kids of my own and I thought I might stay in Arizona and get into the family business. That would have been the safe way to go, but Arizona had become difficult for me. I couldn't go anywhere without people recognizing me as "the girl who got stuck in the snow." Old friends, new acquaintances, and most of the people I ran into knew me as one of the girls who was missing for eleven days and had lost her legs. I'm definitely a "people" person and I've always been friendly, but in Arizona, getting recognized went one step beyond. Complete strangers would come up and talk to me all the time. It's not that I minded being noticed, it's just that I wanted to be invisible sometimes (you know those bad hair days), and I got tired of talking about the past. I needed to break away from people's preconceived ideas about me and start fresh. In short, after all the furor, I wanted to be anonymous.

I got a good taste of that in the summer of '92, when my parents gave me my college-graduation gift—five weeks in a rented one-bedroom condo in Huntington Beach, California. Brittney had moved there the year before, and I missed her a lot, so I was pretty excited when I headed off for California to get away from home during my summer vacation. It was such an active time, so many friends came to sleep in my living room, I hardly ever spent a night alone. And I loved going out to bars and clubs with Brittney; there was a lot of energy there and a refreshing sense of newness. Nobody I met knew who I was or that I'd suffered a tragedy. I was a regular person (sort of) spending time with my friends, and although I went back to Arizona after the five weeks, I knew that eventually I would end up living in Huntington Beach.

Back in Scottsdale, I applied to ASU graduate school to get an advanced degree in Communication. The plan was to take a few extra classes that year, work in the family business, and start graduate school full time in the fall of '92. One of the reasons I felt compelled to stick close to home was my health insurance. As long as I worked in the family business, I had full coverage, which was very important to me since my medical bills were always overwhelming. But once again, the best-laid plans went awry. I liked my courses well enough but I didn't like working in the family business. My job at the lab was to drum up customers by cold-calling people on the phone. I wasn't suited for it; I preferred "hands-on" kind of work, where I could connect with real people. Because work wasn't grabbing me, when I didn't get accepted into ASU graduate school, I wasn't terrifically disappointed. I needed a change and Huntington Beach was the answer.

In June of '93, I rented out my house in Scottsdale and packed up my things, and my dad drove me, my dog Saki—a medium-sized keeshound—and all my stuff to Huntington Beach, where I moved into a two-bedroom apartment. It was important for me to live in a new environment, away from my parents. I had gotten so used to them taking care of things for me, I had no idea how to take care of myself. At twenty-four years old, I needed to become an independent woman, and as long as I lived close to my folks, that wouldn't happen. Either my grandparents, my mother, or my father drove me to the prosthetist whenever I needed to go. It was ninety miles each way and they didn't want me to go on my own, because sometimes I would leave there depressed. I appreciated their desire to save me but this was my life, for better or worse, and I needed to face my challenges and start fending for myself. Moving would mean getting new health insurance, securing a job, and finding a new prosthetist—on my own.

You really need to trust your prosthetist. When you walk into a prosthetist's office, it's like seeing a doctor: you're at the mercy of that person's knowledge, mastery, and moods. There are various kinds of legs, feet, and componentry; some are custom made, others have standard parts, and you're faced with a world of choices based on the latest information, which keeps changing all the time. Each prosthetist has his or her own way of doing things and charges a different amount of money: a good pair of legs can vary from eight to thirty thousand dollars, depending on where your legs were amputated and how you intend to use them. Having a great prosthetist was crucial for me (it always will be), but so far my parents had fought these battles for me. It was time to start fighting for myself.

I was lucky; my mother had worked out an agreement with the insurance company to continue my coverage for a while and I was set with my prosthetics until I found someone new. If I had an emergency, I could always hop on a plane to Arizona, but other things were in the forefront now, like finding a job to pay my rent. I knew that I needed personal contact with other people on a daily basis. Being stuck in sales or on the phone wouldn't make me happy—I'd found that one out the hard way—but what would? Working with children was a logical arena, because if I had to pick anything in this world that I loved the most, it was children, and it still is.

As soon as I got settled in my new home, I went to see Brittney's dad, Bill, about a job. Bill was president of St. Mary's Hospital in Long Beach (a short distance from Huntington Beach) and he'd opened a child-care center there that was a department of the hospital. He was happy to get me an interview for a part-time job. I was accepted; I started out working with the younger kids, ages eleven to fifteen months. I loved them so much, I even liked changing diapers, which some teachers didn't like. It was just so beautiful to watch the kids grow—it happens fast when they're small and I loved knowing that I was helping shape them during their first five years, the most crucial growth period in a child's life.

Each day, I couldn't wait to see my kids, to create a routine for them, to watch them get involved in activities and get excited when story time was coming. We'd all crawl inside a little blue wooden clubhouse in a corner of the room and I'd read them stories and watch their eyes light up. St. Mary's child-care center was a perfect place for me at the time. When someone told me that Cal State Long Beach had a highly recommended child-care development department, I looked into that, too. I found out that St. Mary's would subsidize my enrollment at Cal State if I took continuing courses in child development. In fall of '94, while I was still working at St. Mary's, I also became a full-time student at Cal State Long Beach. Now I was doing what I loved, getting paid enough to cover my bills, continuing earning credits toward my new degree and getting health insurance, all at the same time.

I had become a very busy woman, working, studying, building credits toward my degree, and enjoying full health benefits. The kids gave me so much; I took pride in knowing that while I was changing poopy diapers, I also was stimulating these children's minds and increasing their knowledge while their parents were at work. My life had taken on a gentle rhythm, filled with friends, children, work, and not too many chaotic surprises, give or take an earthquake or two. Yes, I managed to move to California in time for the Northridge earthquake, the big one that shook everybody up and continued with aftershocks that seemed like they would never end.

Southern Californians love to tell "where they were during the earthquake" stories. Here's mine:

I'd been living in Huntington Beach for about six months when Brittney's sister, Kristin, and I went to a bar. We met a few nice new guys; one of them, also named Jamie, was three years younger than I was and we hit it off, not in a romantic way, but as friends. We all came back to my house for a while, I didn't drink, because I was the designated driver, and at about three in the morning, I drove everybody home. I was back home in bed with Saki by four, when everything started rocking and rolling. The sound is what I remember the most—glass and metal clinking and shaking. I grabbed my legs (I can put them on in five seconds when I have to) and got Brittney's husband on the phone. He and Brittney were fine, I was fine, and so was my apartment, except for a few things that had fallen off the dresser. By the time I hung up the phone, the shaking had stopped, all was quiet, and I didn't bother putting on my legs. I calmed down the dog, took a few deep breaths, and went back to sleep. I was unharmed and, in a sense, I felt courageous that I'd gotten through it on my own, another step in finding my independence.

In spring of '95, during my internship at Cal State Long Beach, I began working with toddlers, kids who were eighteen months to three years old. I loved them as much as the younger ones; it was just a different kind of work, like setting up curricula and dreaming up activities to stretch their minds. The atmosphere at Cal State was far less chaotic than at St. Mary's. A child-care center requires a strong business focus; you have to be concerned all the time with ratios of teacher to child and meeting financial goals, or the center won't stay open. Cal State was smaller, it was less chaotic, and it was called a laboratory, not a child-care center, so it was more about the children and less about making sure things were running according to bureaucracy. In fact, they called it a toddler lab and I became head teacher.

I took to it with so much enthusiasm, I decided to challenge myself and move on to the preschool lab. Preschoolers were a whole different story from toddlers and initially I wasn't sure I'd like working with them as much, but I did. They were capable of a lot more than playing games, giggling, and listening to stories. These kids would be attending kindergarten next year and they wanted to learn things, to ask questions, to talk about ideas and solve problems. Before I knew it, I was the full-time head teacher in the preschool lab and I had stopped working at St. Mary's. I was still on call there, and I filled in occasionally when I was needed, but I'd found my niche at Cal State. I earned my second bachelor's degree from their College of Health and Human Services in Child and Family Studies and I was on my way toward my master's degree in child development.

Have you ever noticed when you're living true to yourself, you draw in exactly what you need? One afternoon, when I was happily running from school to work, I ran in to a 7-Eleven in my shorts to pick up a bottle of water and a banana. I was at the counter paying when a polite, older man approached me. "I hope you won't be offended," he said, "but I have a daughter who's a double amputee. Do you have a good prosthetic man?"

We talked a moment; it was obvious he knew what he was talking about, and I felt at ease with him. When I told him I hadn't yet found a prosthetist in the area, he told me about Carlos Sombrano, the man who worked with his daughter. He gave his clients a spray that made the prosthetics look like real skin instead of shiny and plasticky. I took Carlos's phone number and went to see him a few days later. I liked him right away. He was on the cutting edge of the industry and, unbeknownst to either of us, he was destined to help me form my future into something I could never have predicted.

PART THREE

The Real Bionic Woman

20
Saying Good-bye

IGRADUATED FROM CAL STATE LONG BEACH IN SPRING OF '96, CUM laude. I loved working with children so much, I'd buckled down and graduated with honors, proving to myself that all I'd ever needed was passion for what I was doing. Now that I'd graduated with honors, my plan was to continue working as head teacher in the preschool lab. Next year, I'd take the graduate program and work toward my master's degree.

In October of '96, I went to see Carlos for a routine adjustment on my legs. He'd turned out to be a wonderful addition to my life, and thanks to him, my prosthetics were contemporary, manufactured according to the latest technology. He worked out of Torrance, about forty minutes from my house. My body had become more steady and my fittings were far less emotional than they used to be. I actually enjoyed the rides there and back; they were relaxing and meditative, only forty minutes each way, and I was fine going alone.

On this particular visit, Carlos had just returned from Atlanta, where he'd been an observer at the 1996 Paralympics. He was very excited about what he had seen; disabled athletes had set world records and won gold medals, and they were showing the world just how much an amputee could do. He talked about one girl named Aimee who had run on carbon flex sprinters—he called them cheetah legs—made by a great company named Flex-Foot. He suggested I look into running, maybe I would like it. I was a little surprised—I had never thought about running—but I also was intrigued. His enthusiasm was contagious and I told him I'd consider it. On the ride home, I thought about how ironic life was. There was a day when the idea of going to the gym was laughable to me. Now, a confirmed gym rat, I was considering running. What would show up next?

I found out all too soon. About three weeks before Thanksgiving, my roommate, Jenny, was driving me to Orange County Airport so I could fly to Phoenix, meet my parents, and fly on to Chicago for a cousin's wedding reception. I treated Jenny to coffee and bagels on the way to the airport, and after she dropped me off, I discovered I'd left my wallet at the bagel counter. There was no way I could get on the plane without an ID. I was terribly upset and I also thought it was odd—with all the traveling I'd done in my life, I had never forgotten my wallet. The real reason I wanted to go to Chicago was to see Poppy; he hadn't been well, and I was concerned. I'd been aware his health was failing for quite a while. I didn't know exactly what was wrong with him but I really wanted to see him. I thought about taking a later plane, but when I called my parents, they encouraged me to stay home.

"Don't worry," my mother said, "you'll be seeing Poppy in a few weeks. He and Grandma are coming to Arizona for Thanksgiving."

I decided to skip the trip. I didn't want to try to catch another plane; it was too much rushing around, and Thanksgiving was around the corner. But life had something else in mind. It was a tough weekend for Poppy; he was really sick. In fact, his condition worsened so much, he never went to my cousin's wedding reception. He sat in a chair all weekend and he was not himself at all. The next day, he went to bed and stayed there, and he died two days later with his wife and his children by his side. I was not destined to watch him die.

The phone call came early in the morning. I'd been awake for about an hour and Jenny answered the call. She was white as a ghost when she handed me the phone. It was my mother and I knew what had happened the moment I heard her voice. Poppy had been sick with a blood disorder for several years, but my grandma was the only one who knew how serious it was. The last year and a half had been bad; his condition had deteriorated into leukemia. We knew he was ill by then but he had done such a good job of hiding it, none of us realized how critical it was.

My heart was broken and I started packing immediately. I felt bad leaving the preschool lab so suddenly, but I had ten or so competent teachers working under me who could take over without much problem. They understood; they knew how much Poppy meant to me. I stumbled into the shower, turned it on, and stood under the nozzle, sobbing loudly. This couldn't be real. What would the family do without Poppy? How could I go on without him? He was my strength and my comfort. He had been there for me during every difficulty in my life, and when I lost my legs, his blood had been transfused into me. How could he be dead? His blood was flowing through my veins.

I threw my stuff in the car and drove to Scottsdale that afternoon while arrangements were being made for Poppy's remains to be flown in from Chicago. He wanted to be buried in Arizona and that's where the funeral would be. I stayed with my parents for a couple of days. When my grandma arrived from Chicago, I stayed with her every night for the next few weeks. She'd been married to Poppy for fifty years, they had been inseparable, and now she would have to go to sleep alone, wake up alone, and be strong alone. I slept in bed with her, I talked to her about how strong she was, how much I loved her and that I would always be there for her. It was an important time for both of us; I needed to say these things as much as she needed to hear them. We reminisced about my childhood and how much I had depended on Poppy, starting when I was very young and timid.

The first house I remember was our duplex in Des Plaines, Illinois. I was three when my parents bought this four-bedroom, two-story house with a small backyard and a basement that was always filled with toys. Before Jason turned two, my mother had to make him wear a name tag with his name and address on it because he was always wandering away. I was the exact opposite, content to be home, willing to stay with my parents and only a handful of select relatives in whose company I felt safe. Poppy was at the top of the list, and if anybody else tried to take care of me, I would cry hysterically, especially if they were men.

The truth is, I used to be afraid of my own shadow. To look at me now, that's hard to believe, but back then I was a quiet little girl who wouldn't leave my own backyard. Our neighborhood was residential; there were kids everywhere and they used to gather at our house to play. When they suddenly ran down the street like kids do, to play in somebody else's yard, I stayed behind. I was too scared to leave.

Despite my shyness, I had a happy childhood and my family has always been a present and positive force in my life. I never knew my dad's mother—she passed away when my dad was four-teen—but Joe, my father's father, is still around at ninety-six years old and has outlived three wives. He used to live in Florida so we didn't get to see him often, but he's a strong, wonderful man whom I love very much. Poppy and Grandma, my mother's par-ents, lived a stone's throw away when I was growing up and we saw them every day.

From the time I was a baby, I adored Poppy. My mom had Jason and me when she was very young—we were Grandma and Poppy's only grandchildren for sixteen years, and every Wednes-day night after dinner they would take us to the store to pick out a new toy. Whatever was going on, Poppy was in control. He was the undisputed patriarch of the family and he did anything he wanted to do. When Jason was three, Poppy deliberately taught him to say, "Oh, shit." My mother was appalled when she heard her sweet little son cursing, which only encouraged her father to urge him on at the most inappropriate times. He loved getting a rise out of people and Jason's new words were a sure thing.

We moved to Arizona when I was eleven but Jason and I went back to Chicago every summer to visit Grandma and Poppy. We cheered our baseball team at Wrigley Field, we shopped with my grandma, we went to amusement parks, and we spent time with my aunt and uncle, who were living nearby. In the winters, Poppy and Grandma came to Arizona, and for Jason's bar mitzvah present, they took us kids on a trip to Tel Aviv. Poppy hired a personal tour guide who drove the four of us across Israel for ten days and showed us a brand-new world. I was sixteen, a little too young and full of teenage angst to fully appreciate the opportunity, but I was impressed with the mountain vistas and the military men standing on street corners holding automatic rifles. I also loved traveling through the countryside, taking in the historical essence of what Israel is all about.

Poppy exposed me to worlds I had never seen. I can't say enough about him except that he was my hero. I know I wasn't the only one who felt that way; Poppy knew people wherever he went, he was loved by everyone, and he adored his wife. My mother had a couple of great role models for relationships; maybe that's why she and my father are so much in love after thirty-five years and still go out of their way to spend time together. Poppy showed everyone how to go through life in the most honest, playful, responsible, and loving way. He affected all of us so deeply that when Jason and his wife, Judi, had had a son, they'd named him Shawn. The first letter was the same as the first letter of Poppy's real name, Seymour, and in Hebrew the two names are identical.

Without Poppy, all of his loved ones were utterly grief-stricken, and his death threw a monkey wrench into my plans for the future. They shattered into a million pieces and when I returned to California, the fragments didn't fit back together anymore. I never attended graduate school. I finished up the semester at Cal State and kept training at the gym, but nothing felt the same. What better time to look for something completely different? I called Carlos to discuss running. I'd been thinking about what he said; I'd decided to go forward and to compete in the Paralympics in four years. That was just like me, jumping in with both feet when I hadn't even tested the waters, but I'd made up my mind. Why learn to run if I didn't have challenging goals? That was how I lived my life these days. Everything mattered, since I'd been spared, so what did I need to do to make this happen?

Carlos told me all about the company, Flex-Foot, which was

located in Alisa Viejo, California. It seemed that Van Phillips, an amputee athlete, who founded Flex-Foot, hadn't been satisfied with the available running prosthetics on the market, so he decided to engineer his own. After years of work, he invented carbon flex sprinters called cheetah legs, which most of the Paralympic runners used in '96 in Atlanta. Van was constantly utilizing the latest technology to remodel the legs and improve their spring. Why didn't I get in touch with him and have my own pair made?

Wayne Wilkerson, a prosthetist who worked with Flex-Foot, had a facility in Escondido, just outside of San Diego. I went to him for a casting, the first step in getting my very own cheetah legs. I had no idea how I would pay for them, because each time I got a new pair of legs I had to justify them to the insurance company. A pair of prosthetics usually lasts from three to five years, depending upon your activity levels, because the components gradually wear down from use. I wasn't an athlete yet so how could I justify the cheetah legs? These legs were in a whole different category of pricing. I knew they ran anywhere from five to ten thousand dollars. I'd have to figure out a way to pay for them, but I'd manage somehow. After all I'd been through, I'd seen that things had a way of taking care of themselves; my job was to concentrate on getting fitted for my new legs and training myself to use them.

I was amazed at the way these prosthetics looked, with long lines and curved arcs for feet. Very high tech. Flex-Foot was having a race in San Diego in April, the first time they were offering a monetary reward to the winners. Wayne understood the importance of training toward a goal, and he could have my legs ready right after the holidays. How would that suit me? It sounded fine to me. After a few more fittings, I headed home to Arizona to have my first Christmas without my grandfather.

I stayed with Grandma and we talked a lot about Poppy. We're not a family to stuff sorrow in the background and pretend it doesn't exist. If we were, I wonder how we'd have gotten through our trials. During that holiday season, we all cried together—we still do. We told stories about Poppy and we talked about his legacy. I know that I'm a better human being for having known him and for having been loved by him. I told my grandma that as much as I miss him every single day of my life, I feel fortunate that I had him for so many years.

I like to think that Poppy's blood flowing through my heart has made me a more loving human being. Just recently, I was in Santa Monica with Jason, walking along the Third Street Promenade, when I saw a man without legs, begging for money. I flashed back to when I was in the hospital after the amputation, and I remembered Poppy urging me to get up and work on myself. I didn't want to but Poppy never gave up on me. If he hadn't been there at the hospital, if he hadn't picked me up each morning and driven me to my aunt's swimming pool for physical therapy, would I be walking like I am today? Would I have the same degree of self-value? Maybe not. I stopped and gave the man some money. It's impossible for me to judge another amputee, to imagine that if they wanted to walk, they could. How do I know that? What shape would I be in, if it were not for my family?

This is the legacy that Poppy left me and each time I help someone else, I honor him. His existence was a life well lived, and he was a man who made a difference to a lot of people. If I can affect the people around me half as much as he did, I'll know my life was worthwhile.

21

Cheetah Legs

THE BIONIC WOMAN WAS ONE OF MY CHILDHOOD ROLE MODELS. Remember her? Actress Lindsay Wagner played a woman who nearly died in a car accident, so they replaced some of her body parts with bionics. As soon as she got used to her new robotic capabilities, she began to work for the government. Although she was beautiful and put herself together well, the emphasis was placed not on how she looked, but on what she did for the good guys. Oddly enough, her name was Jamie (spelled with an "e"), her boss's last name was Goldman, and I thought she was the coolest girl around.

Besides the fact that my name was all over the show, I was thrilled by the special effects they played when she used her bionics. It seemed like the sound was coming from inside of her, not from a soundtrack, and I got goose bumps every time she did something fabulous against the backdrop of those electronic noises. And still, it wasn't her bionics that excited me the most and made me want to be like her. Granted, her strength was something unusual—women generally didn't body-build or go to the gym. I was intrigued by those things, but what attracted me most was the fact that she was a strong woman, she knew who she was, and she faced off against powerful men with almost no fear. That turned me on because it was so atypical of the image women had at that time.

I liked the original Charlie's Angels, too, for the same reason. They were strong, beautiful, sexy women who battled evil. But the Bionic Woman was my favorite. She was an independent person, she lived and worked on her own, and she went on missions, fighting for what was right and good. I don't remember my friends sharing my fascination with her (makes you wonder, doesn't it?). I was in my own little world when I watched her on TV, cheering her on as she risked her life chasing down the bad guys. She always emerged triumphant, she was humble, and she was emotionally in touch with herself. I related to all of it, never suspecting that one day, she and I would have so much in common.

When I returned to Huntington Beach in January of '97, my new legs were ready. I had no coach, I had never run in my life, but I was determined to compete in the Paralympics that were scheduled three years hence. That would give me plenty of time to find a coach and get in shape. I arrived at Wayne Wilkerson's facility in Escondido pretty excited; I was about to have my very own cheetah legs, which meant I could start running right away. I knew they would take some getting used to, but I was ready to begin. Since custom-made sockets are the foundation for any prosthetic, Wayne tried them on me first. If the sockets don't fit properly and aren't completely comfortable, it doesn't matter what's underneath them, it simply won't work. The sockets start out as clear, see-through molds, and Wayne placed them on my limbs to see where they rubbed and what he needed to adjust. Ninety percent of the changes are done to the clear sockets, since they're easier to change and mold. Once they're ready, they become the final black ones, to which they attach the foot components.

I was giggly when I tried the new legs on, partly because I was excited, partly because they made me nervous. It was so hard to stand up and balance on them, I couldn't imagine being able to run. Wayne held my hand during the shaky walk to the end of a long, narrow hallway where I would run for the first time. A technician stood at the other end, waiting to catch me. "Jog up and down," Wayne said. I inhaled and tried it. It was awkward but I managed to jog in place a little. These legs were definitely built for motion—it felt better to jump around on them than to stand still.

"Tell me when you're ready," he said. Wayne was patient, letting me get my bearings.

A minute later, I replied, "Ready!" Might as well go for it.

Placing my attention on the man at the other end of the hallway, I flew forward with such speed and bounce, I scared myself. There was so much spring, I felt completely out of control, as if the legs might break off right underneath me. I barreled toward the man in front of me, hoping I wouldn't fall on my face before I reached him. Or even worse, I hoped I wouldn't crash into him and hurt both of us.

I didn't fall and he caught me easily—he had obviously done this before—and I burst out laughing. What a rush! It was like a ride on a roller coaster, I felt so exhilarated and filled with joy. I had never imagined running could be so much fun.

"Let's do it again," I roared, instantly filled with the competitive spirit. I was determined to get comfortable enough with my latest tools, my cheetah legs, to get me to the race in San Diego that was only three months away, and then—the big carrot—the Paralympics. I knew it would take trial and error with these legs; I would have to run on them for a while, see where they rubbed, and have them adjusted intermittently. It would require several trips to Escondido and I would have to endure a lot of sores, rashes, and adjustments until the legs fit perfectly. I knew the drill but I didn't care. I had a new goal, something to take my mind off the devastating loss of my grandfather, and I embraced it fully as something to look forward to.

I was excited all the way home, my new legs sparkling in the backseat (my grandma had been kind enough to pay for them), ready to fly me to new heights. All systems were go. I was already at the Paralympics in my mind. I cried a little when I realized that Poppy, the source of my amazing determination, wouldn't get to see me run. I certainly didn't have that kind of one-pointed focus growing up, and I give all the credit to Poppy, my most dedicated and toughest cheerleader, pushing through my resistance with my best interests at heart. Now it was as if he and I had merged, blood, bones, and all, and his dedication and commitment to life had become my own. I wanted to compete for him. I had a goal and nothing would deter me.

Since I had three months to get in shape, I had to find someone to train me right away. I'd been doing my strength training three times a week with a twenty-one-year-old guy named Art who'd been referred by a friend at the gym. During a training session, I mentioned to Art that I wanted to try running. Did he know a coach I could work with?

"I ran in high school," Art said. "Instead of coming to the gym every day, I could meet you outside and train you at the track."

That was a great offer on several levels. Besides having a trainer whom I already liked and trusted, the idea of getting out of the gym and running outdoors was appealing. It was Art's idea to start on the hard-packed sand next to the ocean. I was shaky on my new sprinting legs, falling down was inevitable at the beginning, and I didn't want to get hurt. I fell on the sand plenty of times; these carbon flex legs were a force to be reckoned with, it was hard to stand still on them, and when I wanted to stop moving, I had to grab on to someone or catch myself against a wall. But they really put that speed underneath me. If you ever have the chance to see someone running on cheetah legs, notice how long it takes for her to slow down when the race is over. Able-bodied athletes run faster than disabled ones do, but they can stop faster, too, between digging their feet into the ground and grabbing certain leg muscles to decelerate. Disabled athletes are missing some of those muscles. We depend heavily on hip flexors and the power of the mind.

I got more confident as time passed, and one day I was ready to try the grass. I fell on the grass, too; I had so many bruises when I was first learning, I looked like I'd been in a fight. I would eventually get spikes on the bottom of the cheetah feet, which would help me dig into the ground for traction. For now, I had to keep falling down and feeling my way, getting accustomed not only to the speed, but also to the intricate balance these legs required. Art had no idea how it felt to run on prosthetics (how could he?), and I had never run before, with legs or without. We were quite a pair. We were both charting new territory, but I needed Art. He understood basic track training, especially how to run sprint breakdowns, so we figured it out together.

I loved the feeling of running right from the beginning; the speed and motion required the same kind of control as skiing, but it was much harder work. When you ski, you might hit a rock and get thrown off balance for a minute, but if you discipline your mind to stay in control and stay in contact with your leg muscles, you can regain your balance and get down the mountain. In the same way, I would trip sometimes and lose my balance when I ran, but if I kept my mind strong and centered, I could regain my balance in a split second and get to the finish line—but without the help of calf muscles or feet. Have you ever stopped to consider what your feet do for you? I never thought about it until I tried to run without any. The strength and control switches to the mind and it becomes a matter of mental discipline to stay upright and get to the finish line. I liked building that kind of internal strength and I loved being outdoors, so running took over, filling the hole that a lack of skiing had created.

I had tried skiing about a year after my accident. I was with Darren then—he loved to ski and we decided to go together. It was a big step for me. I remember Grandma being really nervous but she didn't get in my way. She knew it was important for me to see that I could still carry out activities that I'd done before. I loved skiing again, it helped me feel free and strong, but I stopped when Darren and I split, mainly because it was an expensive activity and most of my friends didn't do it. I never realized how much I'd missed it until I started running, which was a lot more fun than basic indoor gym training.

Of course, I had to keep going to the gym in order keep my upper body strong enough to support my weight, but running outdoors was a welcome change from my usual routine. With my sights set on the race in San Diego in April, a U.S. National competition in June, an international race in Germany in August, and finally, Sydney in 2000, I had a full schedule of training ahead of me. I trained on the track with Art almost every day, trying to tame a pair of legs that made me feel like I was riding a bucking bronco. I focused on my time, speed, and stamina and on coming off the starting blocks. I didn't practice with a starting gun; we didn't have one, so Art would stand behind me, clap his hands next to my ears or yell loudly, and I would practice my starts. We did it over and over again while I worked on technical skills like arm placement and body angles. I got home at night in such a state of exhaustion, I barely had the energy to fix myself something to eat before I fell into bed, exhausted and ready to sleep like a baby. I loved every minute of it.

I wasn't dating much at that time—I was occupied with my training—but I did notice Beau, Jamie's brother, who happened to be Art's best friend. I'd met him when Jamie was my roommate, and he came by a few times when Art and I were working together. We'd never really talked, we just smiled at each other, but for some reason, he intrigued me. Beau and I couldn't have been more different. He was seven years younger than I was, he had a girlfriend, and I was seeing a few different people, but I wasn't serious about anyone. Since Darren, no one had really touched me deeply, so I guess the guys I dated for a short time were more of a convenience than anything else.

The problem was, I was finding out that being someone's convenience really blows your self-esteem. My athletic endeavors were making me feel so strong, I decided I'd rather be alone than be with a guy who didn't mean that much to me. I still wanted a relationship and a family, but that would have to wait until the right man showed up. In the meantime I stayed away from meaningless relationships and kept my sights on my immediate goal— the Flex-Foot race at the ARCO Olympic Training Center in Chula Vista, California.

22

Getting Wings

THE CAMPUS OF THE ARCO OLYMPIC TRAINING CENTER SPANS 150 acres of land, including fields and tracks, dorms for athletes in training, and the beauty of the Otay Lake Reservoir. Located in Chula Vista, California, adjacent to San Diego, this extraordinary facility has a huge archery range, an all-weather field-hockey surface, four soccer fields, a fifteen-thousand-square-foot canoe, kayak, and rowing boathouse, four tennis courts, a four-hundred-meter running track, a cycling criterium course, and six acres dedicated to field events. I never had imagined being part of such a place, but there I was, the girl who previously didn't like to sweat, ready to take part in an international race.

At this fabulous training center, U.S. athletes hone their skills for international competitions while they get inexpensive room and board with access to an on-site sports medicine and rehabilitation center—an athlete's dream. As hopeful Paralympic athletes, all participants were invited to stay on the grounds at the training center for several days to compete in a race for amputees that was sponsored by Flex-Foot.

It was both thrilling and intimidating to walk across the grounds and be with so many serious athletes. Aimee, a double amputee like me, was there. I'd spoken to her when I was getting fitted for my cheetah legs and I'd met her several times during the last few months. Although I didn't know her well, I was glad to see a familiar face. Some of my other competitors were single amputees; unfortunately we all compete against each other, because there aren't enough of us in each category, single or double, to have our own events. Double BKs (below the knee) run slower than singles, but single AKs (above the knee) have more trouble getting their weight beneath them because they're missing a knee. The truth is that the playing field is never level; we all have different obstacles to overcome, so it's tough to discern who is at the greatest advantage or disadvantage.

It doesn't matter in the end. We all run because we love it and we're grateful for any opportunity to compete. I was certainly grateful in April of '97, when I arrived at this facility to compete in my first race, ever. My event was scheduled for Saturday morning but I arrived on Thursday to take part in the opening ceremonies. I got to meet athletes from all over the world: Australia, Germany, France, Austria, Switzerland, Sweden, Italy, and several countries in South America. Many of the participants knew each other, they had competed together before, and the truth was that I didn't officially qualify. Having competed in at least one national race was a requirement to take part in this one, but Flex-Foot was kind enough to bend the rules a little for me. Everybody knew I'd never raced before but nobody minded; there was a terrific camaraderie among the athletes. I found them to be wonderful people and I especially enjoyed meeting two guys, a discus thrower and a runner, who were each missing one leg. I had no idea there were so many disabled athletes. I hadn't had a chance to meet them before, it was a real eye-opener, and it made me feel much less alone.

Opening ceremonies centered around children, which was right up my alley. After processions, music, and announcements, we each got assigned a group of local grade-school or junior-high kids, with whom we spent time talking and answering questions. I had a great time with them, and then, during the next few days, I immersed myself in the activities, training when I could and watching other people race. I had never been involved in anything remotely similar, I got hooked on the energy and I was pretty excited when my family and friends showed up on Friday.

There are strict rules for disabled athletes, just as there are for able-bodied athletes, so they can keep the playing field as level as possible. That meant examinations of our prosthetics for classification purposes. On the day of my event, several officials checked my limbs and the height of my prosthetics to make sure my equipment qualified for the competition. I have to admit, I was a bag of nerves when I got onto the track. I've never been the superstitious type, so I carried no charms and did no incantations. I just warmed up and prepared myself mentally. I'd only been running for three months and I had no illusions of winning or coming in second or even third. All I wanted was to remain upright; I was so afraid I'd fall down, embarrass myself, and not be able to finish.

My internal dialogue was in full swing: What had I gotten myself into now? I thought, jumping up and down on my new legs. I wasn't used to them yet. Would I be able to keep still until the gun went off or would I move prematurely and have a false start? Damn, I had to pee. I just peed a few minutes ago. Better not think about it. Instead I watched everyone else warming up, stretching, jumping, and I followed along, pretending to be a part of it. I tried to remember all the things Art had told me. "Don't look straight at the finish line," he'd said, "or you'll come up short. Pick a point beyond it, that's where you're heading, and keep your eyes focused straight ahead of you. Don't let up until you pass your target."

There was a line of trees a few hundred feet beyond the finish line. That would be my focus and I wouldn't slow down until I reached those trees, no matter how I felt. Aimee was warming up next to me. I thought about my family and friends in the stands. My parents, my grandma, my aunt and uncle, and my cousins Mackenzie and Tyler were all there. I really wanted to do well for them, to give them something to celebrate. This could provide the happy ending we all deserved. Or maybe it was just a new beginning.

"Runner to your marks." I heard the command from the official.

I walked to my starting blocks, jumping up and down, shaking with anticipation.

"Set!"

This one's for you, Poppy, I thought as I crouched low in the starting blocks, waiting for the crack of the gun. In a sense, I already had won, just being there. Now I would see how fast I could pull off the hundred meters.

The hundred-meter dash goes by like a lightning flash. It all happens so quickly, there's no time to think. I concentrate on my form, working to keep my arms swinging correctly, and the speed just comes. I imagine someone is behind me, giving me that extra push. I raise my legs high like Art showed me and I feel the muscles in my behind and my hips working overtime. I guess I'm compensating for not having a calf muscle, something I didn't think about until I became a runner and hit the limits of my prosthetics.

When I first got my legs, I didn't analyze the mechanics or wonder how I was able to walk. I just wanted to get where I needed to go and I didn't care how it happened. Since I had begun training, though, I had become intensely interested in how my muscles worked in conjunction with my brain, where the signals came from and how to maximize the capabilities of my cheetah legs.

I thought about these things constantly when I was training, but when I actually ran, it all fell away. It felt like all body parts were merged into one big muscle that worked all together. The race itself was a blur that day. I know I wasn't the fastest one off the blocks, I had a lot of work to do in that area, and still, I got wings and sailed the hundred meters with all the energy I could muster. The biggest surprise was halfway there when I looked to my side and saw that I was catching Aimee, who had competed in the Paralympics the year before. That meant I was fast, didn't it? I had no more time to think about my speed because the next thing I knew, I lost my footing and tripped on one of my legs. I thought I was going down, I saw the ground getting closer, when I caught myself almost magically, and regained my balance. When the race was done, I had come in fourth, and Aimee had beat me by only two one-hundredths of a second.

I was sobbing with joy when Aimee came over to hug me. "I told you you could do it," she said. She was a lot younger than I, and not only had I finished without falling but I'd almost matched her time. What a beginning! My parents rushed out on the field to hug me. My dad was crying, which was no surprise. Ever since my accident, the dams had opened up and he cried at a moment's notice. He wasn't like that before, but now he sobbed through movies and books, and he said he even cried all by himself when he thought about me.

When my eleven-year-old nephew, Tyler, ran over to hug and congratulate me, I was overjoyed that he could see me like this. Tyler had been born a few months before my accident so he knew me only as an amputee. In fact, he used to play with my prosthetics when he was a baby; it all seemed completely ordinary to him. I grabbed his hand and we jogged around the track together for my cooldown lap.

"Jami," he said, "I have something to tell you. You know when you tripped?"

I nodded.

"Well, Poppy caught you. That's why you didn't fall."

"How do you know that?" I asked him.

"I just do. I felt him."

I sensed it was true. I'd asked Poppy to give me a signal so I'd know he was there. Maybe that was it. Although I don't often articulate it, even to myself, I've always sensed a spiritual component to running or any other athletic event. In the scheme of things, we human beings are the size of a pinhead compared with the universe in which we live, so it's not that much of a stretch to think we're being guided by an invisible force. I say this because when I run, something indescribable takes over, an energetic power that wasn't there a few minutes before. It's almost like catching a wave and soaring, when effort ends and something carries me to my destination. Why couldn't Poppy have caught me and set me back on my center? He'd done it so often when he was alive, why not now?

Later, when I saw a photograph taken during the race, I'd been ahead of Aimee at one point. I actually had overtaken her right before I tripped and my time was better than I expected. That was all I needed to see. Sure, I could have been faster, you can always be faster, but when I discovered that my "first-race nerves" hadn't affected my time by much, I was encouraged. I decided right then and there that I would train as hard as I could and next time, I would do better. Eventually, I would win. My competitive edge had been awakened and I was on fire!

I stepped up my training. I was headed for the U.S. National competitions in Springfield, Massachusetts, when I got a phone call from Dream Street, an organization started about thirteen years ago by Billy and Patty Grubman, a brother and sister. They held summer camps for kids with catastrophic illnesses. Two years prior, during a vacation with my mother at Canyon Ranch in Tucson, our visit had overlapped one of their camp sessions. Canyon Ranch donates space and services to Dream Street, so kids were everywhere, playing ball, hanging out by the pool, some bald, some in wheelchairs. I'd met Lenny Roberts, a staff member who had been volunteering at Dream Street for about ten years, when I was moving between the pool and my deck chair, letting my prosthetics hang out.

"Have you ever worked with kids?" he'd asked me.

"Actually, I have," I said. "I have a degree in child development,"

"Would you be interested in being a volunteer counselor for Dream Street? It's a fabulous experience."

I told him that I would, we exchanged numbers, and they contacted me the next year, but camp times had conflicted with my tenth high school reunion. When the call came again in June of '97, the timing was just right—my first race was over and Nationals weren't happening until July. Dream Street held camps all over the country, and the younger kids, the ones they had in mind for me, were having a week-long camp in Malibu in June. There would be close to a hundred kids, about the same amount of counselors, and a full medical staff. I couldn't imagine a better way to spend a week, and I could fit it all in. At the beginning of June, I borrowed a sleeping bag, bought a ton of toys, and drove to Malibu to go to camp.

The kids' ages varied from six to sixteen, there were no real little ones, nobody was in diapers, and they were all in various stages of illness and recovery—some very sick, some not so sick. I saw them take their medications, some of them were bald from chemotherapy, and some couldn't walk, but I never knew exactly what was wrong with any particular kid. They could have had cancer, leukemia, sickle cell anemia, HIV, or full-blown AIDS, but we were told not to bring up the topic of their illness unless they brought it to us. Most of them didn't choose to talk about being sick; they were busy being kids at camp and they didn't want to think about anything else, particularly sickness and pain.

The first night in my cabin, before the kids arrived, I met an extraordinary woman counselor named Zonnie Theirbach, who'd been volunteering for Dream Street for many years. We just clicked, and when we got up in the morning, she and I went on a hike through the campgrounds. It was 7 A.M., the air was cool and misty in the Malibu mountains, and, as we walked, we found ourselves face to face with a few deer drinking from a creek. It was pure magic, a perfect way to start my first summer at camp.

The magic arrived full force when the kids checked into their various cabins and found a bag of toys, makeup, or jewelry on each bed, waiting for them. The cabins were rustic, the bunk beds were rickety, the bathrooms were located next door, and still it felt like paradise. I was assigned to a cabin with preteen girls, which meant there was lots of "boy" drama, between the dances they held during the week and the crushes the kids had on each other. I tell you, you haven't lived until you help choose lipstick color for a bald twelve-year-old girl who wants to attract a cute boy she noticed at dinner the night before.

There were activities all day long and the kids could pick and choose what they wanted to do, according to what they liked and how they felt. There were arts-and-crafts tables open every day; there was a ropes course where you could swing from tree to tree wearing helmets. The pool was open in the afternoons, the hot spot for socializing, and there were makeup artists from the Hollywood studios who made up the kids like monsters or any other characters they liked. The kids went on scavenger hunts, they climbed walls and jumped on trampolines, and there were barbecues at night. DJs were brought in for three different dances, and, on the last Saturday afternoon, we held the Dream Street Olympics. There were various events and meets: throwing balls into the center of rings in the pool, water and egg balloon tosses, electronic dart competitions and tug-of-war games, in which we partnered little girls with the big boys and big girls with the little boys, so no one would be at a disadvantage. It didn't matter anyway; everyone got prizes, winners and losers alike.

The truth is that we counselors were the real winners; we all agreed on that. I loved being away from the real world for a week, with no TV, no radio or newspapers, gazing at the stars without neon or artificial lights in the way. It brought me back to myself, slowed me down, and gave me time to think about how fortunate I was. It was such a privilege to dedicate myself to these courageous kids and have them depend on me. They loved hearing about my accident and my running, there was no place I would rather have been, but it was tough to see them suffer. As I watched these radiant children go through their lives, knowing how ill some of them were and being able to do nothing to help them, I got a taste of how my family and friends must have felt when my feet were frostbitten. It's such a helpless feeling when someone you care about is hurting: all you want to do is love and protect them and you can't stop their pain.

All week long, I spoiled those kids rotten; all the counselors did, because we weren't sure they'd be around next year. One night, a small boy who'd hardly left the infirmary was taken away in an ambulance. My heart broke for him; all he wanted was to be at camp. The next year, he was gone. Occasionally, in the periods between camps, I'd receive a simple note letting me know that a child had died. It was the saddest thing in the world. And still, I wouldn't trade being with the kids for anything.

Camp ended with a full-on Saturday night carnival, complete with rides, booths, and all types of games. For me, it was like being a kid all over again as I manned the ring toss and bowling booths, giving prizes to everyone, whether they won or not. When we left on Sunday, I knew I'd be back (I've done it for three years now), but nobody knew which kids would be returning. Life goes on. Some of them make it, some of them don't, but they always remind me to give my husband a kiss, call my mother, or check in with an old friend I haven't spoken with in a while. Most of all, working with Dream Street helps me appreciate my life even more than I already do. That's a gift far too valuable to measure.

23

Two Steps Forward, One Step Back

RUNNING IS A GIFT, PLAIN AND SIMPLE. THE PUREST FORM OF EXHILaration I've ever known, it gives me a sense of freedom as I fly through the wind unencumbered, and a sense of achievement every time I cross a finish line. It's as if nothing can stop me as I push my body to the limit and I revel in the strength and power of my mind. I study other runners' styles, I listen to my coach for guidance, I watch videotapes to correct my mistakes, but when I run, I'm on my own, completely in control of my body and mind, and I like that.

Most of all, running makes me feel secure. I know that if I ever have an emergency like a fire in my home or if I get apprehended by a burglar or worse, I can run and protect myself. When I have children, I'll be able to grab them and get my family to safety, if need be. I'm someone who learned the hard way how precious life is, and if I were confronted with losing it, I would fight with everything in me. Running has given me one more way to protect myself and I feel proud of my independence.

As I trained with Art, I had a lot of things to be proud of: I'd adopted a healthy lifestyle, I exercised, I felt strong and ate well. I've never been a stickler for diets or deprivation, I eat a little bit of whatever I like, chocolate and other sweets included, but I've taught myself to balance it out so I can stay in control of my weight and still have plenty of energy for my training. As I slowly became a real athlete and strengthened my outer self by working on my muscles and increasing my speed, my inner self was getting stronger, too. I came to love the feeling of being powerful, healthy, and accepting of myself as a whole person, unlimited in every way.

Running also put me in touch with other disabled athletes and suddenly I had friends who faced the same kinds of challenges that I did. As soon as I started running, I got the sense that my life was in order and I came away from every competition with a little bit more of myself, unwilling to hide any aspect of who I was. The truth is that I love competing. I've always been a competitive person and I don't consider that a bad thing. It's part of my nature and I think it brings out the best in me. I used to compete with Jason all the time, as most siblings do. I always won because I was older and taller, but that was temporary. Poppy warned me that one day, Jason would be bigger and stronger than me and the tables would turn. It happened like he said it would, so I took my competitive spirit to the mountains to ski. Now, running was bringing out my love of competition more than ever before. It made me feel alive and I knew I would continue.

Art was not an Olympic coach, but he helped familiarize me with the ins and outs of being a runner. He taught me how to evaluate the various tracks, to see how different one was from the next and how each race was different, too, depending on how I felt that day, who my competitors were, and whether or not they were prepared. I practiced coming off the starting blocks, keeping my legs underneath me, determining the most efficient angle of my body, and I gained more confidence every day. When June arrived, I took my newfound confidence and my cheetah legs to compete in the U.S. Nationals in Springfield, Massachusetts.

The same sprinting legs that had started out as a source of great pain, between falls and giving me sores, had become my friends. I counted on them to propel me, support me, and allow me to move with tremendous speed and power. I learned to use their bionic capabilities to my advantage, as they afforded me the freedom to take my mind off speed and place it on technique. I marvel at them still, at how carbon fiber and metal has changed my life so dramatically and given me a new way to challenge myself and become a stronger and more capable human being.

At this stage, a disabled elite athlete cannot run as fast as an able-bodied elite athlete. But if the technology continues to develop at the rate it's currently moving, I wouldn't be surprised if one day, an athlete with prosthetics will be fully capable of beating an athlete without them. Since I started running, the cheetah legs have been revised three times; there have been minor angle and alignment changes, and each time they get more efficient and capable of more speed. I expect the day will come, maybe even in my lifetime, when the Bionic Woman will be a reality. Until then, the gap remains open, but not by much.

Nobody I know has seen prosthetic technology change more than Lindsay Nielsen, someone I met during Nationals. A fellow disabled runner, Lindsay is a great example of stamina and courage. I can't imagine my running career without her in it, but our friendship had a rough beginning. It was my fault: I was annoyed when a forty-year-old single BK amputee showed up at Nationals, someone I didn't know existed, and she beat me. She came over right after the race to talk but I was a real bitch to her. I acted nonchalant, not looking her in the eye or wanting to be cordial. This was supposed to be my chance to come in first. How could this "old woman" show up out of nowhere and run faster than I did—even if she *was* missing only one leg?

At age fourteen, Lindsay had a single "SYME" amputation owing to an ankle disarticulation. It's a rare kind of amputation— only two percent of amputees opt for it nowadays—but when Lindsay was young, it was pretty common. If it hadn't been for Dr. Malone, I would have had two of them, but since he worked with a prosthetist, he steered me in a different direction. I was lucky to have had such superior guidance. Lindsay had no such information; it had seemed logical that the less they cut, the better off she would be. She and her mother had made the best decision they could with the information they had, and Lindsay struggled just to walk for a long time.

She never considering running until 1995, when the technology had improved drastically. At that time she began running distance, which requires a different kind of training and stamina than track. She showed up at the Nationals to challenge herself, never believing for an instant that she would actually beat anyone at a track event. I guess she surprised herself, and I found out later that my attitude surprised her as well. Marathon runners are less accustomed to cutthroat competition than sprinters, and she hadn't imagined she would upset anyone by showing up. I embarrassed myself by acting frosty toward her, but I made sure to apologize the next time I saw her. She responded right away, and since then she's been a great source of comfort and maturity for me. I've come to trust her implicitly. We watch out for each other, which is a far cry from what I demonstrated that day when she first beat me. I don't blame myself; I was just disappointed and my temper flared. It happens, especially under competitive pressure, but I'm glad I apologized and that she accepted. Now, despite our bad beginning, Lindsay and I love traveling together and we are each other's greatest cheerleaders.

I did very well at Nationals, which earned me an invitation to compete in an international event in Germany in August: the Paralympic Revival. It was a thrill when my mother, my grandmother, and I headed to Germany for my third competition. We didn't have to pay expenses when I competed internationally, so we were able to put some extra money toward a few wonderful nights in a German castle with ancient history and great beauty. Three generations of women traveling together, we admired the old furnishings and we loved our freestanding bathtub with hand-carved legs. The trip was a powerful bonding experience for all of us, but it was particularly important for my grandma, who was away for the first time since Poppy died. Unfortunately, I didn't make a good showing in my race because I was injured. Several weeks before the trip, I had attached one of my legs improperly and when I took a step, it popped off. My unprotected limb hit the ground and got badly bruised, which affected my training. I still managed to beat Aimee, my most serious competitor, by over a second, though. That was pretty satisfying and at the same time, frustrating. What if all systems had been "go"? How well would I have done then?

There are so many "what-if"s in this life, you can get exhausted just thinking about them. But meeting Beau, my husband-to-be, felt predestined, because I kept running into him everywhere. It seemed like I saw him constantly, although we made no real contact for a while. The closest we came was when Art, who knew him well, told me that Beau thought I was cute. My heart raced a little bit, but seven years' difference was a big stretch. I was twenty-eight, he was twenty-one. That's young, but at least he was legal.

One night when we ran into each other at a local bar, he challenged me to a spirited game of air hockey. We laughed a lot, we had a few beers, we hung out together, and when it was time to go home, he kissed me. I was surprised and I drove home smiling. Hey, this was almost the twenty-first century. Maybe twenty-one wasn't so young after all; it certainly didn't seem to bother him. The truth was—he had no idea how old I was—he never asked—so it wasn't on his mind.

When we started dating, we never had to discuss my legs, which was a relief. He already knew all about me. At one point we kind of drifted apart. He lived in a bachelor pad with four roommates, he liked his freedom, and we didn't see each other for a few weeks. I decided to continue dating other guys because of our age difference, but I never got intimate with anyone. I could have, I suppose, but I just wasn't interested. One evening, Beau and I got together at a Clippers basketball game and we realized that we wanted to be together. We may have had very little in common on the outside, but understanding someone else's life experiences and losses can create a powerful bond between two people. That night, when Beau told me what had happened to him a few years prior, I understood part of what had brought the two of us together.

During the summer of 1995, he, Art, and a few other guys pulled up their '68 Buick Skylark in front of a buddy's place in downtown Huntington Beach. Art waited in the car behind the wheel, while a few of the guys and Beau ran up to their friend's front door and rang the bell. There was no reply, so they walked back to the car to leave. A group of white supremacists showed up. Art happens to be Hispanic, and this gang who lived behind his friend's house were less than thrilled to see a "beaner" in their neighborhood. Beau quickly got into the backseat while the gang surrounded the car. When he heard them telling their girlfriends to get into the house, he knew trouble was brewing.

He was right; one of the guys pulled out an AK-47 assault weapon and Beau shouted to Art, "Drive away now!" Art started to make a swift exit, everybody in the car ducked, and Beau was almost on the floor of the backseat when he heard the shots. A gang member had emptied his ammo clip in the car's direction and one of the bullets that hit the car had punctured the trunk and penetrated the backseat. When the bullet hit a two-inch piece of metal inside the car, it exploded and the shrapnel flew into Beau's back. Twelve shots had been fired but Beau was the only one hit.

They rushed him to the emergency room and found two large pieces of shrapnel lodged in his back with a multitude of smaller pieces creating small dark dots all over his skin. During the forty-eight hours he was in the hospital, he realized that if he had sat up in the car, he wouldn't be alive, that he'd been given a second chance. He's fine now; you can see the shrapnel in his back but it doesn't limit him in any way. He jumps when cars backfire or when he hears other loud noises—the experience made a permanent impression—but he walked away with his life and a powerful reminder of how fragile it all is. In that way, he and I share a common understanding that makes everything else seem insignificant.

On the other hand, our family experience is very different. Beau comes from a small family, so the enormity of my extended family must have overwhelmed him at first, it was so opposite from his world. I wasn't sure how he would deal with it, but I watched him respond positively to my parents, brother, cousins, aunts, uncles, and all the rest of them. As each of my family members embraced him, he opened up to them too. He was wonderful with the nieces and nephews and I was feeling better and better about being with him. The truth is, I was falling in love, but I didn't realize it.

When we began to date seriously, it was absolutely wonderful.

I'd never felt so comfortable with anyone. He was fun to be with, we had a lot to talk about, and he showed up for me in a big way. Since my leg had popped off, I'd been getting epidural injections in the end of my limb, which were excruciating and weren't helping at all. The limb was so swollen and it hurt so much, I went to see Carlos to figure out what was going on. He said that it was changing shape, just as Joe Leal had warned me, and I needed to see a specialist. In January of '98, a plastic surgeon to whom I'd been referred took some X-rays that revealed a new bone spur. He felt it was important to remove it as soon as possible and he offered to do the surgery himself. I didn't want to go through another operation, especially with the second Flex-Foot competition only three months away, but he assured me it would be a simple operation and I'd be healed in time to compete in the race.

I trusted him—I had to do something because the pain was interfering with my training—but I should have gotten a second opinion. The surgery appeared to go fine and I was healing pretty well during the week that my grandma came to take care of me. I felt hopeful, and while she was there she saw how loving Beau was. When she got back to Arizona, she gave a glowing report to my parents, which was very important to me. How could I ever get close to someone who didn't get along with my family? I seemed to be doing pretty well, but a week after my grandma left, the pain was not only back, it was worse than before. The plastic surgeon announced, rather casually, that I had a bad infection. Nothing serious, he said, but when he squeezed the end of my limb, the sutures popped and the infection oozed out. It looked awful, it hurt like hell, and there was no way I could get a cheetah leg over my limb. It would be another month before I'd be able to walk on it at all, and I had to go through a round of intense antibiotics. I was pissed off, partly at the surgeon, but mostly at myself, that I hadn't looked for a doctor with more experience. These decisions were so hard to make and the healing process always ended up taking longer than I expected—this one was a good six weeks.

Beau was a godsend during my recovery. I hobbled around on

crutches and he was there for me whenever I needed him. He carried me around when it was inconvenient to use my crutches, and he and I become the best of friends. His actions proved that he might be young in age, but he was a lot more mature than some of the older guys I'd dated. We spent most of our time together and he showed me, in no uncertain terms, that whatever happened to me, he would be there, steady and strong. From that time on, we spent most nights together, at his apartment or my house. I started training again but I could forget the Flex-Foot race, I'd lost too much ground. Even if I hadn't, there was no way I could get a cheetah leg over my limb on race day. I entered the race in everyday prosthetics at the urging of one of my doctors. I guess he thought it would be good for me to show up, but I wish I hadn't. I ran without the help of any sort of racing gear. I ended up doing so poorly, I walked the last part of the race, which undermined my confidence. It was another lesson about listening to myself and not allowing anyone to manipulate me.

It was a strange day all around. I'd practiced throwing the javelin a few times during the previous year, because if I turned out to be any good at it, it could have been another opportunity to get to Sydney. When I competed in javelin at the Flex-Foot event, I didn't do very well and I managed to pop my shoulder out again. I was a mess; I was hopping around on one prosthetic at the gym, the other leg was off completely, I had two sore shoulders, and all I could do was stretching and some simple upper-body weight training. My resilience always showed up and got me going again, but I so hated being out of commission, especially since my racing schedule was getting full and Sydney was fast approaching.

Between my training and dating Beau, it was pretty clear that I was in Huntington Beach to stay, so I put my Scottsdale house up for sale. I was stunned at how quickly it sold, and I found my next home in Huntington Beach two weeks later. It's a wonderful one-story house where Beau and I still live, with a long front porch and plenty of space. By June, my limb had healed enough so I could compete in my second Nationals competition at George Mason University in Virginia. I was the only double amputee there and I was forced to race against five single-amputee women. I came in fourth, which wasn't bad considering my disadvantage, and soon I was on my way to England to compete in a race sponsored by the International Sports Organization for the Disabled (ISOD).

The race in Germany had been only for amputees, so England was my first ISOD event. Athletes from all over the world with different types of disabilities were gathered and I was at the track every day for four days, supporting other athletes and watching the events. I saw amazing feats of courage; along with amputees, there were people in wheelchairs with degenerative diseases like cerebral palsy, and still, spirits were high and the competitions were intense. I competed with all my heart, had a great time, and made new friends. A brand-new world, one that I had never fantasized, had opened up to me and I couldn't get enough.

I did okay there, nothing to write home about, but I met two new prosthetists, who turned out to be significant in my continuing search for better legs and better ways to run. Tom Guth, owner of RGP Prosthetics, and his friend Michael Stull, who worked for him, had been flown in from San Diego to assist the U.S. team. We got chummy during the event and they told me about a new kind of prosthetic called Vertical Shock Pylons (VSPs), made by Flex-Foot. I'd heard about these jogging legs that also could be used for everyday and I wanted some, but I had no health insurance at the time. I was looking for a new company that would insure me on my own and I hadn't found one yet. When Tom heard that Flex-Foot was willing to donate the components to me, he offered to make me a pair of VSPs as a favor. I gratefully accepted and I got home from England with a new prosthetist, Michael Stull at RGP.

All work and no play is not a good way to live, so in the fall, after so much training and competing, I decided to do something purely for fun. I'd heard about a disabled ski event they held in Breckinridge, Colorado, and I thought I'd see how it felt to get back up on a pair of skis. When I got there, I was surprised to find that they were offering adaptive snowboarding lessons, something I'd never considered. I'd figured since I had no feet, how could I snowboard? The answer was: The same way I did everything else—trial and error.

I didn't ski that weekend. Once I got on a snowboard with a special pair of poles, it was such a rush of energy, I was hooked right away. Although you don't go as fast as skiing, it's the same sense of freedom, so I've continued doing it. The toughest part for me is getting on and off the ski lift, something that isn't easy with prosthetics, but I keep trying because I want to be independent, and snowboarding is so much fun. That's one of the biggest changes I've gone through—I care more about pure enjoyment than I ever did before. When I skied as a teenager, it was about getting down the hill as quickly as possible so I could get back up there again. Today, life is less about getting the job done quickly and more about enjoying the process as I go along. I take care to enjoy each day, each event, each moment slowly but surely, as it arises, and life gets better all the time.

I had a lot of fun in Breckinridge, but it was not without its problems. Toward the end of the trip, while I was manipulating the poles, the snowboard, and the ski lift, I popped out my right shoulder again. It was extremely painful and when I got home it was still sore. Pain was a known commodity by then, an old friend I could live with, and I refused to think about surgery or letting my shoulder get in my way. I settled into my training, pain and all, and I watched the beautiful unfolding of my relationship with Beau as it slowly and steadily gained momentum.

24
Running for Adidas

B EAU WAS A GREAT FAN OF SNOWBOARDING, AND WE'D GONE TO Mammoth together over New Year's. I saw Beau's extreme generosity and kindness during that trip. He'd done a great deal of snowboarding and he was accustomed to being with his friends and really giving it his all, but he stayed close to me, so I wouldn't feel alone. I know he sacrificed some of his private time, slowing down to help me, and I was grateful. In the end, we both had fun, but I popped out my right shoulder again. It was becoming a pattern; I did it twice more, once in Tahoe two weeks later when I was attending a bachelorette party for a friend, and again in Telluride during her wedding.

It was time to do something. Running was becoming difficult; the back-and-forth motion of my arms aggravated my shoulder and it was hard to concentrate on anything else. Surgery was inevitable. In February of '99, I was referred to some new doctors named Warren and Sten Kramer, orthopedic surgeon brothers who shared a practice and became my attending physicians. I did my homework this time—I'd learned not to rush into anything after the bone-spur fiasco—and these men had performed successful surgeries on a number of professional volleyball players and windsurfers. When you consider the burden those athletes put on their shoulders, not to mention all the other crazy things they do with their arms, a runner's arm movements are mild by comparison. But my pain was bad, the shoulder kept dislocating, and the X-rays showed that surgery was necessary.

I was hesitant for several reasons. The operation itself was unpleasant to think about and so were the five to seven weeks of rehab, but I could deal with that. I was more concerned about recovering swiftly and completely because I didn't want anything to get in the way of training for Sydney. And then, I hated the idea of wearing a sling for six to eight weeks, which would fix my arm against my body at a ninety-degree angle and disallow use of one hand. How would I put on my prosthetics? I probably could have managed, but the tricky part was pulling on the sleeves that held the sockets onto my legs. They are constructed of a silicone-type material, and if you stretch them too far or in the wrong direction, they can rip. I really needed help and I disliked being dependent upon other people.

Beau offered to live with me and be my caretaker but I declined. We were getting closer all the time but we weren't living together yet and I didn't want to push anything. Breaking up with Darren had felt so much like a divorce, I wasn't sure I ever wanted to live with anyone again unless we planned to get married. I couldn't imagine anything breaking up Beau and me, but I felt that our age difference made it doubly important to let things build naturally. I thought it would be unwise to place an unnecessary burden on our relationship, which was still in its growth stages.

As always, my wonderful family showed up. My mother offered to come live with me in California for a month so she could help me with my legs, but I thought that recovering in Arizona was a better plan. My closest friends were in Scottsdale and I could be close to my parents and Grandma. It would be hard to be away from Beau for a month, but he could come visit and so the decision was made. My mom spent two days with me in Newport Beach while Dr. Warren Kramer performed my surgery. When she was sure I was fine, she flew home and my dad arrived in California to drive me to Arizona so I could have my golden retriever, P.J., with me. My dad and I always loved going on road trips together, but this time it was hard because I was uncomfortable from the surgery. I slept most of the way, lying down across the backseat while my dad drove and P.J. rode shotgun.

Under the loving care of my parents and my aunt Tona, I gradually regained movement in my wrist, while I kept the arm in a sling. Between my parents, my aunt who lived next door, Grandma, and constant telephone communication with Beau, I had a terrific support system. It was a peaceful time: I walked a little, I saw my friends and family, and fantasized about the Paralympics, willing my shoulder to heal.

One day, when I checked my E-mail for the first time in three weeks, I found that Disabled Sports USA, the national governing body for my athletic organization, was holding a conference call the very next day. The business at hand was to discuss the fact that the International Paralympic Committee (IPC) was offering U.S. disabled athletes only thirty slots for the Paralympics in Sydney. I was terribly upset, considering the fact that all U.S. disabled athletes, whatever their disabilities, were in contention for those same thirty slots. If I competed in my own category, I would have come in among the top performers. Against all disabled athletes in the United States—that was a different story.

About ten of us participated in that highly emotional conference call. So few amputees would be able to go to Sydney, many of us felt like we'd been training for nothing. My world was falling apart—what about my dreams and goals? What would keep me going for the next year? While someone was commenting on how sad it was that there was so little support for disabled athletes, my cell phone rang.

I was in a bad mood, I didn't feel like answering it, but for some reason, I laid down one telephone without hanging it up and picked up the other. It was Tiffany, the secretary from the Disabled Sports USA office.

"Hi, Jami," she said much too cheerfully for my taste. "How are you?"

"I'm okay," I answered in a far less upbeat voice. "I'm on the conference call, you know, about the slots for Sydney? Isn't it a drag?"

"Oh, yeah," she said, "I forgot about that. Listen, I just got a call from Adidas. They're looking for disabled athletes for a TV commercial. Are you interested?"

This was a strange turn of events. I wrote down the number, hung up the cell phone, picked the other one back up without missing a beat, and finished the conference call. There was nothing we could do about Sydney except voice our disappointment and pray that something would change. If it didn't, I sure as hell wouldn't be competing "down under" in 2000. I hung up the phone and sat there, dazed. I could hardly believe that after all this time and focus, so much training, several surgeries, and keeping the Paralympics in the forefront of my efforts, Syndey was moving out of my reach. Maybe I should just quit running altogether; it was such hard work, and if there was no payoff at the end, why go on? My disappointment was talking, I know, but it was hard to watch an opportunity getting snatched right out from under me.

I stared at the phone number I'd jotted down. I really wasn't in the mood, but I might as well see what this Adidas thing was all about. I dialed the number, feeling like I'd swallowed a lump of lead. I learned from a casting agent that the Adidas people planned on filming a group of disabled athletes playing softball. I was concerned because my arm was still in a sling, but I didn't say anything. I listened, acted interested, and sent them the materials they requested—my bio, my résumé, and some pictures—while I worried about my shoulder. What if I had to swing a bat? At least it was taking my mind off the bad news I'd just heard. When I told my surgeon about the possibility of playing softball in a commercial, he said if I tried to hit a ball with a bat before my shoulder was healed, he'd disown me. I was torn; I hated missing any opportunity for my sport, because they just didn't show up that often, particularly now that Sydney seemed to be dissolving. But I didn't want to injure myself. I'd just have to wait and see what happened.

A week later, Adidas called back with encouraging news. They'd scrapped the softball idea, changed it to a running commercial, and they'd narrowed it down to ten athletes. I was on the list. Did I have any additional promotional materials or photographs? I dug up a few more pictures, sent them, and another week went by with no word. I was on pins and needles; I really wanted to do this commercial, I needed something to look forward to, and my shoulder was healing.

Then one day, the call came. "Guess what?" the casting director said. "You got it. We're going to film you running. Just you, alone."

I was relieved. It's not that I didn't care about the Paralympics anymore; I just needed to move on as Poppy had taught me, and here was my next source of motivation. It had arrived quickly, too. I love it when life works that way and a lost opportunity is replaced by a gain. If I've learned anything in this unpredictable life, it's that rewards are often riding on the back of disappointment. You just never know what's around the next bend in the road. This time it was Adidas, and they were shooting the very next week in Los Angeles. I felt that it was a sign from God, that no matter what happened, Paralympic slots or not, I couldn't give up on running. Besides, the conference call wasn't the final word. There were thirty slots and I could still get one of them. I'd seen miracles happen before.

I stared at my sling and I knew I could manage the commercial, now that it was running instead of playing ball. Enough time had gone by, I was getting stronger every day, and although I hadn't actually started training again, I was riding the bike and lifting weights. I packed a bag and had drinks with some friends the night before the shoot. I was happy to have something new to think about. The next day, Adidas flew me from Arizona to Los Angeles. Jason, who was living in LA, didn't have to work that week, so he offered to go with me to the shoot in case I needed help with anything, like moral support.

I needed plenty of that. This was the first time I would have my sling off since the operation and I was a little scared. Jason and I showed up at a church somewhere in suburban Los Angeles, where they were in the midst of shooting a commercial with a Hispanic soccer player whose shoes (Adidas, of course) were getting blessed by a priest. The talent coordinator told me I could watch the other shoot, eat from the catering truck, and hang around until they were ready for me. Then we would all go over to the college track to film me running. I didn't eat too much, partly because I was about to run, partly because I was nervous. They'd asked me to bring my cheetah legs and I couldn't imagine how I would fit a pair of Adidas track shoes over the carbon Flex-Foot components, which were nothing at all like a real foot. I'd brought my VSP legs, too, the ones Michael Stull had made for me, in case I could talk them out of it.

I stood at the church waiting, my arm free for the first time in close to two months. It felt vulnerable hanging there, but I didn't want anyone to see the sling, so I didn't even bring it with me. When they were finished with the soccer commercial, the crew, Jason, and I went over to the track while an assistant explained the financial arrangements to me:

There would be no residuals, which meant I would not get paid each time the commercial ran. Instead, they were offering me a reasonable buyout. I had no agent or financial spokesperson, so I agreed right away. Whatever they offered, I was prepared to accept; I felt it was fair because they were taking a risk with me. It really was a long shot for them to film an unknown running on prosthetics, and it would be a real boost for disabled athletes. I wanted the experience and the exposure and there was no way to know how extensive that would be. In hindsight, it probably worked out best for all concerned.

The wardrobe girl handed me some Adidas workout clothes to change into, a pair of black stretchy shorts and a dark tank top. Unfortunately they offered me very few choices. The shorts fit nice and tight, but when I pulled the top over my sports bra, staying mindful of my shoulder, the tank hung on me like a sack. I wonder how large they thought I was—that top must have been three sizes too big and it hung to the side when I ran. But that was the least of my worries.

When I first stepped onto the track with my cheetah legs and we tried to fit shoes on them, it was impossible, just as I had suspected. I finally managed to lace up a pair of shoes over one of the sprinting foot components, but it looked pretty silly. Then there was the difficulty in balancing while I stood around. When I showed them the VSP legs, my jogging prosthetics with feet, they were delighted and so was I. The Adidas track shoes fit over them perfectly—they were made for shoes—and standing around in between takes was much more comfortable. Now everybody was happy.

I ran back and forth on that track for about three hours while they considered angles and points of view and kept on shooting. It was intense, mainly because I hadn't run in such a long time. But as luck would have it, the sun was glaring on the track, so I had to shorten the length of each run. That made it slightly easier, and believe me, I needed every break I could get.

It was a matter of what they saw was what they got—on so many levels. It was bare-bones, no frills at all, which was why it worked out so well and looked so real. For starters, the only makeup I wore was the little bit I'd arrived in, which I sweat off in the first twenty minutes. There was no script and no words—only the sound of my feet on the track and my breath. There were no storyboards, because in essence we were all creating the action together, making it up as we went along. It was just me, the director, the camera, and the track.

Jason, my quiet, steady, hardworking brother, is a softy just like my father. An awesome father himself these days and a great husband to Judi, his wonderful wife, he was an angel to me throughout that shoot. I was getting really tired toward the end and although I didn't let on, Jason knew. I could tell by the look on his face that he was concerned, but he kept quiet about it. He just parked himself beside my starting mark and cheered me on. "C'mon, Jami," he whispered in my ear, "you can do this. It's almost over now."

Over and over again, I ran when they yelled "Action," and I stopped when they called out "Cut!" I never knew how the commercial would look and they didn't either. When they wrapped the shoot, I had no idea what I would see on TV, but I was relieved and proud of myself. I had been a trouper at a very difficult time, my shoulder had held up beautifully, and I'd gotten through it without complaining. I'm glad I hung on to that tank top; it reminds me of something wonderful in my life.

25

Compassion

Ｈow many times have you heard someone say, "He's really not my type, he's so different from the other guys I've dated"? And then they end up marrying him. That was me, with Beau. He was so different from my other boyfriends, it surprised everyone when he moved in with me. Brittney told me she had never expected it to go that far, and I admit, it was a big step for us. At the same time it was the most natural thing in the world, since we wanted to be together so much.

When I went over the standard list of "what I wanted in a man," he didn't exactly fit. He was young for me, we grew up in different kinds of families, we were not the same religion, and we had different life experiences. And yet, I loved him, he loved me, we shared the same basic values, we adored being in each other's company, and he was completely responsible and dependable. I had never met anyone who was more willing to move out of himself and be there for me. Most of all, it was the first time I'd wanted to say "I love you" to anyone in many years. Beau was the man for me. I was ready to see where we could take our relationship, and so was he.

It was three weeks after the Adidas shoot, and Beau had just moved in, when the producers called. The commercial was edited and they were planning to start showing it in a few days. The first airing would be during the 1999 NBA playoffs and I was thrilled! I'm an avid basketball fan; it's the only sport I like to watch on TV, and Beau loves it too. I suppose the biggest problem in our household is the fact that he roots for the Los Angeles Lakers and I'm a Phoenix Suns fan, but we live with it! Loyalty aside, the idea that my commercial would show during the playoffs between the Lakers and the San Antonio Spurs was a huge bonus, since millions of people across the country would be tuning in. What extraordinary exposure for me, for disabled athletes everywhere, and for my sport! I was jazzed to say the least, and amazed that they had gotten it ready so soon.

The day of the airing, a video copy of the commercial arrived at my house by FedEx. I'd gotten up early that morning and gone to the gym, and when I got home, there it was. Beau wouldn't be home until later, so I watched it with my friend Romy. I was stunned when I saw what they had done:

They started on a tight close-up of my face with light birdsong in the distance. As I started to run, you could see me from the waist up, breathing and moving forward with tremendous focus. The cameraman panned down until the frame included the bottom edge of my shorts as I continued to run, accompanied by two sounds: my footsteps on the track and my breath. Now the camera moved backward, stopping the frame at my knees, which showed my silicone sleeves. Finally, it pulled all the way back, revealing my entire body, including my VSP prosthetics with a pair of Adidas track shoes laced on the foot shells. In the last few seconds, you saw me stopping, turning back to face the starting line, checking my watch and then walking with my hands on my hips, breathing hard. When the words "Long Live Sport, Adidas" flashed on the screen, these extraordinary thirty seconds had imparted a powerful message—without a word of dialogue!

Romy burst into a cheer and gave me the thumbs-up. I wasn't too sure; it had been shocking to see myself, mainly because all I did during the shoot was run back and forth. I really had no idea what they would do with it, and although it seemed a little on the weird side, I had to admit that I liked it. When I saw it again, with Beau this time, during the playoffs, I got the full impact. It would most definitely make an impression, that was obvious, but I had no idea how much and whether it had longevity.

The commercial aired every day that week, and they played it so many times after that, I lost track. Everyone called; they had seen it and thought it was terrific. They did heavy rotation on it during the spring and summer, and because there were no words, it played all over the world. Within days of the initial airing, letters and E-mails poured in and people began to recognize me in the grocery store, at the movies, wherever I went. I didn't mind; it was different from being known as the girl who got stuck in the snow. Now I was being recognized for something positive that was happening in the present, and I loved hearing how it was affecting people's lives.

It was around this time that I stopped caring about always wearing cosmetic legs and I wore what was easy and felt best. When I got my first prosthetics, I was concerned with the toes looking like everybody else's, and I was always judging the texture of the skin and the curve of the calf muscles. If the cosmetic aspect of a pair of legs didn't meet my expectations, I would get them changed. It's only natural; my real legs had been shapely and slim and people used to kid me that they were the most delicate and beautiful part of me. Once they were gone, I missed them and there were times I didn't want to admit that I had prosthetics. If someone asked me about a bumpy area at my knees under my jeans where the sleeves fit over the sockets, I might say I'd had knee surgery or act like nothing unusual was going on.

Once I shot the commercial, though, my attitude changed. Suddenly my prosthetics were an asset, not a liability, and they helped define who I was. I wore whatever felt good; that was mostly the VSPs. They were impossible to cover; they had springs on the sides that bowed out and if I tried to make them into a cosmetic leg, my calves would have looked as big as my thighs. I didn't bother; I had achieved complete acceptance of my prosthetics. I started jumping in the car as I was, wearing whichever legs I had on and walking through the streets, the video store, or the mall with my sockets, metal, shocks, and silicone sleeves all in clear view. I didn't do it to get attention, I just didn't want to take the extra time. Of course people stopped to look. How could they not? When was the last time you saw someone in shorts, looking like the Bionic Woman, picking up a few things at the grocery store? Probably never, and if you did, do you think you would notice? Anyone would, that's human.

I believe that the extensive exposure I got from Adidas and the subsequent interviews in newspapers and magazines has molded me into a different caliber of person, one who is less self-conscious and more accepting of myself and other people. I still receive notes from amputees and their families who were inspired and encouraged after seeing me run. When I write back or visit them when I travel, I see that I've affected their lives in a positive way, something I always wanted to do. That's another goal of mine: being a role model on a daily basis and furthering awareness about people with different abilities.

And then there were the unlikely spin-offs from shedding my need to wear pretty legs. I'm talking about the element of choice, of wearing them or not wearing them, according to what I wanted in the moment. For example, when Judi, my brother's wife-to-be, approached me about their wedding, I reclaimed another piece of my freedom. I'd let go of wearing cosmetic legs and high heels, it was too much trouble, but for the wedding, she asked me what shoes I wanted to wear. It was up to me, she didn't care, so I thought about it. It was a special event and I wanted to wear high heels again.

When I first got my prosthetics so many years prior, I was very concerned about being able to fit in and wear heels like everyone else. I made sure the feet on my prosthetics were capable of changing angles so I could wear dress shoes, but it was so difficult, I gave it up for close to eight years. Now I wanted to try it again. My prosthetist said it was no problem. If I gave him a pair of cosmetic legs that I especially liked and was comfortable in, he could permanently change the angle of the foot with some special equipment from Flex-Foot to accommodate high heels. When I put on dress shoes for the first time in so long, I was thrilled. It was like revisiting an old friend. But this time I was wearing the heels not because I needed to fit in, but because I truly wanted to feel that womanly feeling again. I'd almost forgotten how much fun it was to be a girl and go shopping for pretty shoes. I wore my high-heeled legs with pride for my brother's wedding and I was grateful to my new sister-in-law for reminding me that being really comfortable with myself meant more than not wearing heels. It also meant wearing them, too, according to exactly what I chose at any given time. That was a new sense of freedom and I liked it a lot!

The rewards continued. A week or so after the commercial aired, I was contacted by an organization representing the Department of Veterans Affairs (VA). Prosthetics had been born at the VA, for vets who lost limbs in the war. Now they were disturbed that a bill funding research on the continuing development of prosthetics was in danger of being revoked. They wanted to fly me to Washington, D.C., so I could speak at a congressional committee hearing on the benefits of continuing research and development in the area of artificial limbs.

When I agreed to go, they provided me with research materials on topics they wanted me to cover in my speech. I also did some research of my own. My talk would include how Flex-Foot started out and branched off, who engineered the first energy-storing foot, and the amazing opportunities prosthetics had provided for me. Four other speakers and I would take the podium, and my talk would cover the growth of prosthetics over the years, starting from its earliest developmental stages up to the present.

The best part was traveling with my dad, just the two of us. At the airport, someone stopped me and asked if I was the Adidas girl (my prosthetics were a dead giveaway) and my father absolutely beamed. When he sat in on the hearing, he must have been amazed to see his daughter at a congressional committee hearing, addressing senators' and congressmen's aides, urging them not to cancel a bill that provided amputees with necessary funding.

In researching the talk, I'd learned that the problem had gone way beyond the needs of veterans alone. Under our current health-care system, too many amputees could not afford personal health plans and had no choice but to go to the VA for help. Even with the current bill in place, they weren't getting the same kind of care that private insurance could offer. If research stopped and there was no more funding for their only available option, prosthetic development at the VA, where would they turn? How many of them would end up in wheelchairs for the rest of their lives and be grossly limited when it wasn't necessary? I felt passionately about the topic; I so resented the times I was confined to a wheelchair. It was one more reminder of how lucky I was to have a supportive family and adequate finances to make my life a little bit easier.

It was my first talk generated by the commercial, and the response was overwhelming. Many people in the audience had seen me on TV; a number of them congratulated me and requested signed pictures for their kids. I didn't have press photos but I took names and addresses. All in all, it was a great experience for both my dad and me. Neither of us cared much about sightseeing—he'd been there recently with my mom and they'd visited all the tourist spots—so he and I used the time to just be together. The afternoon after the hearing, since it was hot in D.C., we took in a matinee of *American Pie,* which my mom probably wouldn't have seen. My dad and I have the same sense of humor, and we laughed our way through it. When I got back home, I sat for a photo session, signed the pictures, and mailed them out. This was new; I felt like a celebrity, only better, because it wasn't about anything superficial. I was inspiring people and helping them feel better about who they were, just by being myself. The high was terrific.

I want to take a moment here to mention a man named Doug Martin, another angel in my life. He worked in San Francisco for an ad agency called Leagas Delaney, which produced the Adidas commercial, and he and I developed a great long-distance friendship. He proved that he literally would do anything for me, as he went out of his way to help me put together a professional-looking press packet with a huge binder filled with my ads, articles, and photographs. We've still never met in person and he didn't have to help me, but he acted out of the goodness of his heart. I hired an agent to round up more talks, but no one showed up for me like Doug did. I eventually asked him to take on the job of acting as my liaison. Now, besides helping me with my press packet, he fielded my Adidas calls, he assisted in getting me the products that were part of my original deal, and he helped me book talks and lectures across the country.

Nothing pleases me more than speaking to kids at their schools. I write out an outline and bring it with me so I'll feel secure and organized, but I never use it. I just talk from my heart about what I've had to overcome, how my life circumstances have changed me, and I share my plans for the future. I want to offer the kids awarenesses I never had, so I talk to them about incorporating physical activity into their lives, nourishing themselves, and becoming well-rounded healthy people. I try to impress upon them that you don't have to be an athlete to embrace a healthy lifestyle. It's a worthy goal for anyone to eat well, to exercise, and to become strong enough to support his or her own body weight.

Mostly, I want to encourage kids to care about other people and to accept them for who they are—no matter how they look or what disabilities they might have. I led such a sheltered life when I was growing up, I wasn't exposed to people with different abilities. I don't remember anyone in my high school using a wheelchair, so I didn't have feelings for or against them. It just never came up. Today, the circumstances of my life have made me a more compassionate person and that has spilled over into the rest of my family. When my father sees a car parked in a disabled spot with no placard, he leaves a gentle reminder like a note on the windshield, reminding them that a disabled person might need that parking place. He never thought about it before, but it's amazing what a little awareness can do.

That's my job with the kids—to make them aware of things they've never considered. I don't know about reincarnation or an afterlife, but I believe that we are all souls that came from somewhere, and these bodies just carry us along. That makes someone in a wheelchair just as important a human being as you are. If you can't accept other people's misfortunes, how will you accept yourself if something tragic happens to you? I like to encourage kids always to help each other, to carry someone else's books if they have a bad arm, to push a person in a wheelchair, to be a friend to anyone who needs it. It's all about being a good person on the inside and sharing that goodness with everyone, no matter their outer situation.

Because I lost my legs at age nineteen, I didn't have to endure teasing from my schoolyard peers. Many of my disabled friends were not that lucky. They waged a constant battle to be accepted while they were growing up, and I use their stories when I talk to the kids. Children want to feel like they fit in. When they wear glasses, grow taller than their friends, gain weight, or have a disability, they often suffer humiliation. I don't think kids intend to be cruel to each other, they just don't know they can make different choices. For example, one of the kids in my cousin Mackenzie's school has a prosthetic arm. The other kids used to make fun of her—they called her a robot—and Mackenzie stopped them. "My cousin Jami has two prosthetic legs and she's cool," she informed them, "so stop making fun of my friend." She even brought me to school to show them.

I wore jeans that day so they didn't know anything until I rolled up my pant legs. Adults get quiet when they see my legs, afraid of offending me or being disrespectful, but not the kids. They not only wanted to see my prosthetics, they wanted to touch them and they wanted to see my real limbs—my "little legs." They needed to process the information visually and I was willing to show them, but I warned them first that my little legs, although they're not grotesque, bloody, or bruised, are not very pretty—at least not in the terms they're used to.

Mackenzie was proud of her cousin that day, because the kids were riveted. My talks are usually pretty provocative, especially when a kid asks to see my real limbs. I give them permission to turn away if they should become upset, but they hardly ever do. I think it's because I'm so comfortable with myself, they don't get a subliminal message from me to be afraid. With the youngest kids, I don't show them my naked limbs even if they ask to see them. What they really want is to see me crawling around the floor like a baby, which I do for them. They like seeing me the same size as they are, it makes them giggle, but I leave the socks on my limbs because I don't want them to have nightmares that the same thing might happen to them. I assure them they won't wake up one day with frostbite, it doesn't happen like that, and they usually relax. I don't know what they think about it after I leave, but I know for sure they're going to remember me for the rest of their lives.

When I show the older kids my limbs, the oohs and aahs flow freely. They're so ready to accept new ideas, and they ask questions like: Do your legs get rusty in the rain? Can you wiggle your toes? If you scratch an itch, does it really feel like you're scratching? Then there's the all-important question that kids ask me so often: Do you wish you had your legs back?

I joke a little at first and say, "No way. Then I'd be short again." They laugh but the truth is that at this point in time, I would not want my legs back, and I tell them that. "I never would have chosen to lose them," I say, "but if I had my legs back right now, I wouldn't be sitting here, my life would have turned out completely differently, and I like the way it is."

A child once asked me, "What's your job?"

"Being here today is my job," I told her. "My life is my career." It's true. I wake up each day with appreciation and I get ready to accept my life exactly as it is and to take care of business. Whether that means going to the gym, giving a speech, or seeing the prosthetist or the doctor, my goal is to put a smile on my face and be present for my life, just like anybody else. That's what I want to impress on the kids, that we don't always get to choose the circumstances of our lives but we do get to choose our attitudes. If I can be a positive role model for kids and teach them to have compassion for other people, especially for those less fortunate than they, I will have put in a good day's work.

I never considered a career in public speaking when I was looking for my vocation in high school. I really had nothing in particular to say back then, but I was always strong-minded and I spoke out when I had an opinion. I majored in Communication because I liked the idea of speaking my mind. Today, I have followed through on that. I recently spoke at a one-day seminar in Ohio for a group called Project Understanding. They hand-picked kids from all over the state, not necessarily for their grades but for their willingness to take on the responsibility of spreading the word. They bused them in from across the state, some disabled, some not, and I spoke about disabilities and accepting people who are different. Their assignment was to show up, to listen, and, most important, to relay the information to their schoolmates when they got back home. Judging from their high degree of interest and the thoughtful questions they asked, I know they did a good job.

Not too long ago, I did a motivational speech for a group of corporate workers at Goodwill Industries. I also spoke at a Thanksgiving prayer breakfast in Buena Park, California, for five hundred people. During these talks, I can't tell you how often people say to me, "I saw you running in that commercial and I feel so guilty because I'm twenty pounds overweight and I can't get off the couch. My back hurts, my legs hurt, I just can't exercise. I'm so lazy, all I do is eat. Tell me what to do."

They want me to advise them, but I can't, mainly because I view these things differently than they do. I wouldn't dream of putting anyone down for what they do or don't do, or encouraging them to use me as a barometer for how their lives should look. Why waste time comparing ourselves with other people? We are all individuals with different purposes for being on this earth, we are responsible for our own self-esteem and we have our personal histories. Who am I to call you lazy? More important, who are you to call yourself lazy? Maybe you had a rough childhood, I have no idea. Maybe you had polio when you were a kid and you *can't* exercise. Does that make you lazy or worthless? Not in my book.

People say to me, "I never could have survived what you did. I would have fallen apart."

I once heard an adage that goes something like: Do not judge another man until you have walked a mile in his shoes.

I haven't walked a mile in your shoes and you definitely haven't walked in mine. No matter what you might imagine, there's no way to know how you would handle what happened to me. If anyone ever told me that I would have to give up my perfect little legs, the only small things about me besides my height, I never would have thought I could go on. But I have gone on, we all do, each in our own way, and I think people have the wrong impression of me. There are times I wake up in the morning and I bitch and complain—just ask Beau. I say things like, "I don't want to put on my legs, I don't want to go to the track today." And when I get to the track, I'm annoyed about having to go through this long process of changing my legs, making sure they're right when I start running, and then going through tearing a sleeve or falling down and getting a bruise. Sometimes it puts me in a bad mood. I'm only human, I have my off days, and I can be plenty crabby. But I move beyond it and try to remember that I'm alive. It usually brings me back.

I don't know what your individual trials are—they may be a lot worse than mine—and I can't tell you how to handle a crisis. That comes in the moment, and I hope you never have to find out. The one thing we all have in common is our capacity to open our hearts, so if you want to have compassion for others and for yourself, I can tell you who I am, what I've done for myself, and how I access my energy and strength. I can also let you know what your support does for me. If any of that helps, I'm happy to offer it.

I was especially honored to be a guest speaker at a monthly Flex-Foot luncheon for a large group of assembly-line workers who spend their days putting the parts and components together that allow me to walk and run. These are the people behind the scenes, the ones nobody thinks much about. But I do, because where would people like me be without people like them? I loved having the opportunity to let them know how much their work has done for me, and encouraging them to take pride in what they do every day of their lives, even though it may feel ordinary and repetitive while they're doing it. They help people all day long and they so rarely get to see the results of their labors. For this reason, they were especially thrilled to see the commercial—it was meaningful to them on a personal level.

Although I know the Adidas commercial affected many people I will never meet, I got one personal reward, firsthand, that stands out above all the others. A year after the commercial aired, my disabled teammates and I were given a rare opportunity to run in an exhibition race at the Olympic trials in Sacramento. When the eight of us finished the race, I changed my legs and took a front-row seat in the stands to watch the women's hundred-meter sprint. I could hardly believe I was right up front while the great athlete Marion Jones qualified for the Olympics. It was a dream come true. She won easily and there I stood in my shorts on a very hot day, watching her run her victory lap. I snapped a few photographs as she got close to me and when she was about ten meters past me and my friends, she ran a few steps backward, stopped in front of me, and reached out her hand to shake mine.

"I loved your commercial," she said, running in place. "My husband and I watched it as much as we could, it was great." And she kept on running.

I was floored. Marion Jones had just stopped during her victory lap at the Olympic trials to take the time to congratulate me. She touched my heart and I will never forget it. I was aware that Brian Frasure, a single BK, one of the fastest disabled athletes in the world, trained regularly with Marion in North Carolina. Knowing him on a personal level must have made her more aware of how hard disabled athletes work and what we have to overcome, but taking the time to connect with me during her victory lap was above and beyond anything I ever expected.

When she was well past me, I grabbed my camera and walked in her direction. I wanted a picture with the fastest woman in the world. She disappeared behind the stands, probably to take her mandatory drug test, and I waited in the midst of her agents, her friends, and loads of reporters. Then I walked behind the stands—I've always been pretty good at maneuvering myself where I'm not supposed to be—and I found her walking back and forth, talking on her cell phone. When she was through, I asked her for a picture, which she was happy to pose for. It was a boost for me, not only because she was the number-one sprinter in the world. I also admired her because she set such tough goals for herself, like wanting to win five gold medals in the Olympics and talking publicly about it. Later, when she didn't achieve her goals completely, I saw that she took pride in what she *did* achieve. I'm sure she was disappointed to some extent, but she was proud of what she'd accomplished and she'd been human enough to stop and acknowledge me.

It was the highlight of my summer. I may not have it in me to be the fastest woman in the world, but that has never deterred me from being a fierce competitor. Once I started running, nothing has changed my focus from working toward a dream and achieving it. And thanks to Marion Jones and a lot of other people, I've been lucky enough to receive recognition and compassion from unexpected people and places. That's what makes life fulfilling.

26

Running Around the World

DURING THE YEAR AFTER THE COMMERCIAL AIRED, I DID SO MUCH press, I've lost track of it all. Reporters did numerous stories on me in newspapers across the country. I was written up in *Women's Sports Illustrated, Sports and Fitness* magazine, *USA Today,* and the *Los Angeles Times,* to name a few. I was on every network TV station in Los Angeles, and I also did a segment for CNN and *Time* that was viewed by people all over the world. I received an E-mail from a woman somewhere in South America, an amputee mother of three, who wanted to commend my accomplishments and let me know that it was not painful for an amputee to give birth. I really appreciated that.

I was also featured in Oprah Winfrey's magazine. They originally had planned to include me with three other women in the very first edition. Later, they decided to feature me in my own issue. A freelance writer, whom I liked very much, arrived in Huntington Beach to do the piece. She stayed in a hotel nearby, interviewed me extensively, watched me run at the USC track and met all the guys I trained with. We had a terrific rapport and she put out a wonderful article that really made me proud.

The Queen Latifah show was one of my most exciting appearances, because they had prepared a surprise for me. A woman named Veronica Copeland, who lived in New York, had a daughter named Bryanna, who lost both legs above the knee when she was six. Veronica was excited when she saw the commercial, amazed to learn that there was hope for her daughter. She wanted to meet me very badly, so she contacted the Adidas people, who put her in touch with Doug Martin, who played me a very moving voice message she'd sent him. I wanted to speak with her, too, so I got her on the phone. Bryanna was on crutches, which limited her movement drastically. All this child wanted to do was play with her friends, but her mother was not informed as to the latest developments in the area of prosthetics.

Over several telephone conversations, I advised Veronica about the state-of-the-art technology, and helped her find a prosthetist in her area to update her daughter's legs. We became very close, and when I was contacted to do the Queen Latifah show in New York, I called Veronica to set up a time to see her. She sounded terrifically disappointed when she told me that it was short notice and she had to work. I thought it was too bad, I so wanted to meet her and Bryanna, but little did I know they had some wonderful mischief up their sleeves.

Apparently, I had mentioned Bryanna during the initial interview with the producers of the show, and they had found Veronica. Unbeknownst to me, the entire family of four—mom, dad, Bryanna, and her brother—were sitting in the studio audience during the taping. When we were about to go to a commercial break before the last segment of the show, Queen Latifah said, "We're going to break right now, and when we return, Jami, we have a surprise for you."

I had no idea what to expect, but as soon as we were back on the air, out walked Bryanna, a crutch in one hand, a handful of flowers in the other. I knew it was Bryanna right away; they were still making her new prosthetics and she usually needed two crutches to walk, but she was balancing on one so she could manage the flowers and hand them to me herself. The show had sent a car to pick up her family and bring them there, and I couldn't have been more surprised. They rode with me to the airport so we could all spend some extra time together, since this was the first time we'd met in person, and when I took off and headed home, I felt like I had made a big difference in this family's life.

It made me want to keep training and competing all the more. In June of 1999, I returned to George Mason University in Virginia, to compete in Nationals for the third time. My two single-amputee friends, Sarah, an AK, and Lindsay, a BK, ran the race with me. I always lose to Lindsay, I was ready for that, but three women showed up whom I'd never seen. One was a single BK, but two were double amputees like me. Shea was younger, Colleen was older, and the competitive bar suddenly had been raised.

I was not amused. It's always unsettling when perfect strangers show up, just when you've studied your opponents and you think you know what to expect. Now I had to evaluate, on the spot, two women about whom I knew nothing. It made me anxious. At first glance, I saw that Colleen had her first pair of cheetah legs and she wasn't too sure on them. She probably would be no threat. The younger one, Shea, who had just started competing, was jogging on everyday legs. She didn't even have a pair of sprinting legs yet, so I figured I had a viable chance of beating her.

I read it correctly: I came in third in both races, the hundred and the two hundred meters, beating the other two double BKs as I'd hoped. But I was surprised and not too thrilled when Shea, the young beginner, came in only one second behind me. That was pretty amazing, especially since she'd run the race in jogging legs. She most likely would become a force to be reckoned with in the future, but on that day I'd won in my class and I would take home a gold medal!

How can I describe what it's like to win a gold medal? When they place it around your neck, it's the most extraordinary feeling in the world to know that this is something you've trained for and earned by the sweat of your brow. I felt a combination of joy, relief, and total satisfaction when I got my medal. Running is delicious enough by itself; winning a gold medal is like eating a rich dessert after a good meal, having it all to yourself, and then being able to take it home, too.

Nationals had been very good to me. Along with a gold

medal, I'd also earned a place on the U.S. team for the next leg of the circuit—Barcelona, Spain. I was still hoping and praying for a Paralympic slot, even though the odds were against me. I guess you know by now that I've never been the type to give up, so the best preparation was to improve my times with each race. That was my goal in Barcelona. I spent lots of time there with Lindsay and Sarah, and we got much closer as friends. There's a genuine sense of camaraderie among disabled athletes even though we can be fiercely competitive. We run in the same races but we all have different disabilities so we rarely compete against each other for times or rewards. That makes it easier to make room for one another, since we all face different obstacles.

I did very well in Barcelona. Not only did I win three more gold medals for the hundred, two hundred, and four hundred meters; I also set a new world record for the four hundred. In my eyes, though, it didn't really count, because there *was* no official record as yet, and so my time simply became the record. Unfortunately, the wind factor caused my hundred-meter and two-hundred-meter times to be considered unofficial, but there was always Germany, the next venue for an international competition.

I could hardly believe my life; I was seeing the world, competing, and sometimes I was winning. But it wasn't all about competition. Before Nationals, I'd been contacted by the U.S. Olympic Committee, telling me about a yearly telethon in Japan called "The 24 Hour Tele." The Japanese version of Jerry Lewis's telethon for kids with muscular dystrophy, this event raised awareness and money for the disabled in a country where people with disabilities previously were kept "in the closet," so to speak. "The 24 Hour Tele" was largely responsible for bringing disabled issues out in the open in Japan. This year, they were looking for several U.S. Paralympic athletes to make an appearance on the telethon. They knew I was a hopeful, that I'd never competed in the actual Paralympics, but they'd seen my commercial and they wanted to fly me and my mother to Tokyo for six days, all expenses paid, to represent the United States. That would have been a tough offer to refuse. They also contacted Brain Frasure and Tony Volpentest, fellow amputees and record holders, to show up there, too.

I was enthusiastic about going, but I had some concerns. "The 24 Hour Tele" was scheduled ten days before my competition in Germany. That meant I would fly to Japan, stay there for six days, and arrive in Germany three days before the event. If they could fly me directly to Germany and assure me there was a place to train while I was in Japan, I was willing to go. They were happy to accommodate me, so my mom and I headed off to Asia together for an amazing adventure.

When I initially agreed to participate, the telethon sent a Japanese reporter and a cameraman to Huntington Beach to film me in my everyday life, training at the gym, walking my dog, working my old job at Cal State Long Beach with children. They wanted to show the general public that with financial assistance and increased awareness, disabled people can live normal lives. They planned to introduce me to the Japanese people, show the film they'd shot in the U.S., and then the commercial, and finally they would shoot me live, running the hundred-meter sprint all by myself.

It was a great honor to be chosen for this event, and if I had been royalty, there was no way I could have been treated better. From the moment my mom and I landed at the Tokyo airport, they took us under their wing. They put us up at a luxury hotel, transported us wherever we wanted to go, and paid for all of our food. They even gave us our own private translator, who showed up at the hotel each morning and stayed with us until we went to bed at night. We never had to worry about a thing, everything we needed or wanted was provided on the spot, and I will never forget the Japanese people's extraordinary kindness.

When I decided to go to Japan, I'd E-mailed an old high-school friend of mine named Todd, who had married a Japanese woman and settled over there. I'd met his wife when they came to the States for a wedding—she was a wonderful person—and when Todd heard I was participating in "The 24 Hour Tele," he could hardly believe it. It had become such a widespread event, everyone in Japan knew about it, and he promised to meet me at the track where they were shooting my part of the telethon. Todd and his wife lived two hours outside of Tokyo, and they drove to the city to watch me run. On Sunday, the day before I would take off for Germany, Todd, his wife, my mom, and I all went sightseeing together. I was filled with happiness; I was seeing old friends in a part of the world that was brand-new to me, while I was raising awareness for disabled people in Japan. It was everything I had dreamed about. A couple stopped me while we were out shopping—they recognized me from the telethon, because I was wearing shorts—and I realized that, once again, I had impacted people's lives in a positive way. I'd also gotten to spend some time with the other disabled athletes, Brian Frasure and Tony Volpentest, whom I didn't know all that well.

When I arrived in Germany after Japan (my mother flew straight back home), I was so uplifted, it carried right over. I rested for a day and a half in the hotel, feeling secure. I'd trained diligently for the last week, and I was fulfilled because I had given something of myself to a large number of people. I was ready for the German event, which was by invitation, just as it had been when I was first invited in '97, but this time I felt like a seasoned veteran. A prosthetic company sponsored the races and paid all our expenses, with the exception of airfare. That included transportation from the airport to the venue, as well as room and board for the whole time we were there. The prizes were a big incentive; world record–setting athletes would receive a gold bar, which I was hoping to nab.

My sense of readiness and well-being were reflected in my races, even though I didn't get a great start. Coming off those starting blocks was still plaguing me, but the wind was in my favor and I ran the hundred meters in 17.3 seconds. I broke Aimee's world record, officially this time, by a third of a second. When they gave me a gold bar, I could hardly contain myself. All I could think about was showing it to my children one day.

When I got home from Germany in August, I faced a tough decision. The U.S. was sending disabled teams to two more venues: the Southern Cross Championships in Australia and, a week later, the Pam-Am Games in Mexico City. In order to break the two-hundred-meter world record officially and win another gold medal, I needed to attend at least one of these. Of course, I wanted to do both—I was gung-ho at that point and my body was holding up very well—but it was an expensive proposition. I considered the options with my dad: I was attracted to Australia, because it would afford me the opportunity to become familiar with the Paralympic venue. It was irresistible; since I didn't know how good my chances were for a slot in the Paralympics, I decided to go there for the Southern Cross Championships and skip Mexico City. I liked the idea that Lindsay was competing in Australia, too, so toward the latter part of October, Lindsay and I flew to Australia, with my dad following us a few days later.

We stayed in a hotel in Sydney, and each day a bus arrived to take our group of athletes, from across the world, to Home Bush Bay, the Olympic Village city, where the Southern Cross Championships were being held. Stepping off the bus onto the streets of the Olympic Village was like waking up in the middle of a vision. There I was, in a spanking new city within a city, created solely for the upcoming 2000 Olympic Games as well as the Paralympic games. I stared at the massive buildings and newly paved streets that had been constructed in order for us, the athletes, to train and compete at world-class levels. In less than a year, this city would be bustling with the greatest athletes alive, all together in one place to carry on a tradition that began in the fifth century. I hoped I would get to see it in full flower for the Paralympics, but I was a part of it today, about to compete on one of the running tracks in the village.

The Southern Cross Championships was a multidisability event, and there were seventeen hundred athletes competing in fifteen different sport events, so when I wasn't training, I was at the track supporting wheelchair, cerebral palsy, and blind athletes. I fell in love with Sydney, a bustling metropolis where I felt instantly at home. A short distance from the hotel, I could eat in one of a variety of restaurants, take a boat ride along the bay, or listen to music in their magnificent opera house. My dad, Lindsay, and I did a lot of walking around together, and even at night, we felt perfectly safe. During the days, we trained and competed on one of the four Olympic tracks that would register for posterity the footsteps of the fastest runners in the world.

On the day of my competitions, I surprised myself by running the hundred meters in 16.88 seconds, breaking my own world record. I was anxious to see what I could do in the two hunded meters, but when the time came, it was pouring rain. The record for the two hundred stood at forty-six seconds, and I ran it in 39.01, rain and all. The frustration was that I'd nailed it in 36 during practice, but the rain interfered in my time during the actual race. I managed to break the world record anyway, but there was one catch: In order for a record to be set, a minimum of four athletes from three different countries was required. The German women who had registered for the race had been advised by their coach to skip the two-hundred-meter race because of bad weather. Now we were only Americans; we needed at least two runners from other countries in order to have our times officially recorded.

I couldn't let this opportunity pass me by; I found an official I knew who sanctioned the races for ISOD. If I could get two women to run who were not Americans, I suggested, could we do the race over again and consider the new times legal? He agreed and I went to have a talk with Amy, a single-arm amputee friend of mine from Australia. Amy runs with a pylon arm prosthetic, more for balance than anything else. It's tough to run without arms—they set your speed and help you maintain balance—but she has two legs, which makes her faster than I am. I knew she'd beat me but I wanted her to run anyway; it didn't matter who beat whom since we were in different categories. I just needed her to be there, in case I ran fast enough to set a new record.

Amy was willing, and so was a friend from Europe. I ran the two hundred twice that day, doing it for the second time in 38.46 seconds in the pouring rain. That was pretty cool. When I realized that not only had I run in the rain but I'd also broken the world record, I had plenty to be proud of. I took home two gold medals as well as a special certificate declaring me an "all-comer." That meant that I, an athlete from the United States, had come to Australia for the first time and set two world records. My father couldn't get over it and neither could I. I left Sydney feeling as if I was making history while paving my way toward the future.

A world record, however, is a fleeting thing that slips through your fingers faster than you can recite your winning times. I knew this, and still I was surprised at how quickly things changed. I got home pumped up from my success, knowing if I trained really hard, anything could happen. Two weeks after the Pan-Am Games in Mexico, which I did not attend, anything *did* happen, it just wasn't the "anything" I had hoped for. Right before my birthday, I received an E-mail saying that the world record for the hundred meters in my double BK class had been broken by two seconds! It was Shea. She was twenty years old, eleven years younger than I was, so I could understand her beating me. But fifteen seconds for the hundred meters wasn't possible. There had to be some sort of mistake. If not, this was a miserable birthday present.

I E-mailed the same official, asking him if I'd read his message correctly. He repeated what he had written the first time. It was true, Shea had leapt ahead of me by two seconds. What a drag! In less than three weeks, the record I had worked so hard to win was no longer mine. More training was the answer, but it was nearly Thanksgiving, which made the Paralympic trials only six months away. That wasn't much time. Art had been wonderful and he'd given me a great deal, but if I expected to improve enough to be a contender, I needed to get an Olympic-caliber coach. How would I find one?

Deanne Schlobaum, a woman from my gym who was the cross-country running team's head coach at Cal State Dominguez Hills, had asked me to give a speech to her track team before their 1999 season. I spoke to them about running and motivation, and after the speech, I mentioned to Deanne that I was looking for a coach and that time was of the essence. She contacted a woman named Barbara Ferrell-Edmonson, who had trained the track team at USC for ten years. This woman, an Olympic-caliber coach, was currently working at Cal State Dominguez Hills, and Deanne saw her often. She promised to tell her about me. A few days later, Deanne gave me Barbara's phone number, but it took Barbara a month to return my call. I was frustrated, I was losing time, I needed to work with someone really good, and she was the only person I'd found. Why didn't she call me back, even if it was only to turn me down?

She finally called right before the holidays and invited me to the track to watch one of her training sessions with her team of male sprinters. I could meet the guys, she suggested, watch them run, and when it was over, I could run for her. I was scared to have her watch me. She was such a pro and the idea of being evaluated with that kind of critical eye was uncomfortable, but I wanted a coach very badly. I'm happy to say that as soon as we met and I ran for her, we clicked. I had a lot to learn, we both knew that, but she liked my intensity and my energy. I liked her up-front style of communicating and the things she said.

She wanted to know how long I'd been running and how much time I was willing to devote to my training. "Training is a lifestyle," she said, "a commitment to everything you do in your life, that reflects what you do on the track." She told me she'd been hesitant when Deanne told her about me; that's why it had taken her so long to return my call. She'd never worked with an amputee, it would be new for her, but she liked my determination. She ended the conversation by giving me some important things to think over. "How bad do you really want this?" she asked me. "How far are you willing to push your body?"

I called her the next day and told her I wanted to go forward. We discussed finances and she asked me to give her what I could. For her, coaching obviously was not about money. Before we hung up, we made a date to meet at the track, just the two of us, right after New Year's, to start my training.

We began slowly, focusing on technique and breaking some bad habits I'd developed over the years. She said she probably would put me together with her guys at a later date. For now, I had to relearn some of the basics. That was the hardest part, to forget about my gold medals, gold bars, and world records and hunker down on some boring old drills. I'd been running incorrectly for two years, specifically my arm placement and my body angle, and it was necessary to slow way down to make the necessary changes. Running fast and having fun was one thing; being an elite athlete who wins races by hundredths of a second was another story altogether.

It all started very early in the morning, which was unfortunate for me because I've never been a morning person. I became one pretty fast, though, because Barbara expected me to be at the track by 7:30 A.M., warmed up and ready to train. That meant I had to get up at 5:45, eat something, get to the track, deal with my legs, do some drills, and be prepared for training. No excuses. I complained on the inside, but I showed up every day.

Barbara took me to the dirt and started me running up hills with my cheetah legs. I'd never done that before; it was about a thirty-degree incline and it was hard. I'd developed a bad habit in which my left arm tended to swing from side to side instead of front and back, which was slowing me down. My new coach worked with me on arm placement and on shifting my body weight forward. I was accustomed to running nearly erect, which made me feel more secure on my legs, but it was creating resistance to my motion. I needed to find a position that would allow me to roll into the smoothness of my gait. A slight lean is more accepting of motion, it makes it easier to propel yourself, but it initially made me feel like I was about to fall over.

I also needed to lengthen my stride, the longer the better. Barbara encouraged me to take steps that were up to seven strides ahead of myself, instead of the short, choppy steps I was used to. "The longer the stride, the faster the runner," my new coach said. It followed that the taller the runner, the longer the stride, but then, taller people face other challenges that can make a smooth stride more difficult. Besides a long stride, you also need to be muscular, in order to have the power and strength to sprint. If you compare the body of a distance runner with that of a sprinter, you'll immediately see the difference. A distance runner is very slim while a sprinter is denser, with more muscle for propulsion. I needed to build muscles, which took me back to the gym for increased strength training.

Marion Jones has the best of both worlds: she's tall, which makes her fast, she's muscular, which makes her strong, and she's able to lean into and accept the curve during the two hundred meters, without losing speed or balance. Of the two fastest men in the world, Michael Johnson and Maurice Green, Michael is taller, but both men are extremely muscular, which gives them the power and strength to sprint. These are the kinds of things my coach and I discussed to make the time go by, while I trained harder and longer than ever before. More often than not, I'd come off the track so wiped out, I'd eat some protein as soon as I got home and fall into bed for a good hour's nap. But I loved the sense of accomplishment and commitment, and I had great respect for my coach. I worked so hard, I remember falling twice in one day. Barbara made me get up and run again, right then and there. It was all about getting those cheetah legs beneath me, and my coach was going to make sure that I did.

Barbara Ferrell-Edmonson is nothing short of a work of art. She's been running her whole life, she's thoughtful and sensitive, and at the same time she can be as tough as she needs to be. The work was tedious and exhausting but I applied what she taught me as I worked drills and ran uphill. When I heard my times in the beginning, I wanted to quit. It was like going back to negative square one and learning to run all over again, and it was frustrating as hell. But if I wanted to meet my new goals, I had to do it.

27

Trials

THREE WEEKS AFTER I STARTED WORKING WITH BARBARA, I GOT some extraordinary news. The IPC, under pressure from disabled sports organizations across the world, had agreed to extend the number of disabled slots. The U.S. numbers had gone from thirty to seventy-one, which meant the odds of my getting one had increased. Now it was more important than ever to make great strides in my work and to really push myself. It was time for me to run with the guys, a whole new level of motivation.

There I was, trailing behind a group of professional athletic men with two legs who had been running for years. Some were the elite of the elite who trained for the Olympics; they were damned good, they'd been running track since high school, they entered local track meets constantly, and they were very competitive. They pushed me, I pushed them, they inspired me, I know I inspired them, and I improved tremendously. They welcomed me with open arms and they treated me just like one of the guys, exactly the way I wanted to be treated.

What I appreciated most was that they didn't act any differently around me than they did with each other. I saw them have breakdowns, I watched them train with injuries, and I felt the power of their commitment to arranging their lives around running track. It wasn't easy for some of them—they had jobs and responsibilities outside their training just like I did—but we all did our best to leave it behind when we got to the track. Once we were there, we cheered each other up and we cheered each other on. When any of them had injuries, they would slow down their stride and I got the experience of running beside them, a great training tool for me. We staggered our positions when we practiced starts so I had the chance to feel as if I were ahead of them, reaching certain points on the track before they did. It was a brilliant strategy on Barbara's part because it motivated all of us.

The only times I ran with amputees were in actual races. The rest of my training was with able-bodied athletes. With encouragement from my coach, I decided to enter some local meets, to push myself and improve my times against people with legs. The meets lasted all day long. I needed to be there for hours, to warm up, stretch, cool down, and then get another really good warm-up before the race as I acclimated myself to the track. Sometimes Jason came with me, sometimes my parents, and sometimes it was Beau as I ran against myself and the clock, constantly improving my times, never expecting to win against able-bodied runners.

At first, I felt badly being the only amputee. I would be dragging this huge bag that was filled with all my paraphernalia, and I was embarrassed to change my legs on the track. I got over it quickly, though, and at one meet I had a fantastic win that really gave me confidence. The commercial had been running again, and I was doing a lot of interviews for newspapers and television, when I entered a local open meet and beat several high-school girls with two legs. What a rush that was! For this particular meet, they were accepting all comers, which meant disabled, able-bodied, experienced, or inexperienced. Beau showed up to support me. He brought a radio so he could listen to a Lakers game over the long day, and it made me feel secure to know he was there. When I evaluated my competition, the girls were young and strong-looking, so I got ready to run a good race for myself and beat my own clock. Winning seemed to be out of the question.

The hundred meters, my specialty, was the last meet of the day and I was competing against seven able-bodied runners, all much younger than I was. The miracle happened: I came in fourth, beating three girls with two legs. That was about as cool as it gets, and it boosted my confidence for what was coming—the Paralympic trials in June. I hadn't lost hope. I learned a long time ago, stranded in a cold, white world for days on end, that hope is all there is and that miracles *do* happen. I wasn't about to forget it now.

In late February of 2000, the U.S. Olympic Committee gave a grant to Disabled Sports USA to set up a training camp for amputee women. The men already had their training camps arranged, so they set ours up at the ARCO center in San Diego, where I'd run my first official race. Of the eight women who showed up, five of us were intensely serious about our training: myself, Lindsay, Sarah, a girl named Kelly, and Shea. I was keeping an eye on Shea; she was my toughest competitor and I wanted to see how much she had improved. The last three women who made up the eight were just beginning. They were there to have some fun and to learn and we all benefited because they'd be filling in the lanes to make the training more authentic.

When I watched Shea run, I knew I was in trouble. She was a monster, she'd trained very hard, and she was making such good times it scared me. Even though thirty slots had become seventy-one, that number covered all disabled athletes in all categories in the United States. There were fewer double BKs than singles, so even if I beat the best times in my own category, I still might not qualify, because there were so many other disabled athletes. I felt torn; I wanted my friends, even Shea, to do well, but that could mean losing a personal opportunity. I know we all felt the same way; it was hard to think that the better your friends did, the slimmer your chances of earning a slot.

I tried to stay focused on my training. When I do a particularly strong workout on the track, I sometimes get transported into "the Zone," a place where all effort disappears and I begin to soar. That's where I wanted to be, and I reached it as much as I could during training camp, while I paid attention to my weak points, like coming off the starting blocks. Another focus for me was learning to judge my exact times without checking my watch.

I also had to work on sensing what percentage of my energy I was using. When Barbara said, "Give it seventy-five percent," I couldn't be sure whether or not I was doing that or giving it my all. While I worked on my weaknesses, I kept my two goals in mind:

1. I wanted to make the team, that was first and foremost.
2. If I didn't, I wanted to utilize the enormous amount of energy generated by the trials to set a new personal best for myself.

It's so easy to fall on cheetah legs. A little bump in the ground, a less than solid placement of a foot and you're down. When you fall, not only do you risk getting injured but you can rip a sleeve, which will put you out of commission. There are an enormous number of things to remember in the heat of competitive tension: I did my best to stay in the present moment, working hard and getting strong and always, always remembering to keep my legs underneath me.

In May, with only two months before the trials, I got a phone call from a casting agent who had seen my commercial. There was an open call for amputees to play robots in a big-budget Hollywood movie. There was a speaking role, there were parts for lots of extras, and there was one role that involved running, which was why she'd thought of me. Was I interested?

Why not? She faxed me my lines. I had no idea who was producing or directing the film; I only knew it was a huge production and the auditions were the next day. I pulled into the lot at Warner Bros., walked into the designated office, signed my name at the end of a long list, and entered an inner waiting room. It was a major cattle call. I was surprised and I looked down at my skirt, my jogging legs and tennis shoes. Cattle calls by themselves were hardly unusual for Hollywood, nothing to be surprised about—except this time the cattle were all amputees. People with combinations of missing arms and legs or both were chatting together. I recognized a friend, Melanie, a swimmer I'd met in San Diego who was missing all four extremities. I knew no one else in the room, but most of them seemed to know each other.

Then I realized that they were all actors. This was how they made their living, sitting in casting offices to be hired as extras when a movie needed someone missing a limb. Perhaps they enjoyed it, how could I know, but I felt awfully happy that whatever happened in this audition, my future didn't depend on it. When my name was called, I went in to read for a "principal" role. They told me this was a Steven Spielberg film, they videotaped me, and I read my lines, in which I was supposed to be flirting with someone. When I was through, they said, "You were great! We'll call you."

When I didn't hear anything for several weeks, I figured it was all over, so I forgot about it. In the meantime, I was doing lots of publicity, not the least of which was a piece for "60 Minutes II," about my past and my Paralympic aspirations. I always had liked public-interest spots about people with Olympic dreams and I was excited to be one of them. I just didn't realize how much work a short segment would require.

My schedule already was packed, the trials were two weeks away, when I did the first day of running and interviews with the CBS crew for "60 Minutes II." I wasn't spending as much time with Beau as I would have liked, but he was patient. We'd gotten very close and our values had aligned so well, it was pretty obvious we wanted to spend the rest of our lives together. He supported my training completely, I supported him in the same way, he loved me unconditionally, he could put up with my moods (which were considerable sometimes), and when need be, he was able to put me in my place. I would nag him about keeping the house clean and complain that he wasn't working out enough and he never held a grudge. He knew how to calm me down and he was even getting used to my huge family. In fact, they'd embraced him totally, recognizing how right we were for each other, and he had embraced them.

At the end of a long day at the track in San Diego, running and doing interviews with the "60 Minutes" people, I called Beau to tell him I wouldn't be home for dinner. It was after six, I couldn't get back to Huntington Beach before eight anyway, and the crew had asked me to join them for a bite.

"Oh, Jami," he said, "why don't you just come home? I've already cooked, I thought you'd be tired."

That wasn't unusual—Beau was thoughtful—and the idea of kicking off my legs and relaxing with my love was irresistible. I told him I'd get home as soon as I could. I made my apologies to the crew, said I'd see them in the morning, and I got on the road. It was after eight when I walked in the door. Dinner was great; Beau had made king crab legs, salad, and asparagus, some of my favorite dishes. He was acting particularly sweet that night, and after he cleared the dishes, I told him I was going straight to bed. I had to be up early in the morning to put in another long day with CBS.

"Just a few more minutes," he said. "I made dessert."

"Why?" I said. "I'm too full and I have to work tomorrow."

"No, no. Just wait right there."

He bustled around in the kitchen for a few minutes and returned to the table holding a plate with two small pies on it. He'd written something on them with a cake icer and he'd covered the perimeter of the plate with white swirls of whipped cream. A mini Snickers candy bar sat in front of the pies, and I thought, How lovely and unusual. But why was he was so nervous? I was so busy wondering what was wrong with Beau, I hadn't read the words yet. I tuned in to the writing. Oh, my God, it said, "Will you marry me?" I caught my breath as he broke open the Snickers bar and produced a sparkling diamond ring. He got down on one knee and said, "Jami, will you marry me?"

When I said, "Yes," he put the ring on my finger. It fit perfectly and it was beautiful, my taste exactly.

He'd taken me completely off guard. We'd discussed marriage extensively, we both wanted it, but I didn't expect to get engaged until the end of the summer, when all my competing was over. We cried for joy. He had created a precious moment that I will cherish for the rest of my life. When I called my parents to tell them the news, they were delighted but not surprised. My mother had helped Beau pick the ring and my father knew about it too. Still, he was amazed that I would marry anyone, considering how independent I'd become. He told me he believed that Beau was the perfect man for me, that if someone had said, "Go pick a great guy for your daughter," he couldn't have done better himself. I felt great about that, but I had one last person to consult. It was my grandma.

I had to make sure she was okay with my choice, because now she spoke for Poppy, too. When I called her, she was completely supportive; she had seen how Beau had taken care of me after my bone-spur surgery and she really liked him. I cried when I asked her what Poppy would think. Neither Beau nor I were religious people—he was Christian, I was Jewish—and we did not intend to raise our kids according to any particular religion. We both believed in God, we would instill that into our kids from the start, but we wanted to allow them to choose their own religion when they grew up. Would Poppy approve? I would never go against his wishes in a million years.

She assured me that Poppy would approve one hundred percent, that he wanted the best for me, and that as far as she could see, Beau was the best. That was the final word; my entire family had accepted our engagement and I couldn't have been happier. We set the date for April 28, 2001, and that was that. Now I could concentrate on my training, knowing full well that whatever the results of the Paralympic trials, I was set for a beautiful future with a man I truly loved.

In June, I arrived in Connecticut at Connecticut College, the venue for the Paralympic trials. I could hardly believe I'd gotten this far; this would be the biggest race of my life with the most at stake. It had been a long road to get here for all three hundred disabled athletes, including wheelchair and blind athletes. We weren't competing directly against each other, we were running our own races in our classes, but even though we were in a variety of categories, we were vying for the same seventy-one slots. My job was to focus, warm up well, and run to the best of my ability. Beyond that, it was up to the gods.

I kept my personal best in mind and I vowed to give it my all—no holding back, no waiting for another day, this was it. I looked over at Shea warming up. If she was fast, she was fast. What could I do? I was resigning myself to accept her presence when I spotted another woman warming up—someone I had never seen before, a single BK named Elaine. Where the hell had she come from? Under normal circumstances, her time and mine would have nothing to do with each other, because we were in different categories. Today, though, since we were all going for those same slots, I felt like it wasn't fair. But the rules were the rules.

For the hundred meters, I ran a high sixteen, a real stinker of a time for me. I was upset to start with and the new girl Elaine beat me—not by much, but she beat me nonetheless. Shea beat everybody, sailing through in 13.65 seconds. She took it all in her stride, nabbing her Paralympic slot right then and there, but when we saw playback on the video, another girl and I had false-started. I thought so at the time; they should have called us back but they didn't. My bad luck. I congratulated Shea with intensely mixed emotions. She had beaten all the women, even the single BKs, and her times were better than the single AK men. After all the years we'd been told a double couldn't beat a single, along came Shea, who blew everyone out of the water, men and women alike. She really was a phenomenon.

Shea had mostly kept to herself during the trials. Her coach was with her, a wonderful man who also trained Elaine, which was how Elaine had gotten there. She and Shea had been training together for the last several months and had really sparked each other on. Shea had gotten used to winning against a single BK, which had boosted her confidence. I knew the only way I could beat her would be her own error, if she fell or tripped, but I didn't wish that on anyone. I knew how disastrous falling could be to an amputee.

The two hundred meters was the next day. I arrived at the track feeling better than the day before. My goals were to set a personal record and beat Elaine. I simply had to. While I was warming up, I noticed that the end of my limb felt unusually cold. It was two hours before the race, there was plenty of time, so I removed my prosthetic to discover that the liner had ripped and the silicone was coming through. Oh, no, not now! This was the second biggest race of my life and, whatever the results, I needed to finish—for myself.

At that time, I wasn't accustomed to traveling with extra liners. They're not made by Flex-Foot, they're very expensive, and my insurance doesn't cover them, because they're not a medical necessity. They're mainly for runners, and the company that *does* make them has a direct conflict of interest with Flex-Foot. I was screwed.

I found the people who represented Ohio Willowwood, the company that sent the team prosthetists to help the athletes. They had some extra liners with them but they were all too large for me. I was crying pretty hard by now, I just couldn't figure out what to do. Maybe I wouldn't get to run the race at all. We ended up taping the liner together and when I jumped around a little, it felt pretty good. The trouble was, I had to stop warming up so the tape would hold. Now I wouldn't be warm enough. I tried to exercise my upper body as much as I could, moving my arms around, wondering what the hell was going on. It was a scenario I'd never imagined. I had the tape checked right before the race, everything was fine. I watched them putting out the blocks. I took one last look at my liners, just for good measure—and the tape broke. I sat down on the track and sobbed.

The other women were heading for their starting positions. They knew what was happening to me, they were walking slowly so I could gather myself, but everybody had their own problems to deal with and they needed to remain as self-focused as possible. I grabbed an official and showed him what had happened. He authorized an extra two minutes and the prosthetist came over and taped my liner back up. I was a wreck by now, so much so that I false-started. I was so queasy in the stomach, I felt like I wanted to throw up as we all returned to our starting blocks. When the gun went off for the second time, I was so shook up and determined not to false-start again, I lost a half second getting off the blocks. At least I was running.

I called on my higher spirits (just in case there were any hanging around), I found my stride, and when I looked out of the corner of my eye after about fifty meters, I was gaining on Elaine. "I'm going to catch her," I said to myself, "and I'm going to beat her." My determination had kicked back in and I ran as fast as my cheetah legs could carry me. When I came in at 34.15 seconds, the tape had held, I'd run my personal best, and I'd beat Elaine. Considering all that had come before, I was pretty happy.

Shea ran the two hundred meters in under thirty seconds, winning her second gold medal of the day, beating out the toughest women. She'd beat everyone and she'd crushed my two-hundred-meter world record by almost ten seconds. I was bummed and happy for her all at the same time, proud that a U.S. amputee had done so well and disappointed for myself. Lindsay did really well too. She ran her fastest time ever and beat Kelly by half a second. I had to feel proud of her; a woman in her mid-forties, my good friend, largely a marathon runner, had run the two hundred meters fast enough to win a medal and earn a slot for the U.S. She really deserved it—she had worked hard on distance as well as on track. While I'm writing this, Lindsay holds world records in the four hundred and eight hundred meters as well as the marathon. She really wished I could go to Australia. I'm closer to her age than the other girls and she wanted us to room together and share that experience—but nowhere near as much as I did. The day had been disturbing, not at all what I'd envisioned, but once again, I was reminded that there is nothing on the outside that we can count on. It's all on the inside, and I had a great family and a fiancé back home. What could be better than that?

I knew I would keep training to improve my personal best. Maybe in the future, Shea would have a bad day at Nationals and I'd beat her, who could tell? For now, there was a final long shot in August for the Paralympics—something they called "wild-card slots." When the paperwork was turned in to the Sydney Paralympic Committee, they would determine if there were any lanes open for any particular race. For example, there might be only six women across the world registered for the two hundred meters. That would leave two wild-card slots to be filled. "Wild card" was the right word, because the odds were completely stacked against me, but as they say, hope springs eternal. It was almost over but not quite, my future spread out before me in a vast unknown, and in essence everything was still on hold.

28

Layers

D ID YOU EVER NOTICE THAT LIFE HAPPENS IN LAYERS, ONE THING overlapping another and building outward in all directions, like a multi-tiered Rubik's cube? We barely experience something fully before the next layer gets poured on. In the middle, conflicts arise—it's the old round hole, square peg syndrome—as we dance around the puzzle, trying to fit the chaotic parts into a sense of order. One week after the Paralympic trials, while I was still licking my wounds from not getting what I wanted in Connecticut, my own layers began to pile up.

Our extended family had been through a crisis with Brittney's mom, Jeanette, one year prior. It was breast cancer; she'd undergone surgery and chemotherapy and now she was a survivor. Before the Paralympic trials, she and a friend signed up to do the Avon Breast Cancer Walk. Stretching from Santa Barbara to Malibu, thousands of people, mostly women, walk sixty-one miles in three days, sleeping and eating in tents, raising awareness about breast cancer and money to fund research. I wanted to go on the walk too, but I couldn't commit to taking the time until I learned my fate concerning the Paralympics. If I was off to Australia, I would need the time to train. If not, I was free to walk.

Putting aside the highly unlikely possibility of a wild-card slot, I was available. I called Pallotta Teamworks, the production company that was putting on the walk. I explained that I'd waited because I'd been uncertain of my availability, but now I really wanted to be included. They told me that they'd love to include me; they knew who I was, since I'd been widely publicized as a Paralympic hopeful, and the attention would be good for them. But registration had closed. I tried to convince them to change their minds but it was simply too late. I left my number just in case and hung up the phone, sad and rejected. It felt like nothing was going my way.

Then I got a call from the casting agent for Steven Spielberg's film. I was shocked to hear from them, I thought that opportunity was long gone, but they wanted me for the film. Jude Law, from *The Talented Mr. Ripley,* and Haley Joel Osmont, the young boy from *The Sixth Sense,* would be starring in this movie called *A.I.,* which stands for "Artificial Intelligence." They were offering me what they called a "featured extra" role as a robot, which required running. The shooting dates were a full week in October followed by an additional week in November. Could I do it?

I wanted to do it very much, but what if I happened to get one of the wild-card slots? I knew my chances were slim to none, but I'd worked too hard not to be available for Sydney. At the same time, being in the film was attractive. Unlike the Paralympics, it was real, a solid offer with costume fittings, rehearsals, and starting dates. I told them the truth. The casting agent was flexible, she was willing to take a chance, and she made me an irresistible offer. She suggested I come down for the costume fittings and get a cast made of my upper torso and my face. If I didn't win a wild-card slot and I could do the film, they would pay me for my time. If I did get a slot and I was on my way to Australia, they wouldn't pay me and they'd find somebody else. That worked for me.

I arrived at Stan Winston Studios for my appointment with the experts who had done the special effects for *Star Wars.* I was in awe of them; they worked with the man who had created some of the greatest special effects ever shown on film. In my estimation, they were the real thing. One of the technicians placed a blob of the face-casting material in my hands so I could get the feel of it.

"Are you claustrophobic?" he wanted to know.

"No," I said, "not particularly."

The stuff in my hand felt like plaster of Paris, similar to the casting material used to make prosthetic sockets. "It's gonna be cold going on," he said, "and it'll warm up while it forms a hard mold." They would do it in two pieces, covering my upper torso, my back, my shoulders, and the back of my head first. Then they would do the front.

He was right, it felt really cold at first and warmed up on my back in a few minutes. He peeled it off easily and then started on the front part of my body. His assistants placed a trash bag over my chest to protect my skin and they put a bald cap on my head that looked like a section of panty hose, to protect my hair. Then he laid the white plastery, goopy gel all over the front of my upper body and my face. It felt like Jell-O. Someone was constantly wiping under my nose so I could breathe, and they watched me for signs of anxiety. I was fine; if you can deal with a hyperbaric chamber, you can deal with anything. Once my face was covered, they'd gotten some in my mouth but I couldn't talk to let them know. I moaned, "Mmmhh," and somebody got the message.

"Do you want me to take some off your mouth?" an assistant asked.

"Mm-hmm," I groaned.

I felt much better after they wiped my lips off. In five minutes it had hardened and they pulled off a perfect mold of my face. It had been painless, kind of fascinating, because now they could make a plastic mask that looked just like me, to cover my entire face. Then it was onward to the costume shop.

I still didn't know what my role was, but when they put me in a tight red and black corset with a fringed border of soft pom-pom beads that dangled around my waist, I was getting somewhat of an idea. It turned out I was to supposed to be a hooker robot, which I thought was pretty funny. They covered my sockets and legs with black tights so that only my prosthetic feet showed. When I looked in the mirror, I have to say that I liked how I looked. They had me try on some strange robotic-looking face pieces, but they scrapped them, deciding it made me look too space-age.

The second fitting was what they called a "show and tell" for Mr. Spielberg himself. The robots, all twenty-two of us, got into full costume and makeup. They'd put my original face cast on a machine that made a foam latex mask, which they glued halfway down my face, almost to my ears. In essence, I was wearing a mask of my own image. They spiked up my hair, teasing it and spraying on tons of sticky goo, and I had on my cheetah legs. They wanted me to wear these legs for the movie but I was not so sure about it because they were so difficult to stand on.

We lined up to be viewed and approved or disapproved, as Mr. Spielberg stopped in front of each robot individually, staring us up and down. This was the first time I'd seen him; it was pretty impersonal, and I have to say that I felt as much like a robot as I ever had. He approved of my look, all except my hair and a see-through jacket they had given me. I was relieved when they decided on a wig, because even though it was incredibly ugly, it would have been hell to have my own hair beaten up like that every day. Fitting it under a wig was much more "hair-friendly."

When I returned for the next show and tell, eight robots had been cut. Almost everyone's costumes had been changed except one other person's and mine. Instead of the space-agey robots they'd costumed the week before, they wanted the robots to look more humanlike: a butler, a chef, a chauffeur, and me, a hooker. They had kept only five amputees; the rest of the robots had all their limbs. Mr. Spielberg walked back and forth, checking each of us out, never noticing that I was wearing a different pair of legs. I'd been able to talk the Stan Winston guys out of my cheetah legs, explaining that standing on them was next to impossible for any length of time. The tights covered everything but the feet anyway, and I suggested that if I took the foot shells off my VSPs, they looked much more robotic underneath. Lucky for me, they agreed. Someone commented that it would be easier for me to stand in the cage with these legs, where I could hold on to the bars for balance. Now I knew I was a hooker robot in a cage, but that was all I knew.

The Sydney Paralympic Committee never called me to tell me I had not gotten a wild-card slot. When I phoned Disabled Sports

USA to find out what was going on, an executive informed me that the paperwork had gone out days ago. If I hadn't been notified, it was over. So that was that; I was not going to Australia. It was terribly anticlimactic and I was crushed. At the same time, I have to admit that in a certain way I was relieved. Not knowing had been the worst part, but it wasn't like my life had stood still in the meantime. It was time to move on. I had a part in *A.I.*, which, judging from the fittings, would be lots of fun.

The next day, another layer was poured on to my life. It was "Avon calling." They'd reviewed my situation and were willing to make a special concession. I'd be receiving the paperwork the next day. If I could raise the mandatory $1,800 by September 28 (that was less than two months), I could do the walk. In fact, they wanted to profile me, since so many people knew about me, but they warned me to think carefully. I may have been training hard with my track coach, but walking was completely different from sprinting. It used a whole other set of muscles; long-distance required tremendous endurance, and most of the participants had been training for many months. Also, it was a lot of money to raise in a short time. They advised me to think it through.

I didn't need to. "I can do it," I said without a hesitation. I had nearly two months to train and raise the money and it would take my mind off my great disappointment. I almost went to Sydney anyway, just to be there. My friend Sarah, an AK runner who was no longer competing, had graduated from USC in May with a master's degree in broadcasting. She'd been assigned to the Paralympics by a huge media conglomerate called wemedia.com. They would be taping the Paralympic events and sending them back through a live feed on the Internet. Sarah suggested I attend opening ceremonies. I could spend some time in the booth with her, watch a few races, and come right back. I tossed around the idea. I wanted to be a part of it and to support my friends, but sitting it out would be difficult. I decided against making the long trip, and now that I look back, I'm glad. It would have been exhausting and I didn't really need a painful reminder of what I was missing.

It was much more productive to concentrate on the Avon

walk. It would require a new twist in my training, a welcome change. I started immediately, meeting Jeanette three or four days a week for long walks, somewhere between four to twelve miles at a stretch. When she wasn't available, I walked alone. It was a treat to walk and talk, or to think peacefully without being breathless and fatigued at the end of a training session. After running track, everything else was a lot easier, and I embraced my new goal: to make money for breast cancer and be one of thousands of women who were doing the same thing.

At the beginning of September, my work with Adidas sparked yet another unanticipated layer. A television casting agent called to say they were doing a remake of an old game show, "To Tell the Truth." It would be syndicated all over the country, and after seeing my commercial and some of my press, they wanted me as one of the mystery women. I was intrigued when they explained the premise of the show:

Two Jami Goldman look-alikes and I would all claim to be me. John O'Hurley, the actor who'd played Elaine's boss on "Seinfeld," would host the show while a four-member celebrity panel would try to pick out the real Jami. It was up to the three Jamis to trick the panel into choosing the wrong one. The panel would be given an affidavit of my life with sketchy information that mentioned things like: nineteen years old, stranded in a car, amputation, moving back into society, and running. They would ask us questions, but they were not allowed to ask specific dates or names and I was not allowed to lie. The other girls could, though, and we were all encouraged to give vague answers with no elaborating. At the end of the Q&A portion, each panel member and the audience as a whole would cast a vote as to who was the real Jami Goldman—that was five votes in all. For each wrong vote, we'd receive one thousand dollars, which we would split among the three of us. We could make up to five grand and it sounded like fun, especially with money involved as incentive.

The taping was scheduled for Saturday of the next week at NBC Studios in Burbank. One day before, I would meet the other girls to give them pertinent information about me and to plan our strategy. I was a little nervous that Friday afternoon as I set out to meet my alter egos. The producers and I had discussed the importance of finding look-alikes, since I'd been all over the news and the commercial had been so popular. As I parked my car, I wondered how I would feel if they had picked women who I thought were unattractive. Would that mean they saw me as unattractive? What if I didn't like the other girls? Thankfully, my fears were unfounded. Both girls were cute and we all liked each other immediately. That was one hurdle over with. Now I had to teach them about things they probably didn't know.

I was happy to discover they'd done their homework. They weren't actresses: one woman was a massage therapist and the other was an exercise Spinning instructor. They were smart choices; both women were athletic and they knew about the body and exercise, which were huge parts of my life. They knew about me and the accident and we discussed the specifics of prosthetics since we expected those types of questions. We needed to stick with similar stories, because if I gave a technical answer to a difficult question, the other women needed to be able to give technical answers also. If either of them couldn't, it would be a giveaway. We also discussed running—they needed some real information—but beyond that, they were prepared to lie. For example, if they asked one of the Jamis where she went to school, she could say Boston, the other could say Detroit, and I would say Arizona. That wouldn't matter as much as the specifics of wearing prosthetics and being an athlete.

The three of us arrived at NBC Studios early on Saturday morning. We'd all agreed to wear jeans and a fitted, short-sleeved T-shirt, each a different color, that made us look athletic. After we were dressed, the producer taped cardboard under the knees of the other two women to simulate the way prosthetics make pants taper around the knees and then hang loosely at the calves. The women watched me walk and practiced stiffening their gaits slightly so we all moved the same. We had the makeup artist do similar makeup and hair with only slight variations; we were determined to fool the celebrities as much as we could.

The panel consisted of two regulars, comedienne Paula Poundstone and Meshach Taylor from "Designing Women." Bryan

Cranston, the father from "Malcolm in the Middle," joined the panel, and so did Molly Carver from the "Pamela Anderson VIP Show." The host, John O'Hurley, set a great tone with his dry sense of humor.

The show opened on a completely dark set, with a spot-light on each of us individually as we repeated, one after the other, "Hi, I'm Jami Goldman and I run with no legs." I heard Paula Poundstone whisper under her breath to Mishak Taylor, "Oh great, we can't crack any jokes for this one." What did she think, that when you lose your legs, you also lose your sense of humor?

The segment lasted fifteen minutes and each celebrity got two minutes to ask questions. When it was time to vote, Molly Carver was the only one who guessed me. We'd fooled three of the contestants and the studio audience, they showed a clip of my commercial, and we got to divide four thousand dollars among three of us. That's pretty good money for a two-hour taping and a good time.

Before I left the set, I deliberately walked over to Paula Poundstone to chat with her and let her know I was a real person who liked to laugh. She was very friendly, and so were the other celebrities. Beau and I got a free night in a wonderful hotel on the Sunset Strip. All in all, it was a great weekend enhanced by the knowledge that the very next day, I would be back on the road walking many miles for my Avon walk training. Believe me, that really helps you enjoy your time off.

They'd scheduled my segment to air sometime in November, but after they edited the show, they liked it so much that they showed it four weeks after the taping. Ironically, my "60 Minutes II" segment had aired only one week prior, so the layers of my life were starting to intertwine more and more closely and in some cases overlap. I was still let down about the Paralympics, how could I not be, but I took comfort in knowing that if I had gone to Australia, none of these other things would have happened. I was learning that no matter how strongly I wanted something, I didn't necessarily know what would be best for me in the end.

29

Spice Girl

THE FILMING OF *A.I.* WAS AN EXERCISE IN SECRECY. I CONFERRED with the rest of the robots later; none of us had been told anything about the movie and neither had the supporting actors. Each person knew only what he or she was doing right there, right then. In fact, we all had to sign confidentiality agreements that we wouldn't reveal anything about the little bit that we knew or what we did, until after the movie came out. It was like being a spy—you were familiar with your own part and the people with whom you came in contact. Beyond that, you were kept in the dark—the best way to make sure nobody spilled the beans before the premiere.

I was told that I was the Spice Girl Robot and during the first week I'd be shooting scenes from something called "the Flesh Fair." My work began off the set, when all of the robots spent several days in a choreographer's dance studio near Warner Bros. in Burbank. Her job was to teach us to look, move, and act like machines instead of human beings, making staccato movements with our eyes and our bodies. She explained that we'd be required to keep our eyes open for long periods of time without blinking. We needed to practice that, too. After all, have you ever seen a robot blink?

For two days, we walked stiffly, acting as if our limbs were

mechanized. We stood in a row without moving, we ran like machines, and we learned to take on the attitudes of our specific
characters. The butler robot, for instance, practiced standing very
prim and proper, with his hands clasped together behind his
back. Once he had that down, he thought about how a butler
robot might run in a desperate fear situation. The "comedian"
robot was going to be shot out of a torpedo through a flaming circle, where he would catch on fire and splatter across the ground.
He would be in the shot until the critical moment, when he
would be replaced by a real robot. Stan Winston Studios had built
a human-looking mechanical dummy in the butler's image, using
a face mask they'd created from his face. The dummy would get
shot from the torpedo and so would other robots that they scattered among us wearing latex masks of human faces—very eerie
and very cool!

We got into our roles during those two days and really *became*
our characters. As the hooker robot, I was instructed to keep my
hands by my sides with my elbows slightly bent, always acting flirty
as if I were trying to pick someone up. When my character was required to run in fear, the choreographer directed me to keep my
hands on my hips, my wrists bent with my palms facing the
ground, all the time swaying my body back and forth. Even as a
robot running out of desperation, I needed to show it in my
movements, not my face, which was not supposed to register
human emotions, even when the script called for us to watch
other robots supposedly being destroyed.

Early the next morning, we showed up on a set adjacent to
the huge ship, the *Queen Mary,* where we would report for the
next eight days. This self-contained set was a large dome in Long
Beach that previously had housed the airplane the *Spruce Goose.*
My call was between 5 and 6 A.M. each day, because it took them
three hours to get me into makeup. Needless to say, it was an exhausting schedule. I worked from ten to fourteen hours a day,
shooting the Flesh Fair, a completely convoluted sort of cannibal-
istic festival, except it involved robotic mechanized parts instead
of human flesh.

Some days I was on camera all day long. Other days I did

nothing but play cards, read magazines, and try to get to know my fellow cast members. I say "try," because I couldn't speak very well. Some of the other robots had two-piece face masks they could remove when they weren't filming, so they could talk to each other. I, on the other hand, wore a permanent mask that they glued onto my face each morning. Unlike the welder, who had fake oil dripping all over his real face so he could speak and eat normally, I had fake lips glued on top of my own so I could only mumble. There was an opening between the lips where I could fit a straw, but I couldn't chew. I drank smoothies and milkshakes all day, and if I moved my lips too much, I was in danger of cracking my mask along the sides. People were friendly to me although I couldn't respond much, and I managed to mumble my way through our games of blackjack, no gambling allowed!

Our scenes were shot in reverse, the last ones during the first week, the first ones during the last. For my initial week of shooting, while four hundred extras milled around this weird Flesh Fair, I stood in a cage with other robots, including Haley Joel Osmont and Jude Law. The metal cage had a see-through Plexiglas roof on which the heavy metal band Ministry, all dressed up in metal and leather, played ear-shattering music. The idea was that people arrived at the fair to destroy robots for sport according to their method of choice: they could burn us with acid, tear us apart, or toss us in a torpedo (a la the comedian) and watch us fly out and explode into a hundred pieces. I was not to be destroyed, but I had to watch the others.

One day I saw Spielberg's gorgeous wife, Kate Capshaw, when she came to the set, but I barely saw Steven that day. Of course he was always there, he was directing, but it was such a mob scene with so many extras, you could hardly see anyone. During a night shot, we were told to hold on to the bars of the cage and stare out at an audience who were there to witness us being destroyed. We were *not* told that certain members of the audience, who were sitting on risers in the stands, had been instructed to break into a crazed frenzy and storm our cage. Unbeknownst to us, they were to go berserk, pick up isolated mechanized parts from previously destroyed robots that were strewn across the dirt, and start rushing toward us. It was genuinely scary to be stuck in a metal cage with a load of people in strange face masks, getting rushed by a crowd that looked out of control as they screamed and yelled, waving fake body parts around. The first time it happened we were truly shocked, but they went for three or four more takes. I suppose they had technical problems, but once the surprise element was gone, I wondered if the other takes were as exciting.

When the first week came to a close, I had a unique challenge. Because I had removed the foot shells on my prosthetics during the costume phase, my weight was pitched back on my heels when I walked. After seven days of standing around like that, the ground beneath me had eaten away at my carbon fiber heels and I was walking on metal. This was not good; the heels were ruined, my body alignment was thrown off, and my hip flexors hurt. I'd forgotten the delicate balance of prosthetic components; I hadn't anticipated the removal of the foot shells causing such a problem.

The film company was completely gracious; they were happy to pay for any adjustments I needed. Michael fixed the heels and affixed rubber grips on the bottoms of the feet to get me through the next week of shooting, which required running. This ended the immediate problem, but I could no longer wear a shoe with my VSPs. I had two choices: I could remove the grips and have the foot shells replaced, or I could wear them as they were. I actually liked them without foot shells, they were lighter and made it easier to run, so I'd gotten myself a new, lighter pair of jogging legs in the process.

Five robots returned for a second week of work. I was among them, to film scenes that came before the ones we'd already shot. This was to be an action-packed seven days, with a great deal of scrambling around and running in desperation as we tried to escape our captors, the people who would eventually catch us and put us in the cage at the Flesh Fair. Only about thirty extras were called, a far cry from the four hundred or more in the mob scenes we'd shot before, and it was a much more intimate experience.

They had transformed the same set into a dark forest, densely surrounded with trees. In the center of a small clearing was a soggy, deep pit filled with robot body parts. The crew sprayed water in the pit between each take, turning everything to mud, and we were all down in there together, scrounging around the bottom of a muddy pit, picking up arms and legs in an effort to make our mechanical bodies whole. Stunt doubles were in the pit with us, falling and slipping around, and everyone was concerned for me, although I was maneuvering my way in there as well as most of the stunt doubles. I was supposed to be looking for legs while another girl robot, missing her arms, was picking up limbs with her feet. The welder was in there, too, sparks flying from his welding torch while he was diligently welding a white hand onto a black man's robotic arm.

Each person got a close-up in the pit. When my turn came, I opened my eyes very wide as the choreographer had shown me and stared into the camera. Steven Spielberg was standing maybe thirty feet from the set in the midst of his assistants, director's chairs, video cameras, and rows of monitors, watching the action. Each time he changed locations, his crew moved all the equipment too, following him around and setting everything back up wherever he stopped to shoot the next scene. It was kind of comical, as he moved from one place to the next while his assistants carried various parts of his environment closely behind him.

Whatever I did for my close-up must have worked. After he yelled "Cut!" Mr. Spielberg emerged from his bustling "living room" area and walked toward me. He stood at the edge of the pit in a pair of jeans and a sweatshirt, and called down to me. "Great job, Jami!" he said. "That was a terrific shot."

I was thrilled and encouraged; I didn't think he'd ever say two words to me. During another scene in which the moon was rising, we were all supposed to stare up at the sky with a vague sense of fear in our eyes. Again, when he went to me for a close-up, he complimented me when it was through. Unfortunately, a technical error caused them to do another take. It was dusty as hell in that pit and my contacts were making it hard for me not to blink. When my eyes began to water, makeup people came through with eye drops and I had to force my eyes open to shoot the scene again, which made them tear up. It was impossible to keep my eyes clear when I heard the cameraman say, "Rolling," but I did my best. At one point, I blinked with the camera right on me and Spielberg yelled, "No, don't blink! Tell her not to blink," he said to his assistant director.

I felt really bad, but after one more take, he called out, "Cut. That's a print." I knew it wasn't as good as the first one but I was glad to be able to blink my eyes again. On the last day of shooting, we were rehearsing a scene in which several robots were running with Haley Joel Osmont. While they were fine-tuning Haley's directions and setting his marks, I found myself standing right next to the director.

"How did you lose your legs?" Mr. Spielberg asked me.

I was surprised he wanted to talk, but I told him.

He was astounded. "That's incredible," he said.

I agreed. It was getting more incredible every day. I told him I'd been running for three years and explained, very briefly, that sports had been great for me. Expressing myself was no easy task. I couldn't move my mouth and I was mumbling—not the way one might envision having a talk with an award-winning creator like Steven Spielberg.

"You sure get around great," he said, referring to the way I'd been running through pools of water, dirt, and mud.

It was a short conversation between takes but it felt good that he'd taken the time to talk to me. At the end of the last day of shooting, after they had wrapped the scene, he asked me if I'd be at the wrap party that night. I nodded. That was easier than mumbling.

"Please find me and introduce yourself. I'll never recognize you without the mask and the makeup."

I told him I would.

The wrap party was held at Universal City Walk, in order to accommodate the enormous cast as well as all the staff from production, payroll, all the people who come together to create these kinds of megaproductions. Beau doesn't like crowds of people much (that's an understatement), so I asked Jason to escort me. He jumped at the chance because he's always been interested in the movie business.

The party was well under way when we arrived at the large building that was located beside the skating rink on the City Walk. This building had an eight-lane bowling alley, several bars, a dance floor, an arcade, and a large outdoor seating area. I was wearing pants, no one could see my legs, and the other robots had no idea who I was. They had seen each other without masks between takes, but no one had seen my real face so I had to introduce myself to each person individually. It was fun but I looked at Jason at one point and motioned toward the buffet. I'd worked up quite an appetite.

We sat down at one of the outside tables with our full plates. Then we spotted Steven Spielberg walking down a steep flight of stairs that led to the party area. Jason nudged me. "Look," he said, "there he is. This is your chance. Go over and introduce yourself."

"Oh, I can't," I said, feeling suddenly intimidated.

"He asked you to," Jason urged.

I reluctantly got up and walked to the bottom of the stairs. Mr. Spielberg stopped to greet someone and when he was through talking, I touched his arm. He looked questioningly at me.

"I'm the Spice Girl robot from your movie," I said shyly. "Remember me?"

He did a full belly laugh, bending backward at the waist, and I relaxed completely. "I'm so glad you came up and introduced yourself," he said, still chuckling. "I would never have known it was you."

He had a two-minute conversation with Jason, completely embarrassing me by telling my brother all kinds of wonderful things about working with me. It was a real thrill! When we walked away, I'd been a little star-struck because I'd forgotten my manners and I hadn't said to Jason, "This is Mr. Spielberg." I guess he was used to it, people must get intimidated in his presence pretty often, but I was very busy second-guessing myself, wondering if I'd said or done anything wrong.

I forgot about it when I went back to join the party. People were milling around, eating, dancing, and there were a ton of kids I'd never seen, some of them stand-ins for the main players. I didn't see Haley that night, though I'd heard he was there, but I spotted one of his stand-ins, a kid named Kendall whom I'd mumbled at a few times during the shoot. He walked by me and I grabbed him. "Hi!" I said.

He stared at me and then his mom. Neither of them had any idea who I was and she took a protective stance.

"I'm Jami, the Spice Girl robot," I said.

They both burst into big smiles. "No way that's you," Kendall's mom said. "Can we get a picture with you?"

Kendall and I threw our arms around each other while his mom snapped a picture. I was really enjoying myself, but unfortunately I'd committed to making an appearance at the first-ever amputee National Championship half marathon in San Diego the next morning. That meant it was Cinderella time, since I had to be up at 5 A.M.—as if we were still shooting.

On my way out, I spotted Jude Law walking down the stairs with one of his kids. I'd gotten bolder by then so I walked straight up to him. "I'm really sorry to bother you," I said, "but you don't know who I am, do you?"

"No, I don't," he said, looking like he would have preferred to be left alone.

When I told him who I was, he smiled broadly, surprised to see me looking so normal. "Great to see you," he said. I got home feeling pretty happy that night. It had been a great adventure, I'd made some money, and I'd had some terrific exposure. In the not too recent past, I saw a late-night "Entertainment Tonight" segment on TV, spotlighting Steven Spielberg and George Lucas. They'd put together a documentary about the filming of the *Indiana Jones* trilogy, and while Spielberg described the special effects they'd used, I took pride in the fact that I'd worked with this great man and that I was a part of his history.

Maybe twenty years in the future, my kids and I will gather around the TV to watch a documentary on the making of *A.I.* When they see the Spice Girl robot, standing in a deep, muddy pit in the midst of a dense forest, staring wide-eyed at a full moon, they'll say to each other, "That's our mom!" I'll just smile and remember how unglamorous the whole thing was, but I won't let on. Some things are better left unsaid.

30

Walking for Life

WEATHER SEEMS TO FOLLOW ME AROUND IN A TRULY SIGNIFICANT way. On October 27, 2000, the first day of the Avon Breast Cancer Walk, it rained—not a lot, but it was indicative of things to come. Approximately three thousand people would begin in Santa Barbara and cover sixty-one miles to Malibu, an awesome distance when you think about walking it—in the rain. Since I had signed up on the late side, Jeanette, Brittney's mom, had another walking partner for the event, a woman named Traci. They invited me to walk with them; we were all friends and several of us had been singled out by the press.

Each year, in order to create a personal connection for those who weren't walking, Pallotta Teamworks chose a number of women on whom to focus for public-interest stories. The press followed the progress of these particular women all along the three-day walk, reporting on how they were faring and interviewing them from time to time. They thought Jeanette and I were a good story, the cancer survivor and her double-amputee athlete friend, so I walked with Jeanette and Traci and the press interviewed the three of us along the way. Any kind of media attention was a boon, as it brought awareness to the cause.

It was really cold that first morning, just like the two following mornings, so I started out in long pants and I changed into shorts

232

by midmorning. It was less clothing to get wet, and I have the advantage of being able to wear shorts all winter long, since there's only a small patch of exposed skin between my thigh and silicone sleeve. I learned a great deal about breast cancer during those three days and nights and I became more and more passionate about spreading the word. As women shared their stories with me, I learned that no one is immune to the possibility of contracting cancer. It is truly an equal-opportunity disease, no matter your race, your age, how well you care for yourself, or your financial status—not dissimilar to frostbite.

We covered nineteen miles on the first day under a constant light rain. I chatted when I started out, sharing stories and quips until a silence fell over me, a welcome sense of going inside and losing my individuality. I had become a cog in a vast wheel of women, all of us placing one foot in front of the other, moving toward a common destination with one-pointed intention—to show breast cancer and the world that we were not afraid. As in so many profound experiences, I learned why I was there as I went along. Each step was a statement: We walked because we wanted to, because we cared about our friends who were lying in hospital beds, crying, vomiting and losing their hair. We walked to bring attention to women who might have been saved, but they were misdiagnosed or they started on their healing journeys too late. We walked to celebrate life and because we had friends who were no longer among us who would have wanted us to do this. Finally, we walked because we could, and we felt obliged to represent those who couldn't and maybe never would. We could stand up to it, we were united and we would remain so, despite pain, rain, or anything else that tried to get in our way.

I made it through the first day wet and uncomfortable, but without incident. I shared a tent for two nights with a young woman I didn't know and it was fine. We spent our days with our respective friends and met in the tent for sleeping, where I was relieved to pull off my legs and snuggle into my sleeping bag, oblivious to any outside interference. I slept without dreams, as tired as on any day of training with Barbara, but feeling a whole different set of muscles burning. I envisioned myself as a single thread of a three-thousand-person cloth, grateful to be off my feet and out of the wetness that had climbed inside my clothing and my body.

Besides my being more fatigued physically, the second day was better than the first. There was no rain for all eighteen miles as we trudged on, sharing stories, using each other for strength and stamina. I went to sleep that night very tired but hopeful. It was going pretty well; there was only one more day, and if it was anything like today, maybe we'd be crossing the finish line in the sunshine.

I awakened on the third morning wondering about the loud tapping sound overhead. My heart sank when I realized it was rain hitting the top of the tent. The forecast was grim—it was supposed to rain all day long—so I pulled out my bad-weather gear and covered myself up. My body was weary, since I had never walked this far before, day after day, and when I stepped out into the storm, I was disheartened. It was coming down in torrents, each cold drop sharp and piercing and they penetrated my emotions. Maybe I wouldn't make it. I really hadn't considered that until now; doubting flew in the face of my training philosophy and I didn't like the way it felt. When I met up with Jeanette and Traci at the breakfast tent, they were upset too. On this, the third day, we would have to cover the longest distance, twenty-two miles. Jeanette was part of a "survivor's circle" and she had committed to the press that she would be at the finish line at about 1:30 P.M. for closing ceremonies. We were anxious. Time was disappearing as we began making our way through the battering rain toward our destination.

We'd started at about 7:00 A.M. but it was more slow-going than we had expected, even though the rain had abated to a drizzle. At 9:30 A.M., we had covered only about six miles, so we discussed riding to the next pit stop. The Avon people had provided buses but we were hesitant. We wanted to feel that we had completed what we set out to do, but Jeanette had no choice. If she intended to be at closing ceremonies, there was no way she could make it in time if she walked the whole way. Traci and I took the bus with her to the next stop—that eliminated about six more miles—and we ate a midmorning meal. By that time, we really needed the nourishment as we faced another ten or so miles, hoping we could cover them in the remaining hours. "I can do this," I told myself, "the next ten miles should be a piece of cake."

That was only true if you like soggy desserts. We started out at a good pace, not too slow, not too fast, taking some pictures as we walked, feeling weary but suddenly lighthearted. After all, this was the stretch. In less than an hour, however, the heavens opened up and a light drizzle turned into a torrential downpour. Each mile, it got worse. I got wetter and colder, but I was determined to go on—until I noticed that the rain had made it inside my clothing and was traveling down the sleeves that held on my prosthetics.

I turned to my friends, crestfallen, and said, "I have to stop. My legs are wet."

"It's okay, Jami, it doesn't matter," they said, trying to comfort me. "Look what you've already accomplished. Take a bus and we'll all meet at the finish line to celebrate."

Vans were parked at pit stops, providing shelter for people who were waiting for buses to pick them up. In fact, some people didn't walk more than five miles a day because they couldn't. They took lots of rides over the three days, and now that was what I needed to do. I said good-bye to Jeanette and Traci, hugged them, and watched them walk away. When they were out of sight I took shelter inside a van. I pulled my cell phone out of an inside pocket and called Beau and my parents.

"I feel like I failed," I told Beau.

"Jami," he said, "focus on what you did, not on what you didn't do." That was Beau, always there to make me feel better.

My father reminded me that I had no control over the rain. "You don't want to risk injuries," he said. "You were right to stop. The point is, you raised the money and contributed to awareness. It doesn't matter how many miles you covered."

I felt a little bit better and thought about how good it would feel to be dry and off my legs. I talked to other people in the van who were also waiting to be driven the last ten miles to the end. All that mattered now was walking across that finish line and celebrating the contribution we'd all made. I was awfully glad to see the bus when it pulled up. I walked through the rain, got on the bus, took a seat, and began to relax a little. The ordeal was over and in twenty minutes, we'd be there. I exhaled deeply and smiled to myself; this was a success because it wasn't about any one person or about winning or losing. That was the beauty of it—we were all in this together and it was about a collective end result.

I closed my eyes—until a few minutes later when I heard the bus chugging to a stop. We'd covered only two miles when the driver had received a message on his walkie-talkie. Those of us who had boarded this bus were not considered medical emergencies and our vehicle was needed elsewhere. We'd have to get off at this pit stop and wait for another bus. We piled down the stairs and rushed out of the rain into a tent. People who were walking poured inside, taking off their wet shoes to reveal swollen feet and bloody blisters. Most people's feet had gotten soaked the first day and they never dried. I'd had my share of foot pain; I stared at what the rain had done to them and imagined the pain they were in. And they were only taking a break before they got out there to finish the walk. It would be an hour or more before a bus arrived to pick us up. "I have no blisters," I said to myself, "my limbs are dry, and I have no skin breakdown like these other women. I'm mentally and physically depleted, but so are they and they're not quitting. If I keep putting my left foot in front of my right, I can finish this walk, wet prosthetics and all."

It was Poppy, my invisible coach. He had come to be with me, to encourage me, to push me to the next level of my abilities. I removed my disposable poncho and tossed it. It was history. I pulled off my wet sweatshirt and tied it around my waist, noticing a pile of metallic emergency blankets, the kind that are so thin they fold up into four-inch squares. People use these silvery space-age blankets at the end of marathons because they're extremely light, while they hold in the warmth. I grabbed several and stuffed them inside my clothing. With help from the medical aides, I covered myself with a black shiny trash bag, cutting out a hole for my head. They suggested I cut out arm holes too, but I decided against it; I wanted my arms to stay warm and dry. When I exited the medical tent, I was a walking head jutting out of a trash bag, joining a group of other walking heads.

I stepped onto the path, feeling all alone. Maybe I would catch Jeanette and Traci, since I'd ridden a couple of miles while they were walking. I was facing a whole new leg of my personal challenge now and I needed to finish, that much I knew, but I felt unbearably lonely and sad. My body was beaten up, my spirit was exhausted, but when I felt the courage of the women who were walking beside me, how could I give in? Many of these women who were walking on torn-up feet had been to hell and back, nauseated and filled with killer drugs for weeks on end. And they were walking. All I had to do was weather the rain for a couple more hours and it would be all over. What did a few hours of discomfort mean compared with years of medical problems with an uncertain outcome? I refused to allow the rain to conquer me; I would conquer the rain.

I cried the entire eight miles as I walked by myself, calling out to Poppy to give me the strength to keep putting one foot in front of the other. It was gruesome; I've never been a fan of the rain, which is why I've generally preferred desert living. I disliked getting wet on a warm day, and there I was, a walking trash bag, squishing through cold mud puddles with wet shoes, wet clothes, wet prosthetics, and exhausted limbs. But I didn't have cancer or any other terminal illness. I thought about Poppy the whole way. He'd been sick for years and he'd never told anyone. He'd borne the pain and the burden all by himself, with some help from Grandma. His mind was that strong.

I prayed that he would give that strength to me now, so I could make it through the soggy hell of hills and asphalt. As if in response to my prayer, women stepped up beside me and told me how my presence was helping them get from one mile to the next. I walked slowly, I stopped to breathe and cry, my body was sore, my limbs hurt, my head ached, I was cold and wet, and I felt isolated. But it wasn't worse than being stuck in a car in the snow for eleven days or enduring the agony of frostbite. Nothing was worse than that. I could do this.

I stepped across that finish line on my own two feet, wet from head to toe, unable to distinguish the rain from the tears pouring down my face. I headed straight for the special media tent, where I found Traci immediately. She rushed over and threw her wet arms around me as we cried together. We would be seeing Jeanette on stage, since she and six other women, all part of a survivor's circle, were taking a prominent place in closing ceremonies. Arm in arm, Traci and I went back out into the rain to the beach area designated for the ceremonies. It was rigged with a set of curtains that would open as everyone arrived at the end of this long three-day march, a tearful moment for every one of us who had reached our goals. Joy flooded over our bodies and minds in the midst of applause and cheering from the sidelines where people stood in the pouring rain, single-minded in their efforts to support their loved ones.

In the final moments of this event, all the walkers were gathered in one place, standing on the wet sand, allowing their friends and families to demonstrate their love and appreciation. The CEO of Pallotta Teamworks stepped up onto the stage and gave a short speech of thanks and praise not only to the walkers but also to the tireless people who put the event together and volunteered their time to take care of the participants. When he was through, seven breast-cancer survivors, "The Circle Of Life," including Jeanette, stepped onto the stage, holding hands in a circle. We cheered our friend while one of the women stepped up to the mic and spoke about her experience with great pride and courage.

I stood on the sand, exposed to the rain, feeling nothing but joy and relief. It was over, I had done what I set out to do, and nothing had stopped me. Not the weather, not my fear, not the intense physical discomfort that had plagued my every step. I squeezed Traci's hand and smiled out from under my Hefty trashbag costume. "Thanks, Poppy," I said out loud. "I couldn't have done it without you."

I saw his smile and I knew for certain that I'd never have to do anything without him. I knew in that moment that Poppy would guide me through every step of my life, as my future flashed before me in glimmering rainbows, reflected in the crashing tides of the ocean. As I watched the rain fall into the turbulent sea, I vowed to leave a legacy behind, just like Poppy did. I would have a relationship with my children like the one my parents had with me, and a great love with Beau like the one my parents had with each other. I envisioned Beau and me packing up a motor home and traveling up the coast with our kids and a dog or two. I saw my future husband involved in a career that made him happy and I saw us growing old together. Maybe I would run a child-care center of my own. Maybe not, but I would definitely work, because I'd never be content unless I was participating fully in my own life. I would always focus on giving something back, and whatever I chose, kids would be involved.

I would continue running—maybe not always track, though. I didn't know in that instant that very soon I would start distance running with a new invention from Flex-Foot called a "C" foot, which shares some of the angles and dimensions of the cheetah foot, but is a little flatter for the express purpose of covering distance. I *did* know that I'd have to face my friends who got to compete in the Paralympics when I didn't. That would be hard, because when we all met back on the track, they'd have something in common that I didn't share. But I had my own special moments that were unique to me. My task would be to keep in mind that I run for enjoyment first, and to win second, because— I'm alive. That will always be the bottom line of my life. I'll always derive satisfaction from taking risks, I'm wired that way. If I ever feel inferior to anyone, all I have to do is think about what I would have missed if I hadn't gotten a second chance at life.

These were the thoughts passing through my mind as the ceremonies came to a close. I was ready for some hot chocolate and a long nap. It would be good to rest up; it appeared that existence had a lot in store for me over the next part of my life. I'd made it through my first thirty years with flying colors and look what had happened. It ought to be a cinch from here on in, because whatever showed up, all I had was the rest of my life in front of me.

I'm reminded of Anne Morrow Lindbergh, the wife of renowned aviator Charles Lindbergh, who went through tremendous trials owing to the infamous kidnapping death of her first-born child. Anne, an aviator in her own right, a writer and mother of six, and a picture of strength and fortitude, told her daughter at her husband's deathbed in 1974, "Don't worry about me. I'm equal to my life."

I have no idea what's coming next in my own life, which is what makes it so compelling. But in the spirit of Mrs. Lindbergh, I can only say that whatever it is, nobody has to worry about me. I'm ready, I'm waiting, and I'm up and running.

Epilogue

O N APRIL 28, 2001, I MARRIED BEAU MARSEILLES, THE LOVE OF MY life, under the setting sun in Scottsdale, Arizona. Little Savannah, my flower girl, had just finished strewing the white carpet with rose petals so slowly and meticulously, Brittney, her mom and my maid of honor, had to urge her daughter to keep walking forward amid peals of laughter from family and friends. If she had continued at her snail's pace, loath to leave the limelight, we might have been there all night. I wouldn't have minded; I'd waited my whole life to be right where I was, so what difference would a few more hours make?

It had been brutally hot and dry the day before as typical desert temperatures had soared into the hundreds. It was so hot during the rehearsal dinner, my out-of-town guests spent the night fanning themselves, praying for a cool-down the next day. Happily, nature cooperated, which I interpreted as a good omen. Weddings are like that, filled with omens and signs about the future, so if tradition held true and the perfection of the evening was any indication, I was in for a fantastic life.

The ceremony took place in the midst of a botanical garden on the lush grounds of the Phoenician, a sprawling Scottsdale resort hotel. A waterfall thundered over tiers of a jagged boulder wall, spilling into a long, rock-lined brook that narrowed and widened as it ran along, reminiscent of the dips and curves of my life—expanding, contracting, but never shallow. Crimson bougainvillea and weeping willow trees cast their reflections in the shimmering water, while black birds called grackles sang their hearts out during the ceremony as they flitted from tree to tree, heralding triumph and celebration in what seemed like a choreographed symphony.

My grandma walked down the aisle with her arm proudly wrapped around Papa Joe, my dad's ninety-six-year-old father. She appeared radiant and joyful, with tinges of sadness peeking through, due to Poppy's conspicuous absence. My mother had never looked more beautiful in her silvery off-the-shoulder silk gown with a form-fitting lacy bodice. She walked grandly beside my father, his eyes aglow, his face still wet with tears that had started hours earlier, once again demonstrating the Goldman family's unequalled capacity for weeping with joy.

When I reached the chupah that had been elegantly draped in gossamer netting and violet flowers with greenery, I stood in front of the rabbi and faced Beau, my husband-to-be. For many months, I'd wondered what I would be thinking right then. Would I be trembling, exhausted, scared, or distracted? I'm happy to report that I was none of that; I had no doubts, no confusion, no second thoughts. I was fully present in the moment, the world had fallen away, and it was only Beau and me, pledging our lives to each other, ready to take on whatever the world had in store for us—together, forever. Nothing had ever felt more right.

I stood confidently on a refurbished pair of cosmetic legs that RGP had cleaned up for me as a wedding gift. They'd been wonderfully generous, and now they were hidden beneath my beautifully swirled white dress that was spun with silken tulle. This was a moment when all of my worlds were blending together harmoniously. My running friends, Lindsay and Sarah, had flown in and were there among my 170 guests. My trainer, my writer, my family, my friends, and their children were there from Arizona, Chicago, Los Angeles, and Florida.

The ceremony was short, so very sweet, and I gave my audience another laugh when, to Beau's visible chagrin, I adjusted his tie and mopped his brow right during the ceremony. When a friend kidded me about it later in the evening, I turned to her and said, "I know, but I just couldn't resist." I was not in the habit of holding back my impulses, especially where Beau was concerned, so why would I start then?

While my guests, my new husband, and I ate, drank, and danced late into the night and celebrated the future, the past was on all of our minds. How could it not be? Most of the people there had been through it all with me: the ten days when we were missing, the stunning eleventh day when we were found, the hospital time, the amputations, my recovery, the trial, and my new career as a champion athlete. Today, not only was it a miracle that I was alive, it was also a miracle that I had *walked* down the aisle and that Lisa was one of my bridesmaids.

Thanks to my uncle Sid, I have an array of memories of my wedding night eternally etched in mind. "Stop throughout the night," he'd said, "look carefully, then close your eyes and make mental pictures. There'll be tons of people snapping photos, but don't forget to make your own. Watch your parents dancing and remember them. Watch your grandmother and your friends. Then you'll have it all in your heart to bring back whenever you want to see it."

That was the best wedding advice anyone could have given me, and I started practicing the night before. After the rehearsal dinner, Lisa, Brittney, and Kristin were gathered with me in my *casita* at the Phoenician. At 1:30 A.M., I walked Lisa to her car. We stood silently in the dark, breathing in the warm air for a few moments until Lisa said, "I love you, Jami. I'm really happy for you and you're gonna have a great day tomorrow. We all will."

We hugged and Lisa pointed toward the sky. I looked up to see a flock of white birds forming a "V" shape in the sky. They gave off their own light, as if they were glowing from the inside out. I had never seen these birds before in the Arizona desert; they looked like doves, and there must have been thirty of them suspended in space, hovering, changing formation and re-forming into their original V shape.

"You know this means something," I whispered to Lisa, not wanting to disturb the moment.

"Yes, I know it does," she whispered back.

We stood holding hands. This magical moment meant many things—that Lisa and I had survived, that she was driving away by herself because she could, that I'd found the man I wanted to marry, and that I'd be dancing at my wedding on my own two legs. And most of all, it meant that Poppy had found a way to contact me. I'd been waiting for a sign and I knew this was his way of showing me he was there, that he approved, and that everything was going to be just fine.

The birds disappeared into the darkness. Lisa kissed me good-bye and I watched her drive away. Then, feeling like a princess, I floated toward the *casita* where Brittney and Kristin would spend one last night with me as a single woman.

Made in the USA
San Bernardino, CA
04 December 2016